Build-It-Better-Yourself
Storage Around the House

by the Editors of *Rodale's Practical Homeowner*® *magazine*

 Rodale Press, Emmaus, Pennsylvania

The projects and plans presented in this book have been researched and tested, and all efforts have been made to insure accuracy and safety. However, due to the variability of all local conditions, construction materials and personal skills, etc., Rodale Press and the author assume no responsibility for any injuries suffered or damages or other losses incurred during or as a result of the construction of these projects. All instructions and plans should be carefully studied and clearly understood before beginning construction. Follow all accepted safety procedures during construction.

Printed in the United States of America on recycled paper, containing a high percentage of de-inked fiber.

Produced by Scharff Associates, Ltd.
Editor: Keith Mullen
Cover Design: Anita Patterson
Cover Photo: Joe Griffin
Cover Photograph Styling: Troy M. Schnyder

Library of Congress Cataloging-in-Publication Data

Build-it-better-yourself storage around the
    house / by the editors of Rodale's
    practical homeowner magazine.
            p.   cm.
        ISBN 0-87857-753-X
        1. Cabinet-work. 2. Storage in the
    home. 3. Shelving (for books) I. Rodale's
    practical homeowner.
    TT197.B92 1988
    684.1'6—dc19   87-35406
                                          CIP

    2   4   6   8   10   9   7   5   3   hardcover

Contents

Section 4   Bath, Laundry, and Sewing Rooms

Section 5   Garages, Basements, and Attics

Section 6   Workshops

Section 7   Outdoors

INTRODUCTION

"A place for everything and everything in its place" is an old adage that still is very applicable for modern times. Today's family probably has more of "everything" than any society has enjoyed in the past, and one of the most persistent dilemmas is "Where will we put it all?" or worse yet, "Where did I put that?"

If you have been asking these or similar questions, let *Build-It-Better-Yourself Storage Around the House* provide the answers. In its pages, you will find storage projects for every room in the house, as well as projects for the basement, attic, garage, and backyard. Many of the projects are simple and can be made by even the beginning woodworker using only hand tools. On the other hand, many of the projects are as beautiful as they are practical and demand a more professional treatment. However, none of the techniques described in this book are beyond the grasp of even the novice craftsman if sufficient patience and forethought (as well as a little practice on scrap wood) are given to each operation.

Each project suggests a particular type of wood to use in building—usually a readily available grade of pine or interior plywood. However, almost any type of wood—softwoods, hardwoods, plywoods, even particleboard—can be substituted for the suggested materials. The choice of building material should be based on appearance and strength. A particular hardwood might be prettier than #2 pine, but much more expensive. Plywood might be less expensive than solid wood, but the plys will be visible on exposed edges. Unless the project is going to be painted, plywood edges must be banded with strips of solid wood, vinyl, wood veneer, or plastic molding, if appearance is an important consideration.

Strength of the wood is particularly important when building a storage project in which the shelves will be heavily loaded. As a general rule of thumb, the span between shelf supports should not exceed 32" when 3/4"-thick material is used for shelves. If thinner material is used (such as 1/2"-thick plywood), or if a weaker material is used (such as particleboard), shorten the span or add a center support. If spans wider than 32" are necessary, it's wise to dado the shelf into both the sides and back of the cabinet, or add a support cleat under the rear edge of the shelf.

Also keep in mind that plywood is dimensionally more stable than solid wood. Plywood expands and contracts less and resists warpage better than solid wood. Therefore, plywood is ideal for large panels such as cabinet backs or countertops. Wide panels made of glued-up stock tend to warp, but this tendency can be minimized by alternating the direction of growth rings (visible on the ends of each piece) on adjacent boards.

The strength and appearance of any project is also affected by the joinery and fasteners used. Common nails are great for building rough storage projects for the garage and outdoors, but a project intended to adorn a living room demands something finer. Many projects in this book suggest the use of dadoes and rabbets rather than simple butt joints fastened with nails or screws. A dado or rabbet joint increases the glue area, locks the pieces together, and generally strengthens the whole assembly.

Where mechanical fasteners are necessary, the appearance of the project is improved if the fasteners are sunk below the surface of the wood and hidden by plastic wood putty or by wooden plugs or buttons. Be sure to also use the correct size nail or screw. A nail or screw that is too large in diameter can cause the wood to split; one that is too small will eventually fail to hold. A screw or nail should be long enough so that it will penetrate at least two-thirds of the way through the substrate to which the workpiece is being fastened.

Many of the projects in *Storage Around the House* require fastening to a wall. Ideally, the fasteners should be driven into wall studs. Wall studs are usually spaced 16″ on center. However, if the size or planned location of the project does not lend itself to screwing into the studs, you must use a wall anchor specially designed for open cavity walls (or masonry walls, if that is the case).

Many of the projects call for adjustable shelves. There is a variety of hardware available for supporting adjustable shelves. Wooden dowels or manufactured shelf support pins inserted in parallel rows of equally spaced holes provide one simple method for making shelves adjustable. Pilaster standards screwed to the sides of a cabinet or recessed into grooves provide an alternative method.

Doors and drawers can either be made according to the instructions provided in the projects or bought from a cabinetmaker. Always build the cabinet, desk, or shelving unit before building or ordering doors or drawers. Then, measure and cut the doors and drawers to fit the opening, leaving 1/16″ to 1/8″ clearance between them and the adjacent frame or drawers and door.

It is also a good idea to purchase door or drawer hardware before beginning a project. That way allowances can be made for hinge thickness or drawer slides when necessary. This is particularly important when building drawers. Most drawer slides require a 1/2″ clearance between the drawer side and the case or cabinet side. But this clearance dimension varies from manufacturer to manufacturer; so, purchase the drawer slides you need before constructing the drawers.

Each project in this book has a materials list of all supplies needed for construction. A cutting list is also provided with each project. The dimensions for each part are listed as close to the finished size as is possible to describe, and each part is keyed to an exploded view and other detail drawings. Be sure to double-check all dimensions before cutting just in case we have overlooked any errors. Remember, it is always best to measure and cut to fit as you build. If adjustments are necessary, you can make them as you progress.

Before attempting to build any of the projects in this book, we suggest that you review the following tips.

- Feel free to change any of the designs to suit your taste.
- As nearly as possible the finished dimensions of each component are provided in the cutting lists.
- All cutting list dimensions are actual (not nominal) and are given in inches.
- All measurements, unless otherwise indicated, are given in the standard order: thickness × width × length.
- Measurements for rabbets, dadoes, and grooves, unless otherwise indicated, are given in this order: width × depth.
- The materials lists include all the materials (lumber, fasteners, hardware, etc.) needed to build the projects.
- Where needed, scale patterns are provided to make templates for cutting the more intricate components.
- While particular wood products (#2 pine, AB plywood, etc.) are recommended in most of the projects, feel free to use whatever type of wood you prefer. Depending on where you live, availability may well determine what type of wood you use.
- In a face frame, the term *stiles* refers to vertical members and the term *rails* refers to horizontal members.
- Assume that all wood screws are the flathead variety unless otherwise noted. When roundhead or other types of wood screws are required, they will be specified in the materials list.
- When wood glue is required, use a good grade of carpenter's glue, such as aliphatic resin (yellow). If a waterproof glue is necessary, we recommend using a resorcinol glue.
- While some projects recommend specific methods of drawer construction, feel free to use whatever method you are most comfortable with. Remember to leave a 1/8″ gap between the drawer and the frame to allow for expansion of the wood. Additional space on either side of the drawers will also be necessary if drawer guides are utilized. Purchase the guides before constructing the drawers and refer to the manufacturer's instructions for the necessary side clearance.
- In most of the projects, we do not discuss finishing in great detail, since we consider that a matter of personal taste. For help in selecting a suitable finish, consult your local paint retailer or hardware dealer.

Section 1
Family and Living Rooms

The projects you will find in this section are the answer to the books, plants, curios, TVs and stereos, computers and family heirlooms that do not have a permanent place in your present family room or living room. Whether your need is for an entertainment center, a display stand, a bookshelf, or a room divider, you will find that these projects are both beautiful and storage-smart.

Storage units that are not only functional but also look attractive are essential in the living room and/or family room. Unfinished shelves resting on cleats nailed to 2 × 4s are fine in the garage, but in the living/family room, your craftsmanship is constantly on display. Besides the fact that you must look at your handiwork every day, not to mention the poor impression a sloppily made unit will make on your guests, storage units in these more formal rooms must complement rather than detract from the decor. Storage projects fit for these rooms require precision in construction and loving care in finishing.

Many of the projects pictured in this section are made of softwood lumber, but if your budget allows, build them with hardwoods that match your present furnishings. Choose a finish that accents the wood's natural beauty.

Finished edges are a must on projects built for the family and living rooms. On solid wood projects, rout a decorative edge. On panel projects, finish exposed edges with solid wood edge bands or plastic T-moldings. Careful attention to such details will ensure your success in creating "smart storage" that looks smart as well.

FAMILY ROOM DESK AND TV CABINET WITH BOOKCASE

These two wall units will brighten up any family room. The units pictured here were designed as built-ins, but the following plans can be easily adapted to accommodate freestanding units.

Desk

The first step in constructing the desk is to build four frames (A, B). These are the sides of what will be the two cabinets, one on each side of the center opening. Use 1 × 4 pine and cut the vertical pieces 29-1/4" long and the horizontal pieces 19-3/4" long. Connect the joints together with dowels.

Cut the side panels (P) to size. Cut a 3/4"-wide × 3-1/2"-high notch in the upper rear corner of the two center panels. Position the sides flush with the front of the frames. Secure the sides to the frames with wood glue and No. 6 × 1-1/2" wood screws.

Cut ten cleats (C) for use in mounting drawer guides. Position three cleats horizontally inside each frame of the three-drawer cabinet, and two inside each frame of the two-drawer cabinet. On the three-drawer cabinet frames, center the

cleats 6-3/8", 13-5/8", and 20-7/8" from the floor. On the two-drawer cabinet frames, center the cleats 8-3/16" and 19-1/16" from the floor. Fasten the cleats to the frames using wood glue and No. 6 × 1-1/2" wood screws.

Cut a 1 × 4 to a length of 65" for the stretcher (D) that runs across the upper rear of the desk. Fit the stretcher into the notches on the two inner cabinet panels with the outside faces of the panels positioned 28" apart and each 18-1/2" from one end of the stretcher. Fasten the stretcher to the two inner panel-frame units using wood glue and No. 6 × 1-1/2" wood screws.

Now place the two outer panel-frame units at the ends of the stretcher. Holding the upper edge of the stretcher flush with the upper edges of the frames and the ends of the stretcher tight against the panels, fasten the stretcher to the frames using wood glue and screws as before. Each cabinet should now be 19-1/4" in overall width and there should be a 28" space between the two inner panels.

Cut six pieces of 1 × 2, each to a 17-3/4" length, for the cabinet rear rails (E). Fit three rails between the

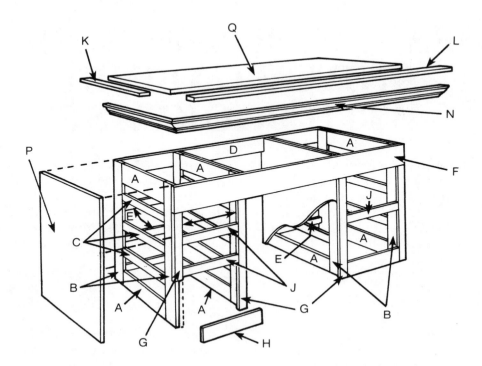

panels at the rear of each cabinet unit. Measuring up from the floor, center the rails on the three-drawer cabinet at 6-3/8", 13-5/8", and 20-7/8"; center the rails on the two-drawer cabinet at 2-7/8", 8-3/16", and 19-1/16". Fasten the rails to the backs of the frames using wood glue and screws as before.

Cut the face frame rails (F, H) and stiles (G) to length. Arrange the pieces so that the drawer openings on the three-drawer cabinet will be 16-1/4" wide and 5-3/4" high. Make the openings on the two-drawer cabinet the same width, but 9-3/8" high. Buy or build drawers that are sized to fit these openings as well as the space between the drawer guide cleats, plus the space needed for the drawer guides themselves.

Attach the face frame to the cabinets using wood glue and 4d finishing nails. Nail into the frame rather than the plywood.

Strengthen the cabinet by installing glue blocks between the face frame and interior frame and between the rear rails and the frame. Be careful to place the blocks where they will not interfere with the operation of the drawers.

Cut the desktop and desktop edge bands to size. Miter one end of each band 45 degrees and dry fit them to the desktop (front and left side edges) to make sure that the miters close up properly. Then, using

MATERIALS LIST (DESK)
3/4" × 4' × 8' sanded plywood (2-1/2 sheets)
1 × 6 × 6' pine
1 × 4 × 8' pine (6)
1 × 2 × 9' pine (5)
4" crown molding (9')
L-brackets (4)
3/8"-dia. dowel pins
No. 8 × 3" wood screws
No. 6 × 1-1/2" wood screws
8d finishing nails
4d finishing nails
Wood putty

CUTTING LIST (DESK)		
KEY	**PIECES**	**SIZE/DESCRIPTION**
A	8	3/4 × 3-1/2 × 19-3/4 cabinet frame rails
B	8	3/4 × 3-1/2 × 29-1/4 cabinet frame stiles
C	10	3/4 × 1-1/2 × 19-3/4 cleats
D	1	3/4 × 3-1/2 × 65 stretcher
E	6	3/4 × 1-1/2 × 17-3/4 cabinet rear rails

CUTTING LIST (continued)		
KEY	**PIECES**	**SIZE/DESCRIPTION**
F	1	3/4 × 5-1/2 × 66-1/2 top face frame rail
G	4	3/4 × 1-1/2 × 20-1/4 face frame stiles
H	2	3/4 × 3-1/2 × 16-1/4 bottom face frame rails
J	3	3/4 × 1-1/2 × 16-1/4 center face frame rails
K	1	3/4 × 1-1/2 × 31-1/4 side desktop edge
L	1	3/4 × 1-1/2 × 69-1/2 front desktop edge
M	1	3-1/2 × 30-3/4 desktop trim (crown molding)
N	1	3-1/2 × 69 desktop trim (crown molding)
P	4	3/4 × 27-1/2 × 29-1/4 cabinet sides (plywood)
Q	1	3/4 × 29-3/4 × 68 desktop (plywood)

wood glue and 4d finishing nails, fasten the edge bands to the tabletop.

Place the cabinet in position against the walls. Fasten it to the wall by driving No. 8 × 3" flathead wood screws through the rear stretcher into wall studs.

Place the desktop on the cabinet and align it with the walls. Secure it to the cabinet using four L-brackets placed inside the kneehole space to avoid interfering with drawer operation.

Cut a piece of 4" crown molding to fit underneath the left end of the desktop. Hold the left end of the molding snug against the wall while marking the other end where it intersects the front edge of the cabinet and the mitered front edge of the desktop. Cut a second-piece of molding to fit beneath the front of the desktop, this time holding the right end against the wall and marking the left end. Miter the ends of the two pieces so that they form a clean joint. Keep in mind that this is not a simple miter joint and the pieces must be cut while held at the angle they will take when installed. After mitering, you may want to back off the rear of the joint slightly with a chisel or block plane to assure a tight fit. Fasten the molding to the desktop and cabinet unit using finishing nails of appropriate lengths.

Set all exposed nail heads and fill with wood putty. The desk unit is now ready to be sanded and finished. The unit pictured was left unstained and finished with polyurethane varnish.

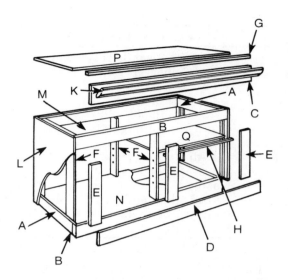

TV Cabinet

Begin construction of the TV cabinet by building two frames of butt jointed 2 × 4s (A, B) measuring 62″ wide by 26″ deep. Use 12d common nails to fasten the pieces together.

Cut the side panels (L), back panel (M), and bottom (N) from 3/4″ plywood. Using No. 8 × 1-1/2″ wood screws, screw and glue the bottom panel to the top of the base frame.

Set the frames up and space them apart so that the back panel neatly covers them. Fasten the back panel in place; the position and fasten the side panels to the frames so that they cover the ends of both the frames and the back panel.

Because this cabinet will be holding the weight of a television, it must be reinforced. Cut six stretchers (F) from 1 × 4s. Drill 1/4″ holes spaced 1″ apart centered in the spacers for shelf supports. Toenail

the stretchers into place with 8d finishing nails, two along each side and one each at the front and back at the center of the frame.

Slide the assembly into place and attach it to the wall by driving No. 14 × 4″ roundhead wood screws through the upper 2 × 4 frame and into the wall studs.

The front of the cabinet is covered by a framework of face boards (C, D, E). Cut the face boards to length and attach them together with dowels. Glue and nail the face frame to the cabinet with 4d finishing nails. Put a glue block in each corner to strengthen the cabinet. The framework leaves two door openings 26-1/2″ by 20-1/4″. Make or purchase doors to fit.

Cut the cabinet top (P) from 3/4″ plywood. Nail the edge strip (G) to the plywood with 8d finishing nails.

MATERIALS LIST (TV CABINET)
2 × 4 × 8' (4)
1 × 10 × 2'
1 × 6 × 6'
1 × 4 × 6' (4)
1 × 2 × 6' (2)
3/4" × 4' × 8' sanded plywood (3-1/2 sheets)
1/4"-dia. dowels
Lazy Susan capable of holding the weight of your TV
No. 14 × 4" roundhead wood screws
No. 8 × 1-1/2" wood screws
12d finishing nails
8d finishing nails
8d common nails
4d finishing nails
L-brackets (4)
4" crown molding (70")
Shelf supports
Wood glue

CUTTING LIST (TV CABINET)		
KEY	**PIECES**	**SIZE/DESCRIPTION**
A	4	1-1/2 × 3-1/2 × 23 frame
B	4	1-1/2 × 3-1/2 × 62 frame
C	1	3/4 × 5-1/2 × 63-1/2 top face frame rail
D	1	3/4 × 3-1/2 × 63-1/2 bottom face frame rail
E	3	3/4 × 3-1/2 × 20-1/4 face frame stiles
F	6	3/4 × 3-1/2 × 21-1/2 stretchers
G	1	3/4 × 1-1/2 × 63-1/2 top edge
H	2	3/4 × 1-1/2 × 30 shelf edges
J	1	3/4 × 9-1/4 × 15 lazy Susan top
K	1	3-1/2 × 63-1/2 cabinet trim (crown molding)
L	2	3/4 × 29-1/4 × 26-3/4 cabinet side panels (plywood)
M	1	3/4 × 29-1/4 × 62 cabinet back panel (plywood)
N	1	3/4 × 26 × 62 cabinet bottom (plywood)
P	1	3/4 × 31-1/2 × 63-1/2 cabinet top (plywood)
Q	2	3/4 × 24-1/2 × 30 cabinet shelves (plywood)

Secure the top to the cabinet top frame with four L-brackets.

Cut a length of 4" crown molding (K) to fit from wall to wall in the built-in. If the sides of your cabinet will be exposed, additional molding will be necessary. Nail the molding to the front of the desk with finishing nails. Cut two shelves (Q) for the cabinet and edge each one with 1 × 2 pine (H). Install the shelves on shelf supports with 1/4"-diameter pins.

Purchase lazy Susan hardware capable of holding the weight of your television. The base of the TV stand can be made from 3/4" plywood or from a 1 × 10 pine board. Cut the base large enough to support the TV and attach it to the lazy Susan. Secure the lazy Susan to the top of the cabinet.

Set all nails, fill the nail holes with wood putty, and sand the unit to prepare it for finishing.

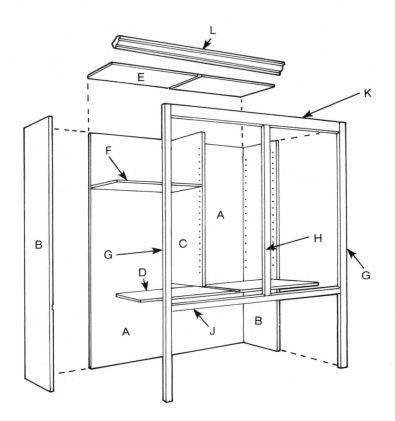

Bookcase

This easy-to-build bookcase can sit on top of the TV cabinet or desk. The bookcase pictured is 72" high. The height of your project will vary according to ceiling height.

Cut the back (A), sides (B), divider (C), fixed shelf (D), top (E), and adjustable shelves (F), from 3/4" birch veneer plywood. Cover edges that will be exposed with iron-on birch edge banding.

Rout 3/4"-wide and 3/8"-deep dadoes across the two side panels and the two back panels, 24-1/2" from the bottom edge of each, to re-

MATERIALS LIST (BOOKCASE)
3/4" × 4' × 8' birch-veneer plywood (3)
1 × 6 × 6' select pine
1 × 2 × 6' select pine (2)
1 × 2 × 9' select pine
4" crown molding (64")
3/8"-dia. dowel pins
No. 10 × 2" wood screws
No. 6 × 1-1/2" wood screws
4d finishing nails
Wood putty
Wood glue

ceive the ends and rear edge of the fixed shelf. Then rout dadoes of the same dimensions across the center of both the fixed shelf and the top

(D, E) to receive the ends of the divider. Finally, rout a 3/8″ × 3/8″ rabbet along the inside edge of each back panel, from the top down to the dado, to make room for the rear edge of the divider.

Drill 1/4″ holes in the sides for the shelf supports. The depth of the hole will vary depending on the length of the support pin. Space the holes 2″ apart and 1-1/2″ from the edges.

Before gluing, dry assemble the unit to check that everything fits properly, then spread a thin layer of wood glue inside each dado and rabbet. Spread another thin layer of glue along each panel edge that is to be fastened. Reassemble the unit, checking to make sure everything is square, and clamp in place while inserting No. 6 × 1-1/2″ wood screws. Run screws through the side panels and top into the edges of the back and through the backs of all the dadoes into the various panel ends. Countersink all screws to ensure smooth surfaces. Once the glue has dried, remove all clamps.

Set the bookcase on the desktop and back against the wall. Check to see if the wall is plumb. If not, use shims as necessary to keep the unit plumb while fastening it to the wall studs using No. 10 × 2″ wood screws. Insert the screws in counterbored holes so you can cover their heads with plugs or wood putty.

CUTTING LIST (BOOKCASE)		
KEY	**PIECES**	**SIZE/DESCRIPTION**
A	2	3/4 × 31 × 72 back (plywood)
B	2	3/4 × 16-3/4 × 72 sides (plywood)
C	1	3/4 × 16-3/8 × 47-1/2 divider (plywood)
D	1	3/4 × 16-3/8 × 62-3/4 fixed shelf (plywood)
E	1	3/4 × 16-3/4 × 63-1/2 top (plywood)
F	3	3/4 × 15-7/8 × 30-1/2 adjustable shelves (plywood)
G	2	3/4 × 1-1/2 × 67-1/2 face frame stiles
H	1	3/4 × 1-1/2 × 41 center face frame stile
J	1	3/4 × 1-1/2 × 60-1/2 bottom face frame rail
K	1	3/4 × 5-1/2 × 63-1/2 top face frame rail
L	1	3-1/2 × 63-1/2 crown molding

Assemble the face pieces (G, H, J, K) into the frame pattern shown in the drawing, using wood glue and dowels to secure all joints. Fasten the finished face frame to the bookcase unit using wood glue and 4d finishing nails. Set all the nails and putty the holes.

Finish the bookcase by adding decorative crown molding across the top. Sand and finish as desired.

ROOM DIVIDER SHELVES

This shelving system can be as large or small as you want it. Because it is built in separate units and hinged together, it makes a terrific room divider and can fit odd-shaped walls. It makes a great bookshelf or decorative unit, and can be made in no time.

Careful design can contribute a good deal to the shelves' usefulness. The basic unit is quite simple to assemble. Keep in mind that some of the shelves are permanently placed and that the width of each unit is limited by the weight you expect to place on it.

For basics, consider 32" about the maximum shelf length and make each shelf from 1 × 10 pine lumber. The height of the overall unit should be limited to 9' or under for stability.

These plans are for construction of one 81"-high unit, with six shelves, but you can build as many as your space requires and modify the design as needed, cutting the uprights to length.

Start by assembling the uprights. Butt a 1 × 3 side upright (A) to the face of a 1 × 4 front upright (B) in an L shape and join the boards using 6d finishing nails and glue. You will need four L-shaped uprights for each unit in the divider.

Once the four uprights are assembled, you must decide whether to have all the shelves (C) fixed in place or to have some of them adjustable. For adjustable shelves, consider the overall stability of the unit. The top and bottom shelves, along with one intermediate shelf, must always be permanently mounted.

To install permanent shelves, first decide the heights necessary to hold the things to be stored. Mark those heights on all four uprights, and mark each leg of each upright for two evenly spaced screw holes centered in the shelves. Drill pilot holes at each mark and counterbore them to accept 3/8" plugs.

Begin assembly by placing the bottom end of an upright on a shelf edge and the other end on a chair or other prop of about the same height. Place the shelf accurately on the marks and drilled pilot holes. Apply a bit of wood glue to the shelf corner, and drive in all four screws.

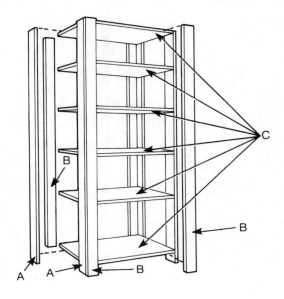

MATERIALS LIST

1 × 10 × 8' (2)
1 × 4 × 8' (4)
1 × 3 × 8' (4)
No. 8 × 1-3/4" wood screws
6d finishing nails
3-1/2" or 4" brass hinges (2)
Shelf supports (optional) (24)
Wood putty
Wood glue

CUTTING LIST

KEY	PIECES	SIZE/DESCRIPTION
A	4	3/4 × 2-1/2 × 81 side uprights
B	4	3/4 × 3-1/2 × 81 front uprights
C	6	3/4 × 9-1/4 × 31-3/4 shelves

Repeat the process for the opposite corner of the same (bottom) shelf. Move on to the opposite ends of the uprights and install the top shelf, repeating the steps.

Gently turn the unit over and install the final two uprights to the top and bottom shelves the same way. Then, install intermediate shelves. The unit is complete, except for finishing.

To make the intermediate shelves adjustable, simply use a piece of 1/4" pegboard as a pattern, and drill 1/4"-diameter 7/16"-deep holes in each upright, making sure they are located directly opposite

one another. Use plug-in shelf supports, two at each corner, to hold the adjustable shelves. Cut the adjustable shelves about 1/2" shorter and narrower than the permanent ones. To hinge two or more dividers together, use a pair of brass or brass finished hinges per pair of uprights. Hinges should be the removable pin type, from 3-1/2" to 4" long. They can be surface mounted or mortised into the upright. All finishing should be done before the hinges are added. Set and putty over set nail heads and plug counterbored screw holes. Sand and paint or finish as desired.

ENTERTAINMENT
CENTER

Here is a project for all types of media lovers. Are you a bookworm? This center makes a spacious bookcase. Do you like musical recordings? Organize your components and speakers on this stereo stand and store records, tapes, and compact discs in the cabinet. Is video your hobby? You can transform this project into a TV stand and VCR rack. There is plenty of room for everything on these easy-to-build shelving and cabinet modules.

The entertainment center pictured was built with standard redwood lumber boards. You can substitute pine boards, if you prefer. The shelves sit in stopped dadoes, but if your equipment is limited, the shelves can be screwed in place.

Each module is supported by four 1 × 6 uprights (A). Cut these to

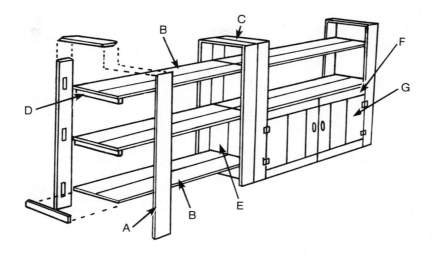

MATERIALS LIST
1 × 8 × 8'
1 × 8 × 10' (4)
1 × 4 × 8' (3)
1 × 6 × 8' (4)
1 × 6 × 6' (2)
No. 8 × 1-1/2" wood screws
No. 8 × 1-1/4" wood screws
3d finishing nails
1-1/2" butterfly hinges (4)
1/4"-dia. × 1-1/2" dowel pins (20)
Latches (2)
Cabinet door handles (2)
Wood plugs
Wood glue

CUTTING LIST		
KEY	**PIECES**	**SIZE/DESCRIPTION**
A	8	3/4 × 5-1/2 × 47-7/8 uprights
B	12	3/4 × 7-1/4 × 37-1/4 shelves
C	4	3/4 × 5-1/2 × 16 top rails
D	12	3/4 × 3-1/2 × 15 shelf supports
E	4	3/4 × 7-1/4 × 23-5/8 cabinet side panels
F	4	3/4 × 3-1/2 × 13 cabinet door rails
G	2	3/4 × 13 × 16-3/8 cabinet door panels

length and miter the top ends 45 degrees to the inside.

Cut mortises in the inside face of each upright to accept the shelf supports (D). The mortises should be 3/4" wide, 3-1/2" long, and 1/4" deep to accept the ends of the shelf supports. Space the mortises 1/4" from the outer edge of each upright. Locate the tops of the mortises 5-1/4", 23-5/8", and 41-1/4" from the bottom edges of the uprights.

Place a bead of glue on the ends of the shelf supports and place them

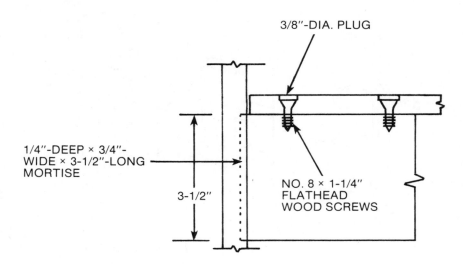

3/8"-DIA. PLUG

1/4"-DEEP × 3/4"-WIDE × 3-1/2"-LONG MORTISE

3-1/2"

NO. 8 × 1-1/4" FLATHEAD WOOD SCREWS

SHELF SUPPORT DETAIL SHELF UNIT

in the mortises. Carefully square the subasembly and clamp the unit together.

After the glue has dried, stand the uprights up, and lay the shelf boards (B) on the shelf supports. Butt the inside edges of the shelf boards together and align the ends of the shelves with the outer edges of the uprights.

Drill and counterbore pilot holes through the shelves and into each shelf support. Screw the shelves to the supports with No. 8 × 1-1/2" flathead wood screws. Fill all counterbored holes with wood plugs.

NOTE: If you want to be able to disassemble the unit, fill holes with buttons rather than plugs, and do not use glue.

Measure across the tops of the uprights on each end and cut the 1 × 6 top rails (C) to fit. Miter each end 45 degrees. Fasten the rails to the uprights with glue and 3d finishing nails. (Predrill to avoid splitting the tops.)

To construct the cabinet module, make the following adjustments to the above procedure. Lay out and cut the mortises for the middle and bottom shelves 3/4" from the outside edge of the uprights rather than the 1/4" setback given for the top shelf. This will allow the 1 × 8s that make up the cabinet sides (E) to be installed flush with the outside edge of the uprights. Cut the bottom shelf 1 × 8 boards 1-1/2" shorter than the other shelves to provide clearance for the cabinet sides. This shelf will be positioned flush with the outer edges of the shelf supports.

Cut the 1 × 8 side boards to length. Butt the top ends of the 1 × 8s under the middle shelf. Drill and counterbore pilot holes through the sides and into the shelf supports. Glue and screw the sides to the supports with No. 8 × 1-1/4" flathead wood screws.

The doors are made to fit flush with the front edges of the uprights and the top of the middle shelf. To make the door panels, first crosscut 1 × 6 stock to four pieces 16-3/8"

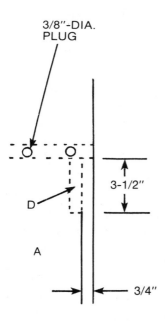

3/8"-DIA.
PLUG

3-1/2"

D

A

3/4"

SHELF SUPPORT DETAIL CABINET UNIT

long and 1 × 4 stock to two pieces 16-3/8" long. Edge glue together two of the 1 × 6 pieces and one of the 1 × 4 pieces for each panel. Trim the panels to 13" wide by ripping stock from the 1 × 4 side. Then, band the top and bottom of the panels with 1 × 4 cut to fit the width of the panels.

NOTE: *This type of door must be made with a dimensionally stable wood such as redwood. Gluing the edge grain of the top and bottom rails to the end grains of the glued-up panels is usually not recommended for wood species that expand and contract excessively. The resulting stresses might warp the door or break the joint between rail and panel. An alternative would be to make the doors from glued-up boards without the top and bottom rail.*

Use flush mount cabinet hinges and secure the doors to the uprights. Sand and finish the storage modules. Install latching mechanisms of your choice. If an additional shelf is desired in the cabinet, screw cleats to the cabinet sides and cut two 1 × 6s to fit.

LIBRARY CABINET

Here is a stately combination cabinet and bookcase that would be perfect in an office, library, or sitting room. It is made of plywood with simple-to-make doweled butt joints, as well as dado and rabbet joints. You will enjoy displaying your books, curios, and other important items in and on the library cabinet. The bookcase pictured here has an angled shelf for holding magazines or possibly a dictionary or atlas. The library cabinet and the computer desk shown on page 27 make a beautiful matched set of storage units.

Cabinet

Begin construction of the library cabinet by cutting the top and bottom frame members (A, B, C, D) to size. Both frames are 33″ wide, but the bottom frame is 2-3/4″ shallower than the top frame to allow for a kick plate and toe space. Butt the ends of the stretchers against the inside faces of the rails flush with the outside edges. Fasten the frame members together with glue and 10d common nails.

Next, cut the cabinet bottom (G) to size. Using glue and 6d finishing nails, attach the bottom to the base frame with the panel flush with the back and side edges of the frame.

Cut the kick plate (J) to size next. Glue and nail it to the front of the base frame flush with the bottom and outside edges of the frame. Use 6d finishing nails.

Cut the cabinet back (F) to size next and glue and nail it (use 6d finishing nails) to the back side of the base frame. The sides of the panel should be flush with the sides of the frame.

Cut the cabinet sides (E) to size. These sides are 26″ wide and 27″ high. Cut a 2″-wide × 3-1/2″-high notch in the front bottom corner of both sides. Position the sides flush with the back edge of the back panel and the bottom edge of the bottom frame. Drill and counterbore pilot holes through the sides into the back and base. Glue and screw the side panels to the subassembly, using No.8×1-1/2″flathead wood screws.Fill the holes with wood putty.

Place the subassembly on its back and position the top frame flush with the top edge of the side and back panels. Drill and counter-sink pilot holes through the sides, and glue and screw the sides to the frame (use No. 8 × 1-1/2″ flathead screws). Turn the unit on its face and screw the back to the frame as well.

Next, cut shelf cleats (K) from scraps or cutoffs for the cabinet shelf. Position the cleats 10-3/4″ from the bottom. Drill and counter-bore pilot holes; then, glue and screw the cleats to the sides of the cabinet, using No. 6 × 1-1/4″ flat-head wood screws. Fill the holes with wood putty.

Cut the shelf (H) to size. Rip the 1/4″-wide shelf edge band (L) from a scrap of 3/4″-wide pine board. Glue and nail the band to the front edge of the shelf, using 1/2″ brads. Place the shelf on the cleats. Secure it to the cleats with 3d finishing nails.

Cut the cabinet face frame rails (M, P) and stiles (N) to length next. Join the ends of the rails to the sides of the stiles with glue and two 3/8″-diameter dowel pins per joint.

Position the face frame flush with the top and outside edges of the side panels. Glue and nail the frame to the sides and bottom with 4d finishing nails. Set the nails and fill the holes with wood putty.

Rip four 3/4″-wide × 3/4″-thick triangular glue blocks to fit between the cabinet top and the shelf and between the shelf and the cabinet bottom. Glue the blocks to the inside front corners to strengthen the face frame-to-cabinet joint.

Cut the cabinet top (Q) to size. Rip 1/4″-wide edge bands (R, S) from 3/4″-thick pine, crosscut them to length, and glue and nail the bands to the sides and front of the top. Install the side bands first, then lap them with the front band.

Position the top of the cabinet flush with the back edge and with a 1/2″ overhang on both sides. Fasten the top to the inside of the side panels with four L-brackets.

Cut the crown molding (EE) to length. Cut a 45-degree compound miter on both ends of the molding. Center the molding under the front of the overhanging cabinet top an equal distance from both sides of the top. Nail it to the face frame and top with 3d finishing nails. Carefully measure the open ends of the mold-ings and cut two pieces of molding (returns) to fit. Carefully glue and

MATERIALS LIST

2 × 4 × 10' #2 pine (2)
1 × 6 × 5' select pine
1 × 4 × 8' select pine (2)
1 × 3 × 8' select pine (3)
1 × 2 × 3' select pine
3/4" × 4' × 8' AB interior plywood
  (4 sheets)
4" crown molding (6')
10d common nails
6d finishing nails
4d finishing nails
3d finishing nails
2d finishing nails
1" brads
1/2" brads
No. 8 × 1-1/2" flathead wood screws
No. 6 × 1-1/2" flathead wood screws
No. 6 × 1-1/4" flathead wood screws
3/8"-dia. wood plugs
3/8"-dia. dowel pins
L-brackets (4)
4" metal straps (2)
Hinges for 3/8" offset doors (4)
Magnetic latches (2)
Door pulls (2)
Wood putty
Wood glue

CUTTING LIST

KEY	PIECES	SIZE/DESCRIPTION
A	2	1-1/2 × 3-1/2 × 19-1/2 base frame stretchers
B	2	1-1/2 × 3-1/2 × 33 base frame rails
C	2	1-1/2 × 3-1/2 × 22-1/4 top frame stretchers
D	2	1-1/2 × 3-1/2 × 33 top frame rails
E	2	3/4 × 26 × 27 cabinet sides (plywood)

CUTTING LIST (continued)

KEY	PIECES	SIZE/DESCRIPTION
F	1	3/4 × 27 × 33 cabinet back (plywood)
G	1	3/4 × 25-1/4 × 33 cabinet bottom (plywood)
H	1	3/4 × 24-7/8 × 32-7/8 cabinet shelf (plywood)
J	1	3/4 × 3-1/2 × 33 kick plate (plywood)
K	2	3/4 × 3/4 × 24 shelf cleats
L	1	1/4 × 3/4 × 32-7/8 shelf edge band
M	1	3/4 × 5-1/2 × 27-1/2 top rail
N	2	3/4 × 3-1/2 × 26-1/4 stiles
P	1	3/4 × 3-1/2 × 27-1/2 bottom rail
Q	1	3/4 × 29-1/2 × 35 cabinet top (plywood)
R	1	1/4 × 3/4 × 35-1/2 front edge band
S	2	1/4 × 3/4 × 29-1/2 side edge bands
T	2	3/4 × 11-1/2 × 75 bookcase sides (plywood)
U	1	3/4 × 32 × 75 bookcase back (plywood)
V	1	3/4 × 15 × 33 bookcase top (plywood)
W	1	1/4 × 3/4 × 33-1/2 front edge band
X	2	1/4 × 3/4 × 15 side edge bands
Y	2	3/4 × 10-1/2 × 32 shelves (plywood)

CUTTING LIST (continued)		
KEY	**PIECES**	**SIZE/DESCRIPTION**
Z	1	3/4 × 10-1/2 × 32 magazine shelf (plywood)
AA	2	1/4 × 3/4 × 32 shelf edge bands
BB	1	3/4 × 1-1/2 × 31-1/2 magazine shelf edge band
CC	1	3/4 × 5-1/2 × 28 face frame rail
DD	2	3/4 × 2-1/2 × 75 face frame stiles
EE	1	3-1/2 × 33 crown molding
FF	4	3/4 × 2 × 10-13/16 door frame rails
GG	4	3/4 × 2 × 14-3/4 door frame stiles
HH	2	3/4 × 11-5/16 × 11-1/4 door panels
JJ	1	3-1/2 × 34-1/2 crown molding

nail them in place with 1″ brads. (Predrill to avoid splitting the returns.)

The cabinet is complete now except for the doors. You can make raised panel doors (as shown in the photograph) or any other type of door you desire. The raised panel doors have a 3/8″ offset that overlaps the frame 1/8″. To make a raised-panel door, rip the rails (FF) and stiles (GG) to width from 1 × 3 boards. Machine 3/16″-wide × 3/8″-deep grooves in the center of the inside edge of each frame piece. Drill 3/8″-diameter × 1″-deep holes in the ends of the rails and in the inside edges of the stiles for dowel pins.

To make the door panels (HH), crosscut a 1 × 4 × 8′ board into eight pieces 11-3/4″ long. Shape glue joints in the edges and glue four of the boards together for each of the panels. Trim the panels to size. Cut raised bevels in the panels with a table saw or a raised panel shaper bit and a shaper.

Assemble the frames around the panels and secure the frame corners with glue and 3/8″-diameter dowel pins. Do not glue the panel edges to the frames.

Set all visible nails and fill the nail holes with plastic wood putty. Sand the cabinet and the doors and finish as desired.

Attach the doors to the frames with two 3/8″ offset hinges per door. Install door pulls and magnetic latches.

Bookcase

To make the shelving unit, first cut the sides (T), back (U), top (V), and shelves (Y, Z) to size. Note that parallel 30-degree bevels must be cut on the front and back edges of the magazine shelf because of its angle of installation, and that its edge banding is different from the rest. If you do not want to include an angled shelf in the case, leave the edges of all three shelves square and cut all the edge banding the same.

Machine a 3/4″-wide × 1/4″-deep rabbet in the inside back edges of the sides. The back panel will fit in this rabbet.

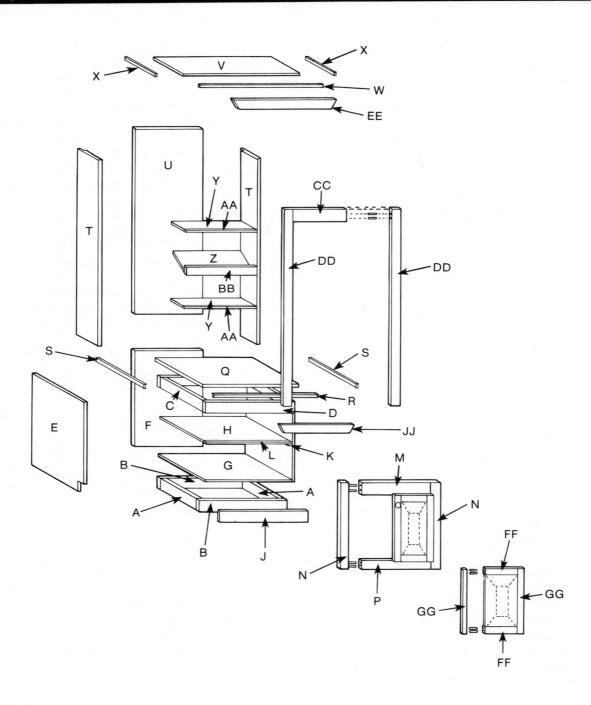

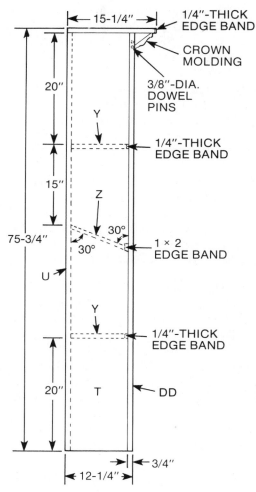

15-1/4"

1/4"-THICK EDGE BAND

CROWN MOLDING

3/8"-DIA. DOWEL PINS

20"

Y

1/4"-THICK EDGE BAND

15"

Z

30°

30°

1 × 2 EDGE BAND

75-3/4"

U

Y

1/4"-THICK EDGE BAND

20"

T

DD

3/4"

12-1/4"

SIDE VIEW OF SHELF

Machine two 3/4"-wide dadoes, each 1/4" deep, in each side panel. Space the lower dadoes 20" from the bottom and the upper dadoes 20" from the top.

Rout a third dado in each side panel as shown for the angled mag-azine shelf (Z). Measure down 35" from the top of the panel along the front edge of the rabbet. From that point, draw a line angled at 30 degrees across the side panel. Rout the 3/4"-wide × 1/4"-deep dado below this line.

Cut the thin shelf edge bands (AA) to size and fasten them to the front edges of the top and bottom shelves (Y) using glue and 1/2" brads. Cut the 1 × 2 edge band (BB) to length and rip a 30-degree bevel on its lower edge. Center and fasten it to the front edge of the magazine shelf using glue and 3d finishing nails. To create the needed lip for holding books and magazines, make sure the beveled edge of the banding is flush with the bottom face of the shelf.

Spread glue in the side panel rabbets and dadoes and on the shelf and back panel edges that will fit into them. Fit the three shelves into place. Lightly clamp the side panels around them across the front while installing the back panel. Use clamps to pull the sides up snug against the ends of the shelves and edges of the back panel.

Check to make sure everything is square and that the backs of the shelves are flush against the back panel, then drive No. 6 × 1-1/4" wood screws through the back panel into the edges of the sides. Drive the screws in straight and countersink them to make them flush with the back of the unit. Leave clamps on the case while the glue dries.

Rip the top edge bands (W, X) to size from a 3/4″-thick board. Fasten the edge bands to the sides and front of the top panel with wood glue and 2d finishing nails.

Position the top panel on the bookcase so that the back edge of the top is flush with the back edge of the case and the top overhangs the case the same amount on both sides. Drill and countersink pilot holes for No. 6 × 1-1/2″ flathead wood screws. Glue and screw the top to the sides and back.

Cut the face frame stiles (DD) to length. Butt the stiles against the underside of the top panel and align them flush with the outside edges of the side panels. Clamp the stiles in position and drill and counterbore holes for No. 6 × 1-1/2″ flathead wood screws and 3/8″-diameter wooden plugs.

Before removing the stiles from the case, measure the distance between the stiles and cut the top rail (CC) to fit.

Join the ends of the rail to the edges of the sides of the stiles with glue and two 3/8″-diameter dowel pins per joint. Clamp the frame together until the glue dries.

Reposition the frame on the case and glue and screw the stiles to the side panels. Fill the holes with 3/8″-diameter wood plugs.

Cut the crown molding (EE) to length. Cut a 45-degree compound miter on both ends of the molding. Position the molding under the overhanging case top an equal distance from both sides of the top. Nail it to the face frame and top with 3d finishing nails. Carefully measure the open ends of the molding and cut two pieces of molding return to fit. Carefully glue and nail the molding in place with 1″ brads. (Predrill to avoid splitting the returns.)

At this point, fill all nail holes with wood putty and sand and finish the bookcase to match the cabinet.

Set the bookcase on the cabinet. Center the two units across their width and make their back edges flush. Secure the case to the cabinet with two 4″-long metal straps screwed to the backs of the cabinet and case.

COMPUTER DESK WITH SHELVES

Bring your imagination to life with these two library wall units. Both make attractive storage units for books, knickknacks, and magazines. One is specially designed for your personal computer, complete with a paper slot cut in the desktop so you can store computer paper behind closed doors and out of sight.

The writing surface of the computer desk is 29" above the floor. A cabinet is built to the right of the kneehole area. Inside the cabinet is a shelf that holds a box of fanfold computer paper. A slot cut along the right rear edge of the desk allows the computer paper to feed up through the desktop and into the computer printer.

Begin the project by removing any shoe moldings found along the wall where the desk will be placed. Retain these moldings for reuse after the built-in unit is complete.

Build an 18-1/2"-wide and 20-1/4"-deep rectangular frame for the cabinet by butting and nailing together pieces of 2 × 4 (A, B). This frame is sized to allow for a 2"-deep kick space at the front of the cabinet.

Cut the cabinet bottom (P) and the cabinet and desk side panels (Q) from 3/4" plywood.

Position the bottom panel so its front edge extends 2" beyond the frame while its other three edges are flush with the frame. Fasten the panel to the frame using 6d common nails.

Cut 2" × 3-1/2" notches in the lower front edges of the three side panels so that when installed they will maintain the kick space between the frame and bottom panel. Also cut a 3/4″ × 3-1/2″ notch in the upper front corner of the inside cabinet panel to make room for the 1 × 4 front frame rail (F).

Cut the four 1 × 4 frame spanners (C), which are installed across the upper sections of the three side panels to add rigidity to

MATERIALS LIST

3/4″ × 4′ × 8′ AA interior plywood (4)
1/4″ × 4′ × 8′ AC interior plywood
2 × 4 × 8′ #2 common pine
1 × 4 × 8′ #2 common pine (2)
1 × 6 × 4′ select pine
1 × 4 × 6′ select pine
1 × 3 × 8′ select pine (3)
1 × 2 × 10′ select pine
1 × 2 × 8′ select pine (2)
3/8″-dia. dowel pins
No. 10 × 2″ wood screws
No. 6 × 1-1/2″ wood screws
No. 6 × 1-1/4″ wood screws
No. 4 × 3/4″ wood screws
10d common nails
6d common nails
4d finishing nails
3d finishing nails
2d finishing nails
4″ crown molding (8′)
L-brackets (6)
Vinyl wood grain veneer tape
2″ hinges (4)
Magnetic latches (2)
Cabinet doorknobs (2)
1/8″ double strength glass,
    2 panes cut to fit
Plastic wood putty
Wood glue

CUTTING LIST

KEY	PIECES	SIZE/DESCRIPTION
A	2	1-1/2 × 3-1/2 × 17-1/4 cabinet frame pieces
B	2	1-1/2 × 3-1/2 × 18-1/2 cabinet frame pieces
C	4	3/4 × 3-1/2 × 21-1/2 frame spanners
D	1	3/4 × 3-1/2 × 18-1/2 cabinet frame rail
E	1	3/4 × 3-1/2 × 19-1/4 kneehole frame rail
F	1	3/4 × 3-1/2 × 38-1/2 front frame rail
G	1	3/4 × 3-1/2 × 40 top face frame rail
H	2	3/4 × 1-1/2 × 22 cabinet face frame stiles
J	1	3/4 × 1-1/2 × 17 face frame bottom rail
K	1	3/4 × 1-1/2 × 24-3/4 desk face frame stile
L	2	3/4 × 11/16 × 23 shelf cleats
M	1	3-1/2 × 40 desk trim (crown molding)
N	1	3/4 × 3-1/2 × 20 kick plate
P	1	3/4 × 18-1/2 × 22-1/4 cabinet bottom (plywood)
Q	3	3/4 × 23 × 28-1/4 cabinet and desk side panels (plywood)
R	1	3/4 × 26-3/4 × 41 desk-top (plywood)
S	1	3/4 × 18-1/2 × 22-15/16 shelf (plywood)
T	2	3/4 × 11-1/2 × 75 shelf unit sides (plywood)

CUTTING LIST (continued)		
KEY	**PIECES**	**SIZE/DESCRIPTION**
U	1	3/4 × 15-1/4 × 41 shelf unit top (plywood)
V	4	3/4 × 11-1/4 × 39 shelf unit shelves (plywood)
W	1	1/4 × 39 × 75-1/4 shelf unit back (plywood)
X	1	3/4 × 5-1/2 × 40 shelf unit face frame top rail
Y	2	3/4 × 2-1/2 × 69-1/2 shelf unit face frame side stiles
Z	2	3/4 × 2-1/2 × 22-5/8 shelf unit face frame center stiles
AA	2	3/4 × 2-1/2 × 35 shelf unit face frame center rails
BB	4	3/4 × 1-1/2 × 14 door rails
CC	4	3/4 × 1-1/2 × 23-1/4 door stiles
DD	1	3-1/2 × 40 shelf unit trim (crown molding)

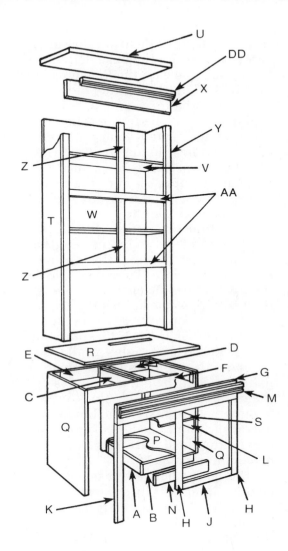

the desk unit. Place one spanner on either side of the inside cabinet panel and one on the inside of each of the other two panels. Set the rear end of each spanner 3/4″ in from the rear edge of its panel and make the upper edges of the spanners and panels flush. Fasten the spanners to the panels using No. 6 × 1-1/4″ wood screws.

Fasten the two outer side panels to the base frame using wood glue

and No. 6 × 1-1/2″ wood screws. Counterbore the screw holes where they will be visible after the unit is installed, so they can later be filled with plugs or putty. Now cut the frame rails (D, E, F) for the rear and front of the unit. Position the inside cabinet panel on the base, leaving 19-1/4" of space on the kneehole side and 18-1/2" on the cabinet side. Make sure the three side panels are plumb, then fit the frame rails into position and fasten them to the ends of the spanners using No. 6 × 1-1/2" wood screws. Run screws only through the upper half of the front rail so they will later be covered by the decorative molding.

Cut four triangular glue blocks out of scrap 2 × 4 to help strengthen the four outer joints of the unit and keep them square. To make a pair of blocks, square the end of a 2 × 4, then square a line across the board 3-1/2" from the end. Draw a diagonal line across the 3-1/2" square and cut off the two triangles. Make a second pair of blocks in the same manner. Coat the adjacent sides of the right angle on each block with wood glue and fasten the block in one of the outer corners of the unit, just below the desktop level, using 6d common nails.

Move the partially assembled desk/cabinet unit into the space chosen for it and fasten it in place by running No. 10 × 2" wood screws through the rear frame rails and the outside cabinet panel into the wall studs. For a neater look, counterbore the screw holes on the kneehole side of the unit.

Cut a 20" length of 1 × 4 to serve as the kick plate (N) and fasten it to the front of the cabinet base using 4d finishing nails. Then construct a

face frame to cover the exposed plywood edges on the front of the desk/cabinet unit. After cutting the face frame pieces to length, butt the face frame stiles (H, K) against the top face frame rail (G) and position the face frame bottom rail (J) between the two shorter stiles (H) as shown in the drawing. Fasten all joints with wood glue and dowels; then, attach the face frame to the desk/cabinet unit using wood glue and 4d finishing nails.

Cut the desktop (R) to size and position it on the desk/cabinet sub-assembly, centered along its length and flush against the wall at the back. Then, determine where your printer will be set over the cabinet and mark the position of the paper slot. To form the slot, drill 1"-diameter holes 20" apart; then, flip the desktop over and draw lines between the top and bottom edges of the two holes. Cut down the lines with a saber saw.

Crosscut a piece of crown molding to a length of 39" and cut a 45-degree compound miter on both ends. Position it under the front of the desktop, centered along the length of the desk. Nail it to the face frame and top with 3d finishing nails. Close the ends of the crown molding with crown molding returns cut to fit.

Cut a shelf (S) to size and edge the front with veneer tape. Rip two shelf cleats (L) from the leftover 1 × 2 and screw them to the sides of the cabinet with No. 6 × 1-1/4" wood screws. Place the shelf on the cleats.

Construct or purchase doors to fit the 17″ × 20-1/2″ opening.

Set all nails. Fill nail and screw holes with wood putty, then sand. After finishing the desk/cabinet unit, cut the original shoe molding to size and replace it.

Shelves

To build the shelving unit, first cut the sides (T), top (U), shelves (V), and back (W) to size.

Machine four 3/4″ × 1/4″ dadoes in both sides, spaced 16-1/2″, 28-1/8″, 41-1/2″, and 53-1/4″ from the top of the sides to accept the shelves.

Machine 1/4″ × 1/4″ rabbets along the rear inside edge of the side panels and the bottom rear edge of the top panel to accept the back.

Fit the shelves into the dadoed sides and counterbore pilot holes through the sides into their ends. Use wood glue and No. 6 × 1-1/2″ flathead wood screws to fasten the shelves in place. Putty over the screw heads.

Position the back panel in the rabbets and fasten it to the sides using wood glue and No. 4 × 3/4″ flathead wood screws.

Position the top flush with the back and centered over the sides. Fasten it to the sides with No. 6 × 1-1/2″ flathead wood screws.

Cut the face frame rails (X, AA) and stiles (Y, Z) to length. Dowel the frame together and nail to the shelv-

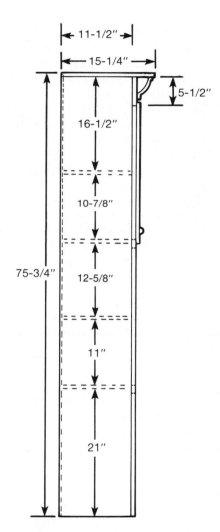

SHELF UNIT CROSS SECTION

ing unit with 4d finishing nails. Set the nails and fill the holes with wood putty.

Cut the crown molding (DD) to length. Cut a 45-degree compound miter on both ends. Center it under the front edge of the top. Nail the molding to the top and face board, and close the mitered ends with mitered returns cut to fit.

Sand the unit and finish as desired. Apply vinyl woodgrain tape to the exposed shelf edges.

The upper two shelves are enclosed by glass paneled doors. The doors fit flush over the face frame. These doors can be purchased from a cabinetmaker, or you can build them yourself. To do so, cut the door frame rails (BB) and stiles (CC) to length. Join the frame members with glue and dowels. Ease all exposed edges with a decorative router bit. Turn the frames over and rout a 1/8"-deep × 1/4"-wide rabbet in the inside back edge to accept the glass. Measure and order glass to fit.

Sand and finish the frames. Install the frames on the shelving unit with 2" decorative hinges. Install the glass, doorknobs, and magnetic latches.

Set the shelving unit on the desk and line the inside bottom edges with 3/4" quarter-round molding stained to match the unit and secured with 3d finishing nails.

STACKING BOOKCASE

Here is a simple adaptation of the ever popular stacking bookcase. This case has the natural warm glow of redwood and is made from standard sized boards. Cleats fastened to the top and bottom of each shelf interlock with "mortises" in the shelf supports. Each shelf is a separate module. The modules can be built as wide as you want, stacked as high as you want, and combined in whatever configuration you want. You can build a single bookcase or design a wall full of shelves. However, if you build any module longer than 48", be sure to include support blocks every 4' to prevent sagging. The cutting list included with this project is for a four-shelf bookcase.

Begin construction by cutting all material to size. Assemble the shelf supports (B) and shelf support spacers (C) with wood glue and 4d finishing nails. Make sure that the 1 × 4 spacers are flush with outside edges of the 1 × 12s.

Cut the cleats (D) to fit snugly in the mortise between the 1 × 4s in the supports. If the boards you are using are well seasoned, the cleats should be 4-1/4" long, but measure the opening in the supports just to be certain.

MATERIALS LIST
1 × 12 × 8' redwood (4)
1 × 4 × 8' redwood (2)
4d finishing nails
Wood glue

	CUTTING LIST	
KEY	PIECES	SIZE/DESCRIPTION
A	4	3/4 × 11-1/4 × 47-7/8 shelves
B	12	3/4 × 11-1/4 × 14 shelf supports
C	12	3/4 × 3-1/2 × 14 shelf support spacers
D	12	3/4 × 1 × 4-1/4 cleats

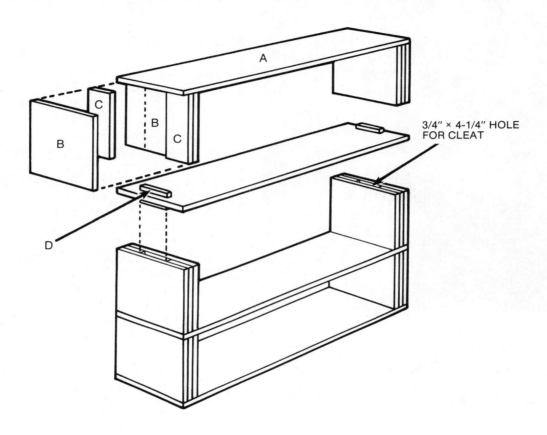

3/4" × 4-1/4" HOLE
FOR CLEAT

Center the cleats 3/4" from the edge of the shelf. Glue and nail the cleats to the shelves (A) with 4d finishing nails. Blunt the tips of the nails before using to minimize chances of splitting the cleats. Fasten cleats to the top and bottom of each shelf except for the top and bottom shelves, which get cleats on one side only.

Finish the modules as desired. Then, stack the modules to create your own shelving system.

GARDEN CENTER

The roomy garden center shown here has four shelves, each 58-1/2" long and 19-1/2" wide, and is an impressive 6' high. There are more than 20 square feet of growing space under three commercially available grow lights. It was constructed with all heart redwood, which has a natural resistance to moisture and water, but you can use any type of wood, stain it if you like, and seal it with several coats of polyurethane varnish.

Begin construction of the garden center by cutting the four uprights (A) to length. Carefully square the ends of each one.

Mark the location of the 1 × 3 shelf supports (B) on the 2 × 4 uprights. The tops of the lower three supports should fall 2-3/4", 26", and 49" from the bottom of the uprights. The top shelf support should be flush with the top of the uprights. The ends of each shelf support will be flush with the outside edges of the uprights.

Use No. 6 × 1-1/2" wood screws and waterproof resorcinal glue to fasten the shelf supports to the uprights. Make sure that the supports are square with the uprights and predrill and countersink pilot holes for the screws to avoid splitting the 1 × 3s.

Cut the side rails (C) to size and mark their positions on the uprights. Each side rail should be 3/4" (or the thickness of the 1 × 4 shelf slats) above the top of the shelf supports. Position the rails flush with the outside edges of the uprights. Drill and counterbore pilot holes to receive 3/8" wood plugs. Glue and screw the side rails to the uprights, using No. 6 × 1-1/2" wood screws. Make sure that the frame is square as it comes together.

Cut the front and rear rails (D) to length. Align these with the outside edges of the side rails. Drill and counterbore pilot holes, and glue and screw the rails to the uprights. Allow the glue to set up overnight before proceeding.

Cut the sixty-four shelf slats (E) that will form the shelves. Position them between the front and rear rails with 1/32" clearance on both ends. Evenly space the boards about 1/16" apart. Glue and nail the slats to the shelf supports with 4d finishing nails. Cut the end slats to fit between the uprights.

Fill the counterbored holes with redwood plugs and finish the center as desired. Purchase three fluorescent grow lamps and install them to the underside of the upper three shelves, following the manufacturer's instructions.

MATERIALS LIST

2 × 4 × 6′ clear all heart redwood (4)
1 × 4 × 8′ clear all heart redwood (20)
1 × 3 × 10′ clear all heart redwood (4)
No. 6 × 1-1/2″ wood screws
4d finishing nails
Redwood plugs
Waterproof resorcinol glue

CUTTING LIST

KEY	PIECES	SIZE/DESCRIPTION
A	4	1-1/2 × 3-1/2 × 72 uprights
B	8	3/4 × 2-1/2 × 57 shelf supports
C	8	3/4 × 3-1/2 × 18 side rails
D	8	3/4 × 3-1/2 × 58-1/2 front and rear rails
E	64	3/4 × 3-1/2 × 17-15/16 shelf slats

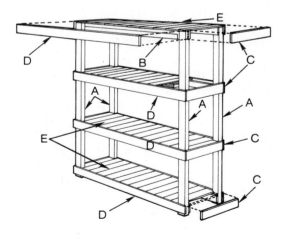

WALL SHELF
WITH MIRROR

Here's a solution to entryway clutter that you will be proud to hang. Not only will your guests have a place to hang their coats and set packages, gloves, and hats, they can also straighten a tie, comb their hair, and otherwise check their appearance.

Begin construction by cutting the horizontal and vertical frame members (A, B) to length. Trim each

piece to a 2-3/4″ width. Round the corners with a radius of 1/4″, using a router and a 1/4″-radius corner round router bit.

The horizontal pieces lap the vertical pieces. Cut the lap joints on the frame members 2-1/2″ from the ends, 2-3/4″ wide, and 3/8″ deep (half the thickness of the pieces).

Cut a 3/4″ × 3/8″ dado across each vertical frame member 2-1/2″

below the bottom of the upper lap joint. The shelf (C) will sit in this dado.

Assemble the frame with wood glue and clamps. Be sure that the frame is square after clamping the pieces together.

After the glue has set up, round the face edges of the frame with a router and corner round bit. Sand the frame until smooth.

Cut notches in the back edge of the shelf so that the shelf fits flush with the back edge of the vertical frame members. Cut the notches 3/8" deep, 2-3/4" wide, and set back from each end 2-1/2".

Round the front corners of the shelf to a radius of 1-1/2". Use the edge rounding router bit to round the face edges of the shelf. Attach the shelf to the frame with glue and No. 6 × 1" wood screws. Drive the screws through the back of the frame and into the shelf.

Make a full-size template for the shelf supports (D). (See the illustration for details.) Cut out the supports from a 1 × 6, round the edges, and sand them smooth.

Attach the supports to the frame under the shelf. Drive two screws through the back of the frame into each support centered in the vertical frame members. Then, fasten the shelf to the supports with two screws inserted through the top of the shelf into each support. Drill and counterbore pilot holes, install the No. 6 × 1-1/2" wood screws, and fill the screw holes with 3/8"-diameter wooden plugs. Sand the plugs flush with the shelf.

Use a router to cut a 3/8"-deep rabbet on the inside edges of the back frame for the mirror. Square the corners left by the router bit with a chisel.

Sand the unit and finish as desired.

Install the coat hooks spaced evenly apart. Install the mirror and hardboard backer. Secure them in place with 1/2" brads.

MATERIALS LIST

1 × 6 × 6' clear all heart redwood
1 × 4 × 6' clear all heart redwood (2)
3/16" × 14" × 26" mirror
1/8" × 2' × 4' hardboard
No. 10 × 3" brass roundhead wood screws
No. 6 × 1-1/2" wood screws
No. 6 × 1" wood screws
1/2" brads
Brass coat hooks
Toggle bolts or expansion anchors (optional)
Wood plugs
Wood glue

CUTTING LIST

KEY	PIECES	SIZE/DESCRIPTION
A	2	3/4 × 2-3/4 × 36 horizontal frame members
B	2	3/4 × 2-3/4 × 24 vertical frame members
C	1	3/4 × 5-1/2 × 36 shelf
D	2	3/4 × 5-1/2 × 12 shelf supports
E	1	1/8 × 14 × 26 hardboard mirror backing

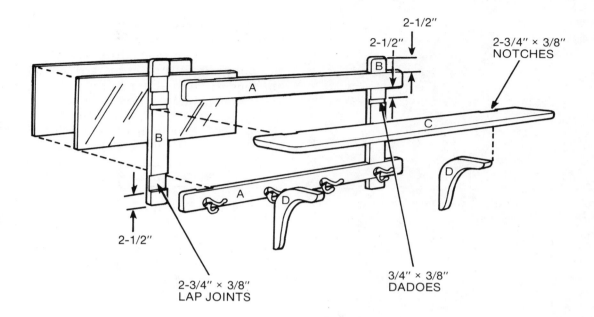

2-1/2"

2-1/2"

2-3/4" × 3/8"
NOTCHES

A

B

B

C

D

A

D

D

2-1/2"

2-3/4" × 3/8"
LAP JOINTS

3/4" × 3/8"
DADOES

Secure the shelf to the wall with the appropriate hardware. Drill the necessary holes into the upper horizontal frame member. No. 10 × 3" brass roundhead wood screws can be used to screw the unit to wall studs, or toggle bolts can be used to attach the unit to drywall or masonry walls.

ONE SQUARE = 1"

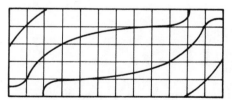

TEMPLATE FOR SHELF SUPPORTS

DISPLAY STAND

Display figurines, plants, books, or knickknacks in style. This free-standing display stand is made of redwood, which lends its natural warmth to the elegant design. Most of the fasteners are hidden under the shelves, giving the stand a clean, untouched look.

The first step in making this display stand is to cut the curved and straight leg members (D, E) to length, width, and shape. Using the template shown in the illustration, lay out and cut the curved portion of the legs. If you cut carefully, the shelf apron side pieces and end pieces can also be cut from the 1 × 8 stock. (See the cutting diagram.)

MATERIALS LIST

1 × 12 × 6'
1 × 10 × 6' (2)
1 × 8 × 6' (4)
1 × 3 × 6' (3)
1 × 2 × 6' (4)
No. 6 × 1-1/4" wood screws
No. 6 × 1" wood screws
4d finishing nails
Wood buttons
Wood glue
Wood putty

CUTTING LIST

KEY	PIECES	SIZE/DESCRIPTION
A	1	3/4 × 11-1/4 × 50-1/2 top
B	2	3/4 × 2-1/4 × 50 top apron sides
C	2	3/4 × 2-1/4 × 9-1/4 top apron ends
D	4	3/4 × 6-1/2 × 53-1/2 curved leg members
E	4	3/4 × 1-1/2 × 53-1/2 straight leg members
F	4	3/4 × 7-3/4 × 32-1/2 shelves
G	4	3/4 × 2 × 7-3/4 shelf apron ends
H	4	3/4 × 2 × 34 apron sides

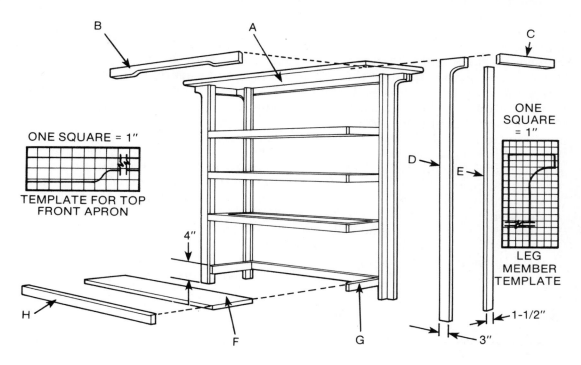

ONE SQUARE = 1"

TEMPLATE FOR TOP
FRONT APRON

ONE
SQUARE
= 1"

LEG
MEMBER
TEMPLATE

1-1/2"

3"

4"

Glue and nail the curved and straight leg members together. Use 4d finishing nails to attach the straight edge of the straight piece to the inside face of the curved piece. Make two left-facing legs and two right-facing legs. Set the nails slightly below the surface and fill the holes with wood putty.

Cut the shelves (F), shelf apron ends (G), and shelf apron sides (H) to length. Rip the 1 × 10 stock to 7-3/4" in width for the shelves. Rip the apron pieces to a 2" width. Glue and nail the shorter shelf apron pieces to the ends of the shelves. Glue and nail the longer shelf apron pieces to the sides of the shelves and

the apron ends. Set the nails slightly below the surface of the wood and fill the holes with wood putty. Round the edges of the apron pieces with a router and edge rounding bit.

Fasten the shelves to the legs, faces flush, with screws inserted from the inside of the shelf apron. Place the first shelf 12" from the top of the legs, the second shelf 24" from the top, and the third 36" from the top. Place the top surface of the final shelf 4" from the bottom of the legs.

Cut the top apron pieces (B, C) to length and trim them to a 2-1/4" width. Cut the curves in the top front apron as shown in the template details.

To assemble the apron, fix the end pieces between the sides. Drill and counterbore holes for No. 6 × 1-1/4″ wood screws through the sides and into the end pieces. Fasten the sides to the end pieces using glue and screws. Fill the holes with wood buttons.

Position the apron over the stand flush with the top of the legs. Drill and counterbore pilot holes through the inside of the legs and into the inside face of the apron sides. Secure the apron to the stand with No. 6 × 1-1/4″ flathead wood screws and fill the holes with wood plugs.

Position the top on the stand so it overhangs the apron 1/4″ on all sides. Clamp the top in position. From underneath, drill pilot holes up through the apron and into the top. Counterbore the holes 3/8″ in diameter and 1-1/2″ deep in the side and back apron pieces. Bore the holes 1/2″ deep through the narrow portion in the front apron. Screw the top to the apron with No. 6 × 1″ flathead wood screws. Fill the holes with 3/8″-diameter wood plugs. Using a router and 1/4″ corner rounding router bit, machine a 1/4″ radius on the top edge of the top panel.

Sand and finish as desired.

MATCHING FREESTANDING AND WALL-HUNG BOOKCASES

Here is a beautiful storage combo that you will be proud to add to your living room, or any room in the house, for that matter. The vertical supports are handsomely arched, and the shelves are dadoed, glued, and screwed for stability. You can make this bookcase duo with standard pine or redwood boards or use a hardwood to match existing furniture in your house.

Freestanding Bookcase

Begin making the freestanding bookcase by cutting the shelves (A), upright supports (B, C), and foot members (D), to size.

Cut 3/4″ × 3/8″ dadoes across the inside face of the uprights. Locate the first dado 1-1/2″ from the bottom, the second 15-1/2″ from the bottom, the third 26-1/2″ from the bottom, and the fourth and last 37-1/4″ from the bottom.

Drill pilot holes through the outer face of each upright and centered in each dado. Counterbore each hole 1/2″ round and 3/16″ deep.

Lay out and cut the arches on the tops of each upright piece. Use the template design given in the illustration. Round the inside edges of the uprights and the facing edges of the shelves using a router and a 1/4″-radius corner round router bit.

Glue and screw the shelves in place, making sure that the middle

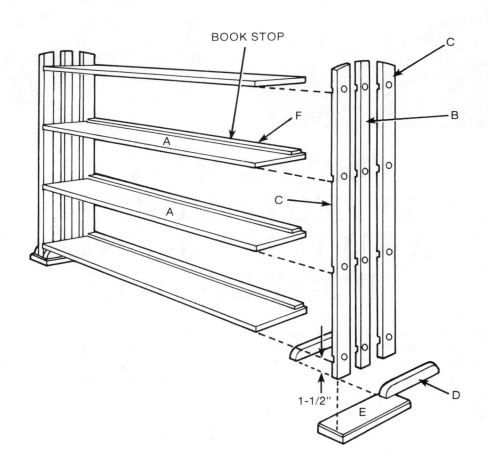

uprights are centered in the assembly and that the assembly is square. Use No. 6 × 1-1/4″ wood screws. Plug the holes with 3/8″-diameter wood plugs and sand them flush.

Cut curves on the top corners of the foot members and round all outside faces except the bottom edges. Attach the inner foot members to the uprights with glue and 2d finishing nails. Set the nails and fill the holes with wood putty. To attach the outer foot members to the out-

side face of the uprights, drill and counterbore pilot holes through the feet and into the center of each upright. Then, secure the feet to the uprights with No. 6 × 1-1/4″ flathead wood screws. Fill the holes with 3/8″-diameter plugs and sand flush.

Rip the book stops (F) to width from a 1 × 2. Attach these flush with the back edges of the three lower shelves with 2d finishing nails and glue. Set the nails, fill the holes with putty, and sand flush.

Round the upper edges of the feet (E). Fasten to the foot members with glue and screws driven from underneath.

Sand the unit and finish as desired.

Wall-hung Bookcase

If you have empty wall space and crowded shelf space, build this attractive wall-hung bookcase. It is made very similarly to the freestanding bookcase. The uprights (B, C) are cut to size, rounded, and curved on both ends. The uprights are also dadoed to receive the shelves (A). Locate the center dado

MATERIALS LIST (FREESTANDING BOOKCASE)

1 × 10 × 6′ (2)
1 × 4 × 2′
1 × 3 × 8′ (2)
1 × 2 × 8′
1 × 2 × 6′
No. 6 × 1-1/4″ wood screws
2d finishing nails
Wood plugs
Wood putty
Wood glue

CUTTING LIST (FREESTANDING BOOKCASE)

KEY	PIECES	SIZE/DESCRIPTION
A	4	3/4 × 9-1/4 × 34 shelves
B	2	3/4 × 1-1/2 × 41-1/2 middle uprights
C	4	3/4 × 2-1/2 × 41-1/2 outer uprights
D	4	3/4 × 1-1/2 × 9-1/2 foot members
E	2	3/4 × 3-1/2 × 10-1/4 feet
F	3	3/4 × 3/8 × 33-1/4 book stops

MATERIALS LIST (WALL-HUNG BOOKCASE)

1 × 10 × 6′
1 × 3 × 10′
1 × 2 × 10′
No. 8 × 3″ flathead wood screws
No. 6 × 1-1/4″ wood screws
Wood plugs
Wood buttons
Wood glue

CUTTING LIST (WALL-HUNG BOOKCASE)		
KEY	**PIECES**	**SIZE/DESCRIPTION**
A	3	3/4 × 9-1/4 × 21-1/4 shelves
B	2	3/4 × 1-1/2 × 29 center uprights
C	4	3/4 × 2-1/2 × 29 outer uprights
D	2	3/4 × 1-1/2 × 20-3/4 mounting bars

12-3/4" from the top of the uprights and space the top and bottom dadoes 2-1/2" from the top and bottom of the uprights. Drill and countersink pilot holes through the uprights

and into the shelves. Glue and screw the uprights to the shelves with No. 6 × 1-1/4" flathead wood screws. Plug the holes.

Mounting bars (D) must be added to the wall-hung unit. Cut the mounting bars to length from 1 × 2 stock and glue and screw them to the underside of the top and middle shelves flush with the back edge of the shelves. Counterbore holes through the mounting bars to mount the unit to the wall. Screw the unit into wall studs with No. 8 × 3" flathead wood screws. Fill the counterbored holes with wood buttons so that the unit can be removed from the wall whenever desired.

TEMPLATE FOR ARCH

ONE SQUARE = 1"

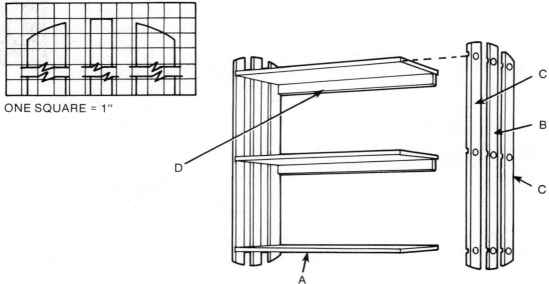

ELECTRONIC
MEDIA CENTER

Electronic gadgetry is becoming a common storage item in most homes. Electronics provide a major source of entertainment: videotapes and recorders, video games, compact disc players, and your favorite TV programs. Computers help balance a checkbook or do taxes, teach the children to spell and count, word process a research paper, and for some, generate an income. "Smart" homes with computer-controlled lighting, heating, and security are not far off in the future. The smart home today, however, has an electronic center to organize it all. You

CUTTING LIST (CORNER UNIT)		
KEY	**PIECES**	**SIZE/DESCRIPTION**
A	2	3/4 × 23 × 72 side panels
B	1	3/4 × 38-15/16 × 78-1/2 top panel
C	1	3/4 × 40-3/4 × 78-1/2 desktop
D	1	3/4 × 33-5/8 × 76-3/8 center shelf
E	2	3/4 × 12-1/2 × 20 shelf supports
F	2	3/4 × 16-7/8 × 20 inner shelf supports
G	1	3/4 × 28-3/4 × 39 center back panel
H	2	3/4 × 35-11/16 × 39 left and right back panels
J	2	3/4 × 12-1/2 × 24 adjustable shelves
K	2	3/4 × 20-3/4 × 28-1/2 file cabinet sides
L	1	3/4 × 16 × 21-1/2 file cabinet top
M	1	3/4 × 14-1/2 × 28-1/2 file cabinet back
N	1	3/4 × 2-1/2 × 16 file cabinet kick plate
P	2	3/4 × 12-15/16 × 16 file cabinet drawer front
Q	2	3/4 × 20-3/4 × 28-1/2 storage cabinet sides
R	1	3/4 × 16 × 21-1/2 storage cabinet top
S	1	3/4 × 14-1/2 × 28-1/2 storage cabinet back
T	1	3/4 × 2-1/2 × 16 storage cabinet kick plate
U	1	3/4 × 16 × 20 storage cabinet drawer front

CUTTING LIST (continued)		
KEY	**PIECES**	**SIZE/DESCRIPTION**
V	1	3/4 × 5-7/8 × 16 storage cabinet top drawer front
W	2	3/4 × 4 × 17 outer valance
X	1	3/4 × 4 × 26-5/8 center valance
Y	2	3/4 × 1-1/2 × 16 desktop outer bands
Z	1	3/4 × 1-1/2 × 24-7/16 desktop center band
AA	2	3/4 × 1-1/2 × 36 desktop outer cleats
BB	1	3/4 × 1-1/2 × 28-3/4 desktop center cleat
CC	2	3/4 × 1-1/2 × 36 top panel outer cleats
DD	1	3/4 × 1-1/2 × 28-3/4 top panel center cleat
EE	2	3/4 × 1-1/2 × 18-15/16 upper side cleats
FF	2	3/4 × 1-1/2 × 11-15/16 lower side cleats
GG	1	3/4 × 16 × 29-1/4 support box front
HH	2	3/4 × 6-1/2 × 29-1/4 support box ends

can build one like the one shown with a minimum of woodworking skills.

This electronic media center is made of waferboard. The desktops and some of the drawers are laminated, and the panel edges are finished in plastic T-molding. The joinery is limited to butt joints that are fastened with glue and

MATERIALS LIST (CORNER UNIT)

1 × 2 × 10′ solid pine (3)
3/4″ × 4′ × 8′ waferboard panels (6)
1/2″ × 4′ × 8′ waferboard panel
1/16″ plastic laminate (21 sq ft)
3/4″ plastic T-molding (43′)
No. 8 × 1-1/4″ wood screws
No. 4 × 3/4″ wood screws
3d finishing nails
Corner braces (6)
Drawer guides (4 sets)
Wood putty
Wood glue

No. 8 × 1-1/4″ wood screws. All screw holes are counterbored for later filling with wood putty. Side and back panels are screwed to 1 × 2 solid wood cleats. Some shelves sit on 1 × 1 cleats. Others are adjustable and sit on shelf pins that fit into 1/4″ holes spaced 2″ apart. Before cutting and assembling the units, measure your equipment and adjust the shelf spacing, if necessary, to best accommodate each piece.

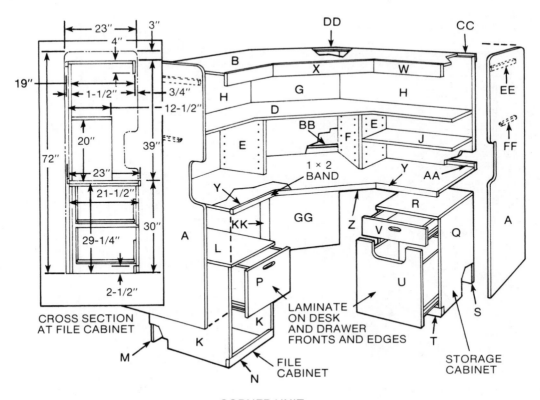

CORNER UNIT

Corner Unit

Begin by cutting the side panels (A) to size. Make the cutouts in the panels and round all facing corners as shown in the illustration.

The top panel (B), desktop (C), and center shelf (D) are irregularly shaped. The cutting list gives the rectangular areas from which each piece can be cut. Lay out each panel according to the dimensions given in the illustrations and cut them to size.

Cut the T-molding kerfs in the facing edges of the top panel, side panels, and center shelf. Use a kerf cutting router blade or a table saw to make the cuts. Be sure to center the kerf in the panel edge. Check the molding manufacturer's instructions for the recommended kerf size.

Cut the desktop bands (Y, Z) and the desktop cleats (AA, BB) from 1 × 2 stock. Miter the ends to fit the 45-degree angles in the desktop. Countersink pilot holes through the face of each band and attach the bands and cleat to the top with No. 8 × 1-1/4″ wood screws.

Cut the top panel valances (W, X) and top panel cleats (CC, DD) to size, and miter the joining edges to fit the 45-degree angles in the unit top. Counterbore pilot holes and fasten the valance to the top with glue and No. 8 × 1-1/4″ wood screws. Fill the holes with wood putty. Glue and screw the cleats to the back edge of the top panel, also.

Cut the side cleats (EE, FF) to length. Drill and countersink pilot holes in the side cleats, then glue and screw the cleats to the side panels 3-3/4″ and 22″ from the top.

Cut the storage and file cabinet panels to size. Cut a 3/4″ × 2-1/2″ notch in the lower front corner of each side panel (K, Q) for the kick plates (N, T). Cut the drawer fronts (P, U, V) to fit flush with the outside edges of the sides. Glue and screw the cabinet sides to the backs (M, S), the tops (L, R) to the sides and backs, and the kick plates to the sides.

To cut the handholds in the file cabinet drawer front, drill 1/2″ holes spaced 4″ apart, 1-1/2″ from the top

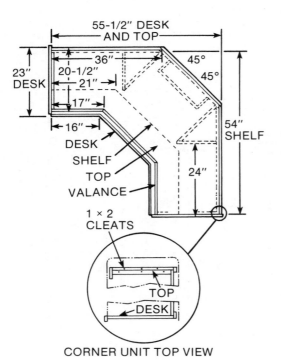

CORNER UNIT TOP VIEW

of the drawer front and 4" from the panel sides. Draw lines connecting the outer diameters of the holes and cut along the lines with a jigsaw.

Cut the 4" × 8" hand space in the storage cabinet with a 1-1/2" radius in the inside corners.

Cover the drawer front faces and edges with plastic laminate. Buy drawer guides for each of the drawers and install the part that fits the cabinet frame. Then, make or buy drawers sized to fit the space available inside the drawer openings. Cut handholds in the drawer fronts and fasten them to the drawers.

Build the desktop support box next. Glue and screw the support box front (GG) to the support box ends (HH). Remember to fill the counterbored screw holes with wood putty.

Place the desktop (C) on the cabinets and support box. Carefully align the edges and screw the desktop to the cabinets through the underside of the cabinet tops. Secure the desktop to the support box with two L-brackets screwed to the underside of the desktop and to the facing panel of the back.

Cover the desktop and its edge banding with plastic laminate.

Position the sides (A) flush with the cabinet edges and screw them to the cabinets from inside the cabinet side panels.

Cut the back panels (G, H) to size. Bevel the joining edges of the panels 45 degrees as shown in the top view. Note that the long sides of the beveled panels face inside. Place the panels in position and secure them to each other and to the desktop cleat and to the side panels, using wood glue and 3d finishing nails. Reinforce the panel joints with metal angle braces bent to fit.

Cut the shelf support panels (E) to size. Miter the facing edges of the inside pieces as shown in the top view illustration. Cut a kerf in the facing edges of the outside support panels for T-molding. Fasten the pieces together using No. 4 × 3/4" wood screws. Secure the supports in position with screws through the back panel.

Install the fixed shelf and the top panel. Screw these to the back panels and the side panels.

Drill parallel rows of 1/4"-diameter holes 3/8" deep into the side panels and shelf supports to receive the 1/4"-diameter shank shelf support pins. Space the holes 2" apart and locate them 1-1/2" from the front and rear edges of the panels.

Test fit your computer components for placement. Mark and drill holes through the back panel for the equipment cables.

Finish the panels as desired. Waferboard can be stained to match your room decor and the plastic laminate or covered with several coats of a transparent polyurethane varnish. After the finish has dried, cover exposed panel edges with T-molding.

Left Unit

The construction procedures used in assembling the corner unit are applicable to building the end units as well. Cut the main cabinet parts to size. Cut the cutouts in the side panels (A) and dividers (F, G, H) as shown in the illustration. Round the corners, and cut kerfs in the panel edges for T-molding.

Lay out parallel rows of 1/4"-diameter holes on the inside faces of the side panels. These holes will accept the shelf supports that support the adjustable shelf (D).

NOTE: *Cut the adjustable shelf slightly undersized so that it can be positioned easily between the side panels.*

Locate the holes 6" in from the back edge of the panel and 3" in from the front edge of the panel. Drill the first hole in each row 8" from the top of the panels. Drill four more holes in each row, spaced 2" on center. Drill the holes 3/8" to 1/2" deep, depending on the length of the shelf support pins.

Rip three strips, each 3/4" wide, from the 8' long 1 × 3. Crosscut one strip 46-1/2" long to use as the rear cleat for the top panel. Crosscut the remaining strips and the cutoff from the first strip into twelve side cleats, each 19" long.

Using glue and screws, fasten six side cleats (U) to the inside

Left Unit Storage Cabinets

faces of the two side panels (A) in the locations where they are needed to support the top panel (B), the desktop (E), and the end shelves (J). Leave a 1" space between the front end of each cleat and the front edge of the panel. Fasten the remaining six cleats to the lower dividers (H) where needed to support the end and center shelves (J, K). Then, fasten the rear cleat for the top panel to the front face of the back panel.

Cut the 1 × 2 cleats (S) to length and cut a 1-1/2" radius on the upper

MATERIALS LIST (LEFT UNIT)

3/4" × 4' × 8' waferboard panels (4)
1 × 2 × 10' solid pine (2)
1/16" plastic laminate (8 sq ft)
3/4" plastic T-molding (52')
No. 8 × 1-1/4" wood screws
Drawer guides (6 sets)
Wood putty
Wood glue

CUTTING LIST (LEFT UNIT)

KEY	PIECES	SIZE/DESCRIPTION
A	2	3/4 × 23 × 72 side panels
B	1	3/4 × 20-3/4 × 46-1/2 top panel
C	1	3/4 × 46-1/2 × 72 back panel
D	2	3/4 × 20-3/4 × 46-1/2 upper shelves
E	1	3/4 × 20-3/4 × 46-1/2 desktop
F	2	3/4 × 20-3/4 × 20 upper dividers
G	2	3/4 × 16-3/4 × 20 upper dividers
H	2	3/4 × 20-3/4 × 26 lower dividers
J	2	3/4 × 12 × 20-3/4 end shelves
K	2	3/4 × 21 × 20-3/4 center shelves
L	1	3/4 × 20-3/4 × 46-1/2 bottom panel
M	2	3/4 × 11-7/8 × 16-5/8 file cabinet drawer front
N	2	3/4 × 7-5/8 × 11-7/8 desk drawer front
P	1	3/4 × 3/4 × 12 lower center shelf rear cleat

CUTTING LIST (continued)

KEY	PIECES	SIZE/DESCRIPTION
Q	1	3/4 × 2-1/2 × 46-1/2 kick plate
R	1	3/4 × 2-1/2 × 46-1/2 bottom shelf rear support
S	2	3/4 × 1-1/2 × 72 rear panel side cleats
T	2	3/4 × 7-7/8 × 20-7/8 center storage drawer fronts
U	12	3/4 × 3/4 × 19 side cleats
V	1	3/4 × 3/4 × 46-1/2 upper shelf rear cleat
W	1	3/4 × 1-1/2 × 46-1/2 edge band

rear corners of the cleats. Spread glue on the facing edge of the cleats and position them against the back face of the back panel flush with the outside edges of that panel. Fasten the back panel to the cleats with No. 8 × 1-1/4" flathead wood screws.

Fasten the supports (Q, R) to the underside of the bottom panel (L). Position the rear support flush with the back edge of the panel, but hold the front support at least 3/4" back of the front edge.

Before assembling the unit, sand and finish the sides, top panel, dividers, shelves, and bottom panel. Begin the assembly of the unit by positioning the rear edges of the side panels flush with the rear edges of the vertical cleats attached to the back panel. Drill and countersink pi-

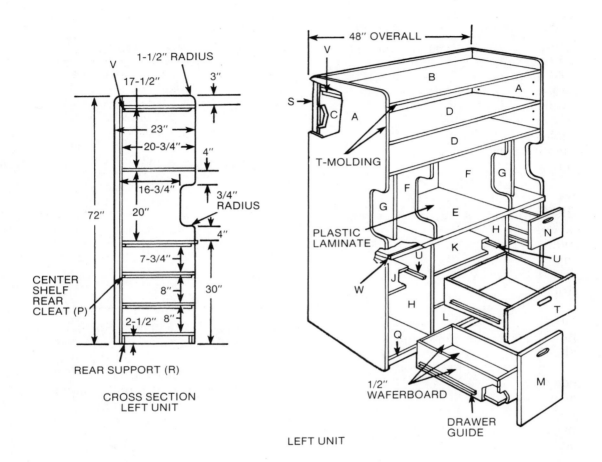

CROSS SECTION
LEFT UNIT

LEFT UNIT

lot holes through the inside faces of the cleats and fasten the cleats to the sides using glue and No. 8 × 1-1/4" flathead wood screws.

Place the top panel (B) and the bottom panel between the side panels, making the front edges of all pieces flush. Then, fasten these pieces together using No. 8 × 1-1/4" wood screws. Counterbore the holes for any screws you want to hide later.

Fasten the edge band (W) to the front of the desktop (E) making the upper edges of each flush. Then cover the upper face of the desktop and the front of the edge band with plastic laminate. Set the desktop in place and run screws up through the side cleats and through the back panel to secure it in place.

Set the upper dividers (F, G) in place on the desktop and position the upper shelf on top of them. Run screws up through the desktop and down through the shelf into the dividers and in through the side panels into the ends of the shelf. Counterbore the holes that will be visible so you can putty over the screw heads.

Use four L-brackets to fasten each lower divider (H) into place, then insert the shelves (J, K) and screw them to the cleats.

Buy drawer guides for each of the drawers and install the part that fits the cabinet frame. Then, make or buy drawers sized to fit the space available inside the drawer openings. Cut handholds in the drawer fronts (N, T) and fasten them to the drawers.

Install T-molding in the kerfs cut early in the edges of the side panels, top panel, dividers, and shelves.

Position your TV, VCR, and stereo equipment in the unit as desired. Mark and drill holes for cables. If necessary, cut the back panel to make room for the TV to sit flush with the front of the unit.

Cut the drawer fronts (N, T) to size and assemble the drawers and file cabinets from 1/2″ waferwood. Install drawer guides and drawers. Finish the unit as desired and install T-molding.

Right Unit

The right side unit is very similar to the left side unit. The side panels (A) and back panel (C) are fastened to 1 × 2 cleats. The top panel and middle shelf sit on cleats fastened to the side panels while the upper and lower shelves are adjustable. The side panels, top panel (B), and shelves (D, E) must be cut with a kerf to accept T-molding.

However, the similarity ends there. The lower portion of the unit contains two cabinets—one is designed for computer paper storage and the other is a rollout unit that can be used as a projector stand or serving cart.

Paper Storage Cabinet

To build the paper storage cabinet, cut the panels to size.

Cut 3/4″ × 2-1/2″ notches in the lower front corners of the sides to make room for the kick plate.

Cut a slot centered in the top and 2″ from the rear edge for the computer paper. To do this, drill two holes, 12″ to 15″ apart (outside dimensions), and draw a line between the outside radius of the two holes. Cut along this line with a saber saw to complete the cutout.

Fasten the kick plate to the cabinet sides.

Position the kick plate in the notches in the cabinet sides and fasten it to the sides with glue and No. 8 × 1-1/4″ wood screws.

Position the back between the sides and secure the panels together with glue and No. 8 × 1-1/4″ wood screws.

Fit the bottom in over the kick plate, push it flush against the back, and while holding the bottom 2-1/2″ above the bottom edge of the back panel, drive No. 8 × 1-1/4″ wood screws through the back panel and

Right Unit

side panels and into the edges of the bottom.

Position the cabinet top (F) on the cabinet with all edges flush. Drill and countersink pilot holes through the top and into the sides and back panel. Fasten the top to the cabinet with glue and No. 8 × 1-1/4" flathead wood screws.

Fasten the edge band (P) to the front edge of the top panel, using glue and 4d finishing nails. Also fasten the 3/4" filler strip (U) in

---

MATERIALS LIST (RIGHT UNIT)

3/4" × 4' × 8' waferboard panels (4)
1 × 2 × 8' solid pine (2)
1/16" plastic laminate (6 sq ft)
3/4" plastic T-molding (38')
No. 8 × 1-1/4" wood screws
4d finishing nails
2" cabinet hinges (4)
L-brackets
2-1/2" casters (4)
Wood glue

CUTTING LIST (RIGHT UNIT)

KEY	PIECES	SIZE/DESCRIPTION
A	2	3/4 × 23 × 72 side panels
B	1	3/4 × 20-3/4 × 34-1/2 top panel
C	1	3/4 × 34-1/2 × 72 back panel
D	2	3/4 × 20-3/4 × 34-1/2 shelves
E	1	3/4 × 12-1/2 × 34-1/2 shelf
F	2	3/4 × 17 × 21-1/2 cabinet tops
G	2	3/4 × 20-3/4 × 29-1/4 storage cabinet sides
H	1	3/4 × 15-1/2 × 20-3/4 storage cabinet bottom
J	1	3/4 × 15-1/2 × 29-1/4 storage cabinet back
K	2	3/4 × 20 × 26 rollout cabinet sides
L	1	3/4 × 17 × 21-1/2 rollout cabinet bottom
M	1	3/4 × 15-1/2 × 26 rollout cabinet back
N	1	3/4 × 2-1/2 × 17 kick plate
P	2	3/4 × 1-1/2 × 17 edge bands
Q	2	3/4 × 1-1/2 × 72 rear panel cleats
R	4	3/4 × 3/4 × 19 shelf side cleats
S	2	3/4 × 17 × 25-1/8 cabinet doors
T	2	3/4 × 3/4 × 34-1/2 shelf rear cleats
U	2	3/4 × 3/4 × 17 filler strip

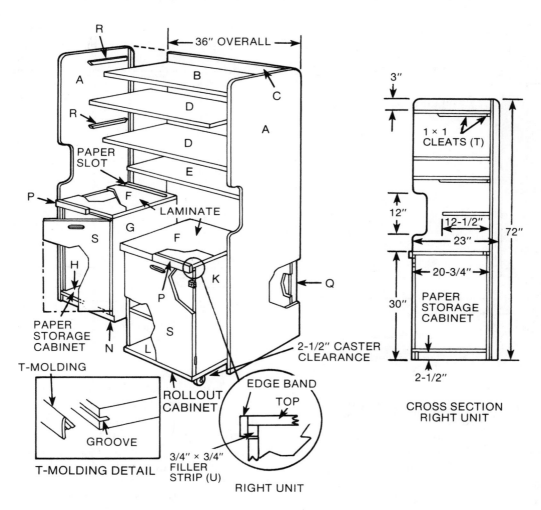

R

36" OVERALL

A

B

C

R

D

A

PAPER
SLOT

D

E

P

F

LAMINATE

G

F

S

H

PAPER
STORAGE
CABINET

N

P

K

S

L

Q

2-1/2" CASTER
CLEARANCE

ROLLOUT
CABINET

EDGE BAND

TOP

3/4" × 3/4"
FILLER
STRIP (U)

RIGHT UNIT

T-MOLDING

GROOVE

T-MOLDING DETAIL

3"

1 × 1
CLEATS (T)

12"

12-1/2"

23"

72"

20-3/4"

PAPER
STORAGE
CABINET

30"

2-1/2"

CROSS SECTION
RIGHT UNIT

place behind the edge band with glue and 4d finishing nails. Cover the top and edge band with plastic laminate.

Cut the cabinet doors (S) to size. They will lap the front edges of the cabinet sides and fit between the top edge band and the bottom panel. Cut out a 3/4"-wide × 4"-long handhold in the doors.

Position the printer and any other electronic equipment in the storage unit. Mark and drill holes for the cables.

Rollout Cabinet

The construction of the rollout cabinet is slightly different than the paper storage cabinet. After cutting the panels to size and banding the

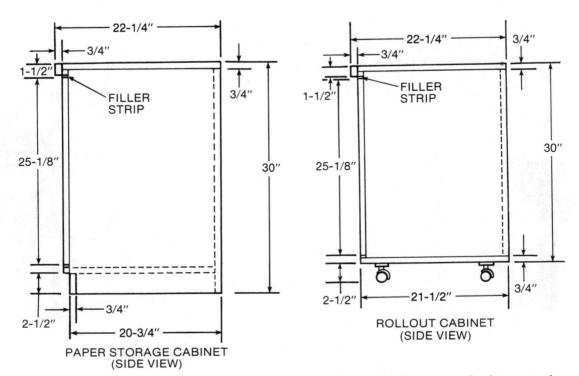

PAPER STORAGE CABINET
(SIDE VIEW)

ROLLOUT CABINET
(SIDE VIEW)

facing edge of the top (F) fasten the sides (K) to the back (M). Then, fasten the bottom (L) to the sides and back. Fit the top over the upper edges of the back and side panels and is fastened to them. Here again a 1 × 1 filler strip (U) must be cut to fill the gap between the side panel and the top. Coat the strip with glue and tack it in place.

Turn the unit upside down and install the four casters. Follow the manufacturer's instructions for installation. Then, turn the cabinet upright and cover the top and band with plastic laminate.

Cut a door (S) to fit the cabinet opening and cut a handhold in it.

Sand the edges of the unit. Finish it as desired and install the T-molding and cabinet doors.

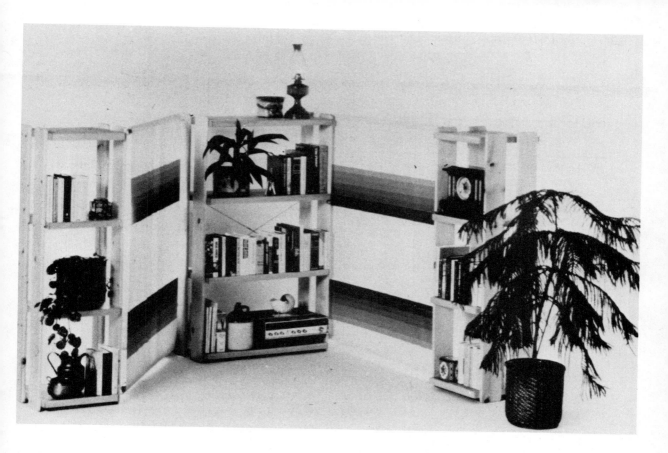

MOVABLE
STORAGE CENTER

Storage can be aesthestic as well as functional. Here is a flexible storage center that doubles as a room divider. Freestanding shelving units are connected by fabric covered stretchers. The stretchers are suspended from L-hooks so that the units can be pivoted to any angle. The storage center combines natural wood finishes, lacquered surfaces, and fabrics. With a little imagination, this project can be adapted to any room decor.

The following instructions are applicable to both the square and the rectangular shelving units. The materials list and the cutting lists provide for one unit of each size and one divider panel. Make as many of each unit as necessary to satisfy your storage needs.

To begin construction of the rectangular shelf unit, cut the side shelf edge bands (B) to length and cut a 3/8"-deep × 3/4"-wide rabbet across the inside face at both ends of each

MATERIALS LIST
(SHELF UNITS)

1 × 6 × 10' #2 pine (4)
1 × 2 × 8' #2 pine
1 × 2 × 6' #2 pine (10)
3/4" × 4' × 8' birch veneer plywood
No. 8 × 1-1/4" wood screws
4d finishing nails
Fabric of your choice
Jack chain (6')
3/16" turnbuckles (2)
1-1/2" L-hooks (4)
3/8" screw eyes (4)
Wood plugs
Wood glue

CUTTING LIST
(SHELF UNITS)

KEY	PIECES	SIZE/DESCRIPTION
A	8	3/4 × 5-1/2 × 60 shelf supports
B	8	3/4 × 1-1/2 × 16-1/2 side shelf bands
C	8	3/4 × 1-1/2 × 32-1/4 front and back shelf bands
D	4	3/4 × 15-3/4 × 32-1/4 shelves
E	8	3/4 × 1-1/2 × 16-1/2 side shelf bands
F	8	3/4 × 1-1/2 × 15-3/4 front and back shelf bands
G	4	3/4 × 15-3/4 × 15-3/4 shelves
H	2	3/4 × 1-1/2 × 46 stretchers

piece. Then, cut another rabbet 3/4" × 3/8" along the top inside edge of each piece.

Next, cut the front and back shelf edge bands (C) to length. Cut a 3/4" × 3/8" rabbet along the top inside edge of each of these pieces, also.

Assemble the shelf bands with the side bands lapping the ends of the front and back bands as shown in the drawing.

Cut the plywood shelves (D) to size. Sand any rough edges smooth. At this time, stain the shelves to suit if a contrasting color is desired between the shelves and the shelf banding frame.

Coat the edges of the shelves and the rabbeted areas of the shelf band with glue. Set the shelves in their band frames and tack them in place with 4d finishing nails.

Rout a 1/4" radius all around the top and bottom edges of the shelves. Sand smooth and finish as desired.

Cut the shelf supports (A) to length, and cut a 3/4" radius on all four corners of each piece. Also, rout a 1/4" radius on all the edges of each piece. Predrill the uprights to accept two wood screws per shelf. Counterbore the pilot holes. Predrill the shelves, as well. Sand and finish the uprights. Then, glue and screw the uprights to the shelves. Fill the counterbored holes with wood plugs.

Next, insert screw eyes into the ends of the rear shelf bands of the second and third shelves (rectangular unit only). Attach chains and turnbuckles to the diagonally opposed screw eyes. Adjust both turnbuckles to stiffen the shelf units.

Now the room divider can be assembled. Start by predrilling through the center of the upright

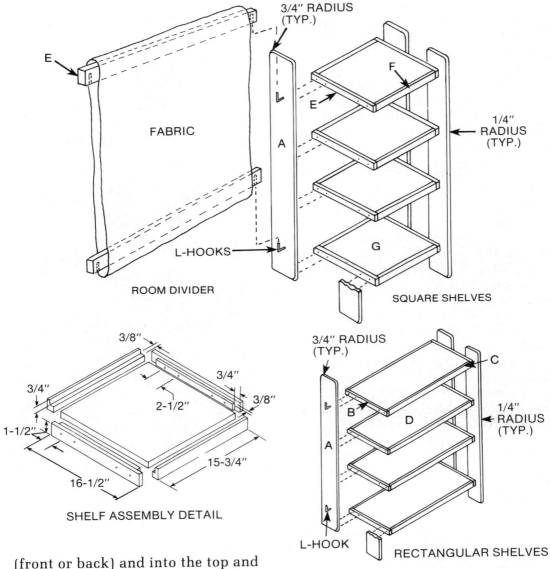

3/4" RADIUS (TYP.)

E

FABRIC

A

L-HOOKS

ROOM DIVIDER

F

E

1/4" RADIUS (TYP.)

G

SQUARE SHELVES

3/8"

3/4"

3/4"

2-1/2"

3/8"

1-1/2"

15-3/4"

16-1/2"

SHELF ASSEMBLY DETAIL

3/4" RADIUS (TYP.)

C

B

D

A

1/4" RADIUS (TYP.)

L-HOOK

RECTANGULAR SHELVES

(front or back) and into the top and bottom shelves. Insert the L-hooks that support the 1 × 2 stretchers. Leave at least 3/4″ of the hook shank protruding from the upright.

Cut the 1 × 2 pine stretchers (E) to length.

NOTE: The length of the dividers can be adjusted to suit. Space the shelving units according to taste and cut the stretchers to fit.

In the end of each stretcher, drill a hole large enough to accept the end of the L-hooks. Locate the holes 1/2″ from the ends of the stretchers.

Sand and finish the stretchers and place them on the L-hooks.

Measure the distance around the stretchers and sew a cloth sleeve to fit over them.

Shelf Insert

If you use the movable storage center in the kitchen, you will want to build the shelf insert shown here in the rectangular shelf unit. The rectangular boxes double the shelf space, and you can modify the dimensions to fit whatever you have to store.

Begin by crosscutting both a 1 × 8 and a 1 × 10 to 66-1/4″ in length. Edge glue the boards together and from the glued-up board, crosscut A, E, and F. From remaining 1 × 10 stock, crosscut parts B, C, and D. Rip part B to 5-1/2″ in width.

Machine a 3/4″ × 3/8″ rabbet across both ends of parts A and F and across one end of part E. Machine a 3/4″ × 3/8″ dado across parts A and D, located as shown in the illustration.

Rectangular Unit with Shelf Inserts

MATERIALS LIST
(SHELF INSERT)

1 × 10 × 8′ #2 pine
1 × 8 × 8′ #2 pine
4d finishing nails
Wood glue

Rout a 1/4″ radius on all exposed edges.

Assemble the shelves with glue and 4d finishing nails. Sand and finish to match the larger shelving unit.

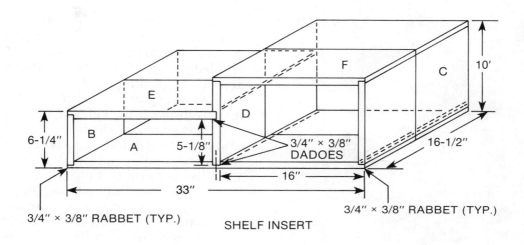

SHELF INSERT

KEY	PIECES	SIZE/DESCRIPTION
A	1	3/4 × 16-1/2 × 33 bottom rails
B	1	3/4 × 16-1/2 × 5-1/2 low end
C	1	3/4 × 16-1/2 × 9-1/4 high end
D	1	3/4 × 16-1/2 × 9-1/4 middle
E	1	3/4 × 16-1/2 × 16-5/8 low shelf tops
F	1	3/4 × 16-1/2 × 16-3/4 high shelf tops

CUTTING LIST (SHELF INSERT)

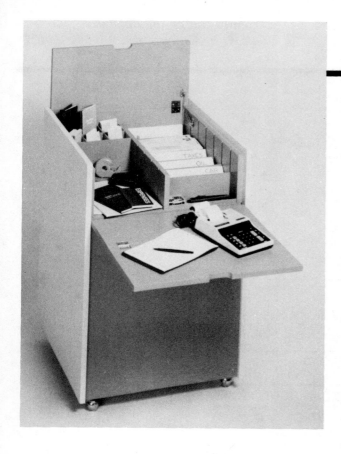

HOME FINANCE CENTER

A home finance center provides a way to stay on top of bill paying and record keeping. The project has a lid that opens into a writing surface on which you can write checks to pay monthly bills. Small compartments on the desktop are designed to hold checkbook, savings book, and payment booklets. Larger compartments on the desktop hold legal-size envelopes for storing receipts, bank statements, canceled checks, and so forth. A calculator and ledger pad fit easily in the open area of the desktop, and a pencil stop will keep writing instruments from rolling off the surface.

At the back of the home finance center (not visible in the photo) are two doors that open into a storage area divided into eight sections. Each storage section is large enough to hold a year's worth of financial information. So, when December 31 rolls around, just bundle up the envelopes from the top compartments you've been methodically stuffing all year and place them in a storage section. Then, if a curious Internal Revenue Service inquires about the three years' worth of records you're required to retain, you'll have them readily at hand. Getting to the storage area in the back is no problem. The home finance center is set on casters, so you can easily roll it out to reach the back doors.

The outside panels of the center are cut from one sheet of birch veneer plywood. The internal panels and shelves are made from a less expensive construction-grade plywood, and the top compartments' divider panels are made of hardboard. Construction of the center isn't complex—simple butt joints fortified with stripping, glue, and nails bring the plywood panels together.

Cut the sides (A) to size. On the sides, lay out the locations of the compartment panel (D), the base (K), the sliding rail panel (L), the front (B), back (C), and the shelf pin holes. Drill 1/4"-diameter holes 1/2" deep for the shelf pins.

Cut the front to size. Lay out and cut two 2-5/8"-deep × 1-5/8"-wide notches in the top edge of the front to allow passageway for the sliding rails (Q). Install two desk hinges on the top edge of the front, setting the hinges 3/32" into the top edge.

Cut the back, the base, the sliding rail panel, and the rail guides (P) to size. Attach the rail guides to the Grade C side of the sliding rail panel with glue and nails.

Cut the compartment panel, the lid stops (E), and the center wall (F) of the top compartment to size. Using an electric iron, apply veneer tape to the top and front edges of the center wall and the lid stops.

Machine parallel sets of 3/16"-deep and 5/16"-wide dadoes on the inside face of each lid stop and the face of the center wall that will be opposite it. Cut enough dadoes for six hardboard divider panels to fit into each side of the top compartment and space them as shown in the section view drawing. Note that the photograph shows several divider panels removed to create room for a calculator, ledger pad, etc.

Glue and nail the center wall to the compartment panel.

Cut the shelf panel (M) to size. Lay out the position of the 1/4" shelf pin holes, and drill them 3/8" deep.

Glue and nail the shelf panel between the sliding rail panel and the base.

Cut corner glue strips (used to strengthen butt joints between panels) to size from scrap lumber. Glue and nail the compartment panel, the sliding rail panel, the base, and the front to one of the sides. Do not attach the back. (You may find it easiest to attach corner stripping to the sides at this time, before assembly.) Then, glue and nail the other side in place. Glue and nail the lid stops in place, as well.

MATERIALS LIST

3/4" × 4' × 8' birch plywood
3/4" × 4' × 8' AC interior plywood
1/4" × 2' × 2' tempered hardboard
2 × 3 × 4' #2 pine
1 × 2 × 2' #2 pine
1 × 1 × 4' #2 pine
1/2-dia. dowel (3')
1/4"-dia. × 2" fluted dowels (4)
6d finishing nails
3d finishing nails
1" wire brads
1-1/2" × 2" (open) brass hinges
1-1/2"-wide offset cabinet hinge for
  3/4"-thick doors (brass-plated)
Right-hand brass-plated lid support
Standard magnetic cabinet door
  catches
2" plate-mounting brass-colored ball
  casters
Plastic shelf pins
3/4"-wide birch veneer tape
Wood filler
Wood glue

KEY	PIECES	SIZE/DESCRIPTION
CUTTING LIST		
A	2	3/4 × 24 × 34 sides (birch plywood)
B	1	3/4 × 22-1/2 × 25 front (birch plywood)
C	1	3/4 × 11-1/8 × 22-1/2 back (birch plywood)
D	1	3/4 × 21-1/2 × 22-1/2 compartment panel (AC plywood)
E	2	3/4 × 7 × 21-1/2 lid stops (birch plywood)
F	1	3/4 × 5 × 21-1/2 center wall (birch plywood)
G	2	3/4 × 10-5/8 × 22-3/8 cabinet lids (birch plywood)
H	1	3/4 × 6-1/4 × 22-3/8 desk panel (birch plywood)
J	2	3/4 × 11-1/8 × 21-1/2 storage doors (birch plywood)
K	1	3/4 × 21-1/2 × 22-1/2 base (AC plywood)

KEY	PIECES	SIZE/DESCRIPTION
CUTTING LIST (continued)		
L	1	3/4 × 21-1/2 × 22-1/2 sliding rail panel (AC plywood)
M	1	3/4 × 20-7/8 × 21-1/2 shelf panel (AC plywood)
N	6	3/4 × 10-5/8 × 21-1/4 shelves (AC plywood)
P	2	3/4 × 3/4 × 21-1/2 rail guides
Q	2	1-1/2 × 2-1/2 × 22-1/4 sliding rails
R	2	1/2-dia. × 13-3/4 cross ties (dowel)
S	1	3/4 × 1-1/2 × 22-3/8 desk panel edge strip
T	7	1/4 × 3-1/2 × 10-7/16 movable dividers (hardboard)
U	2	1/4 × 5 × 10-7/16 storage grid long walls (hardboard)
V	2	1/4 × 5 × 5-7/8 storage grid short walls (hardboard)

Cut the sliding rails to size. Drill two 1/2"-diameter holes through each rail. Locate the holes 1" and 7" from the rear edge of the rails and centered in the rails.

Cut to size the cross ties (R) for the sliding rails.

Drill a 7/8"-diameter fingerhole 1-3/4" deep into the end of each sliding rail. Drill a 7/8"-diameter hole into the bottom of each sliding rail intersecting each fingerhole.

Glue and nail the sliding rails onto the cross ties. Insert the sliding rail assembly between the compartment panel and the sliding rail panel.

Cut the cabinet lids (G) to size. Cut a 3"-wide × 1"-deep finger recess centered in one edge of each lid.

Cut the desk panel (H) and the desk panel edge strip (S) to size. Attach the edge strip to the desk panel by drilling four 1/4"-diameter holes

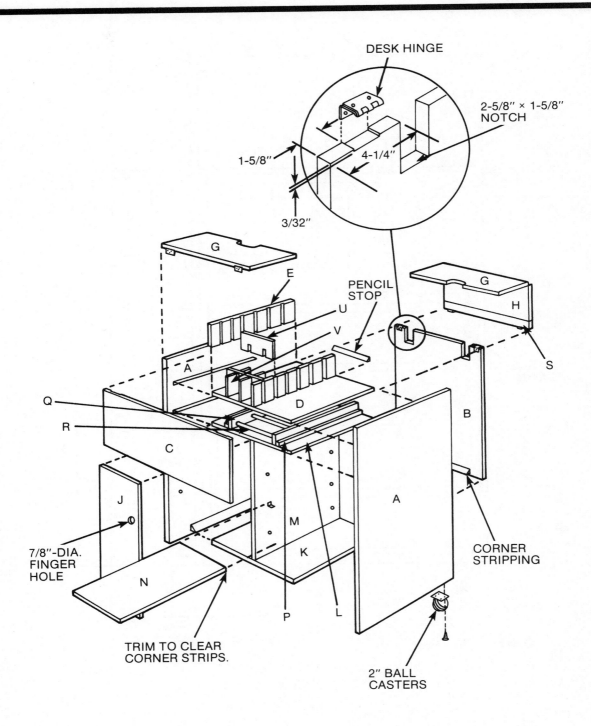

DESK HINGE

2-5/8" × 1-5/8" NOTCH

1-5/8"

4-1/4"

3/32"

G

E

U

V

PENCIL STOP

G

H

S

A

Q

D

B

R

C

J

7/8"-DIA. FINGER HOLE

M

K

A

CORNER STRIPPING

N

P

L

TRIM TO CLEAR CORNER STRIPS.

2" BALL CASTERS

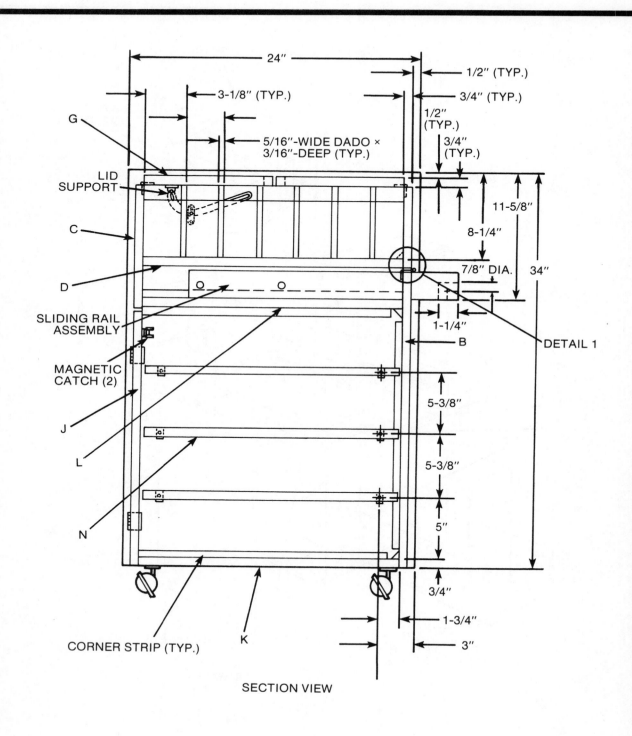

SECTION VIEW

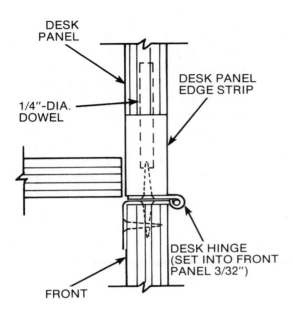

DESK PANEL

DESK PANEL EDGE STRIP

1/4"-DIA. DOWEL

DESK HINGE (SET INTO FRONT PANEL 3/32")

FRONT

DETAIL 1

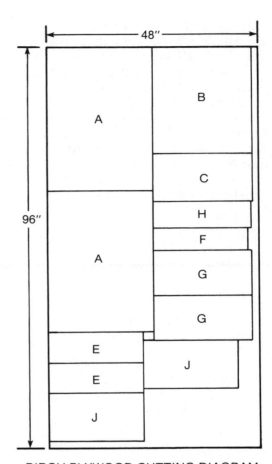

BIRCH PLYWOOD CUTTING DIAGRAM

into each and attaching with the edge strip dowels.

Apply veneer tape to cover all end grain of lids, the desk panel, and the top edge of the back panel.

Hinge together the back panel and one of the lid panels. Set the hinges in 3/32", or until the crack between the two panels is minimal.

Hinge together the desk panel with the second lid, setting the hinges in 3/32". (All lid hinges will be removed for painting.)

Glue and nail the back panel in place.

Apply veneer tape to the exposed edges of the sides.

Cut the shelves (N) to size. Trim one corner of each shelf as needed to clear the corner strips adjoining the front and side panels.

Cut the storage doors (J) to size. Drill a 7/8"-diameter fingerhole in each door.

Cut the pencil stop to size from the corner glue strips. Glue and nail the pencil stop in the top compartment panel between the center wall and the right side wall.

Cut the movable dividers (T) of the top compartment and the long and short walls (U, V) of the check storage grid to size. Cut two 1/4"-wide × 2-1/2"-long notches from one edge halfway across one long wall of the check storage grid. Cut matching notches centered in the short walls of the grid.

Assemble the check storage grid by gluing the long and short walls at the notches to form cross lap joints and by gluing the front wall (U) to the front ends of the short walls. After the glue dries, the check storage grid can be placed on either side of the top compartment.

Apply wood filler where needed, and sand all surfaces until smooth. Paint all parts as desired.

Reinstall all lid hinges. Hinge the storage doors to the sides. Install a magnetic catch for each storage door and a lid support.

Install the shelf pins and shelves; then install the casters on the base.

HOME OFFICE

Running a home is serious business. Banks, insurance companies, and the paper carrier must be paid on a regular basis. The pantry, cleaning closet, and medicine cabinet must be constantly replenished. Home improvements, entertainment, and vacations must be carefully budgeted. And then there are Christmas clubs, IRAs, and other investments that require attention, as well as the inevitable taxes. How does a person keep track of it all?

This project doesn't promise to balance your checkbook, but it will put your bookkeeping supplies in order. It is perfect for the modern home manager who uses a personal computer to track finances. And there is plenty of drawer and cabinet space for storing records and receipts. Whether in a bedroom or in

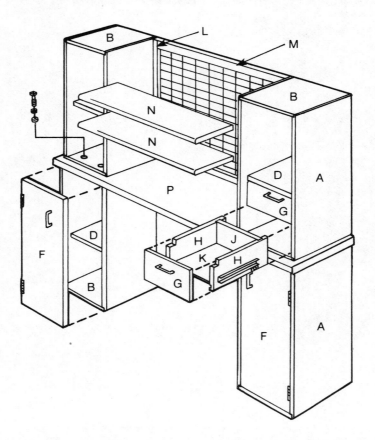

the family den, this attractive knockdown wall system will be a welcomed addition to your home.

Begin building the home office by cutting the box unit sides (A), tops and bottoms (B), back panels (C), and dividers (D) to size. Machine a 3/8"-deep × 3/4"-wide rabbet along the top and bottom edge of each side to accept a top and bottom, and along the back edge of each side, top, and bottom to accept a back panel.

Lay out and machine a 3/4" × 3/8" × 13" stopped dado cen-tered in each side to accept a divid-er. Cut a 3/8" × 1-1/2" notch in the front corner of each divider to allow it to fit the stopped dado in each of the side pieces.

Assemble the box units with glue and clamps. Secure the back panels in place with nails. Apply veneer tape to the front edges of each box unit and divider. Then, paint the box units and back panels with an enamel paint of your choice.

Cut the plinths (E) to size. Spread glue on the tops of the plinths, center the plinths under the

MATERIALS LIST

3/4" × 4' × 8' birch plywood
(2-1/2 sheets)
1/4" × 4' × 8' AC plywood
(1/4 sheet)
5/4 × 4 × 8' #2 pine (8)
3/16"-dia. × 1-1/2" hardwood dowels
(8)
14-gauge × 1" × 2" wire mesh,
31" × 46" in size
16-oz. can of spray paint
3/8" staples
1/4"-dia. × 3" chrome-plated door
pulls (4)
Magnetic cabinet door catches (2)
12" drawer slides (2 pairs)
Flush door cabinet hinges (2 pairs)
1/4"-dia. pin shelf supports (8)
3d finishing nails
No. 10 × 1-1/2" flathead screws (4)
1/4" × 3" machine screws with
washers and nuts
13/16" birch veneer tape (75')
Wood glue

CUTTING LIST

KEY	PIECES	SIZE/DESCRIPTION
A	8	3/4 × 16 × 32 sides (birch plywood)
B	8	3/4 × 15-1/4 × 16 tops and bottoms (birch plywood)
C	4	3/4 × 15-1/4 × 31-1/4 back panels (birch plywood)
D	4	3/4 × 14-3/8 × 15-1/4 dividers (birch plywood)
E	2	3/4 × 14-1/2 × 14-1/2 plinths (birch plywood)
F	2	3/4 × 14-3/8 × 30-3/8 doors (birch plywood)
G	2	3/4 × 7-1/4 × 14-3/8 drawer fronts (birch plywood)
H	4	3/4 × 6-3/8 × 13-1/4 drawer sides (birch plywood)
J	2	3/4 × 5-7/8 × 12-5/8 drawer backs (birch plywood)
K	2	1/4 × 12-5/8 × 13 drawer bottoms (AC plywood)
L	2	1-1/8 × 1-1/2 × 32 wire grid sides
M	2	1-1/8 × 1-1/2 × 47 wire grid top and bottom
N	2	1-1/8 × 10-1/2 × 46-7/8 shelves
P	1	1-1/8 × 17-1/2 × 80-1/2 tabletop

two lower box units, and nail the boxes to the plinths, using 3d finishing nails.

Cut the doors (F) to size. Apply veneer tape to all exposed edges of the doors and plinths. Then, cut two recesses on the outer edges of each door to accept the hinges.

Paint the doors and plinths. Then, attach the doors to the box units, using two hinges for each. Attach a door pull and magnetic catch to each bottom cabinet.

Cut the drawer fronts (G), backs (J), sides (H), and bottoms (K) to size. Machine two 3/4" × 3/8" × 5-3/4" stopped dadoes on the inside face of each drawer front to accept

the drawer sides. Cut a 3/8" × 5/8" notch in the top front corners of each drawer side to allow the sides to fit tightly into the stopped

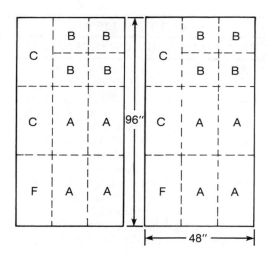

grooves in each drawer front. Machine a 3/4″ × 3/8″ dado across each drawer side, 3/8″ from the end, to accept a drawer back. Machine a 1/4″ × 3/8″ groove 1/4″ from the bottom edge of each drawer side to accept a drawer bottom.

Glue and clamp the drawers together. Apply veneer tape to the edges of each drawer front and to the top edges of the drawer sides. Then, paint the drawers.

Cut the wire grid sides (L) and the top and bottom (M) to size. Half-lap the corners to the frame. Ma-

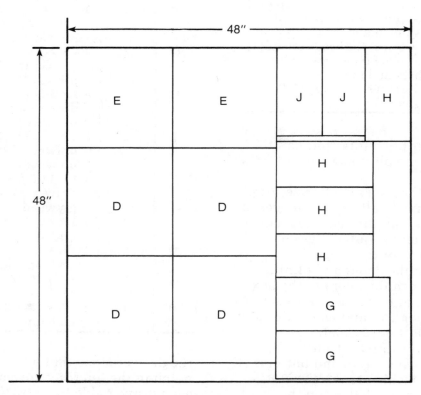

CUTTING DIAGRAM FOR HALF-SHEET

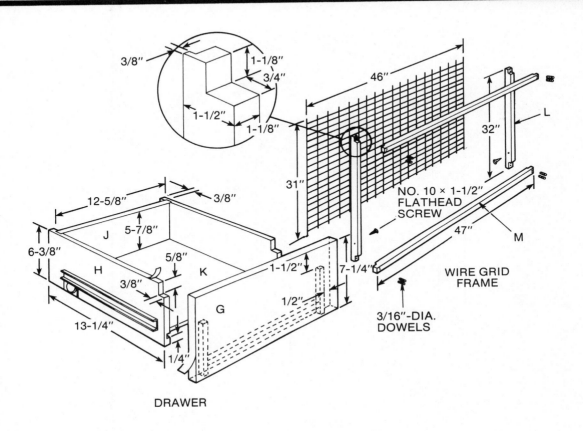

3/8"
1-1/8"
3/4"
1-1/2"
1-1/8"

46"

31"

32"

L

12-5/8"
3/8"
5-7/8"
J
6-3/8"
5/8"
H
3/8"
K
1-1/2"
G
1/2"
13-1/4"
1/4"

DRAWER

7-1/4"

NO. 10 × 1-1/2" FLATHEAD SCREW

47"

M

WIRE GRID FRAME

3/16"-DIA. DOWELS

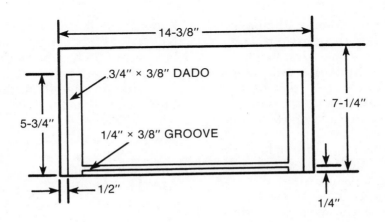

14-3/8"

3/4" × 3/8" DADO

7-1/4"

5-3/4"

1/4" × 3/8" GROOVE

1/2"

1/4"

DRAWER FRONT DETAIL

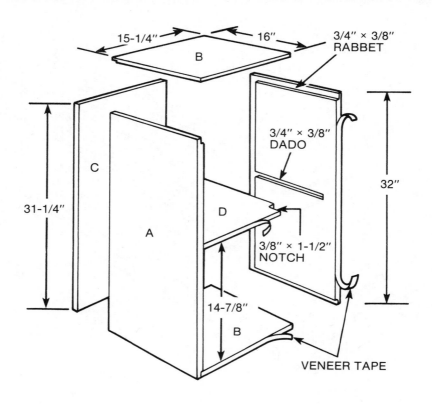

15-1/4"   16"   3/4" × 3/8"
RABBET

B

3/4" × 3/8"
DADO

C

32"

31-1/4"

D

A

3/8" × 1-1/2"
NOTCH

14-7/8"

B

VENEER TAPE

BOX UNIT

chine a 1/4" rabbet along the back edge of the frame's sides, top, and bottom to accept the wire mesh.

Drill two 3/16"-diameter holes through each corner of the frame to accept the dowel locking pegs.

Glue, peg, and clamp the frame together.

Machine a 1/4" radius along the front edges of the frame. Sand the frame and apply a clear finish to it.

Cut the wire mesh to size and paint it. Fasten the wire mesh to the frame with 3/8" staples. Drill four holes through the frame to accept No. 10 × 1-1/2" screws, which will be used to fasten the wire grid frame to the box units.

Glue up enough #2 pine to form the two shelves (N) and tabletop (P).

NOTE: Plywood or particleboard that is 3/4" thick can be used in place of the glued-up pine. If the substitution is made, use a double layer for the desktop.

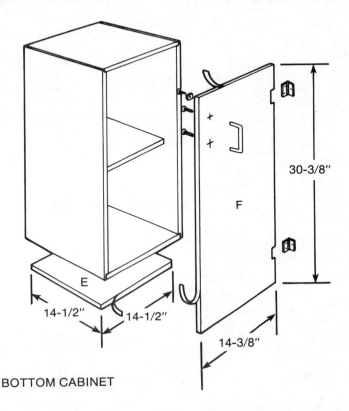

30-3/8"

F

E

14-1/2"   14-1/2"

14-3/8"

BOTTOM CABINET

Machine a 1/4" radius along the edges at each end of the shelves. Machine a 3/8" radius along the front and back edges of the shelves and along all edges of the tabletop. Sand all surfaces of the shelves and tabletop and apply a clear finish to them.

Set the tabletop on the bottom cabinets and set the upper box units on the tabletop. Drill 1/4"-diameter holes from the box units through the tabletop into the bottom cabinets. Be sure all units are positioned properly and clamped before drilling. Countersink the holes and bolt the units together with machine screws.

Lay out and drill 1/4"-diameter holes inside the box unit sides to accept shelf support pins. Install drawer slides and drawers where desired. Mount the wire grid frame between the box units, using No. 10 × 1-1/2" flathead screws. Insert shelf support pins in the holes you drilled for them and place the shelves in position.

Section 2
Kitchens and Dining Rooms

The busiest workshop in any home is probably the kitchen. Hours are spent every day in food preparation, serving meals, and preserving vegetables, fruits, and jams. Wall-to-wall and ceiling-to-floor cabinets with yards of countertop space are necessary for storing utensils, appliances, cookware, cutlery, and dinnerware—not to mention food supplies.

The goal of storage in the kitchen and dining room is efficient use of time and space. Appliances and utensils used most frequently should be stored where they are quickly accessible. Keep knives, mixing spoons, pots and pans, and other items used every day where they can be reached and replaced with a minimum of effort and motion. Utensils used less frequently should be kept above or behind those items in greater de-

mand. Seasonal or seldom used items should be boxed and stored out of the way in a closet.

Related items should be grouped in work centers. For example, rolling pins, cookie pans, flour, baking powder, and other baking needs should be stored in the same area to reduce footsteps and wasted time. Divide your kitchen into mixing, cooking, washing and drying, serving and food storage centers, and organize your storage accordingly. These storage hints will reduce the time and effort expended in the kitchen and make it a more enjoyable place.

The projects in this section will help you realize the goal of "smart storage." Some will help you discover overlooked space. Others will help you organize wasted cabinet space or place often-used items nearby.

SOFFIT STORAGE

If there never seems to be enough space in the kitchen, try looking up—above the cupboards, that is. The space between the top of the cabinets and the ceiling is an ideal place to display baskets, copper pots and pans, pottery, even serving pieces.

In the kitchen pictured, several storage boxes were built to fill the space between the cabinets and an overhead soffit. The boxes were made from glued-up pine stock, but plywood edged with pine strips could be used as well. The instructions given here are for one box 16-1/2" high, 14-3/4" deep, and

12' long. You may vary these dimensions to best utilize the available space in your kitchen. Build as many boxes as necessary and simply butt them together, hiding the joints with lengths of 3/4" molding (E).

Begin by assembling ten 1 × 4 × 12' pine boards into the top and bottom panels (A). Machine glue joints in the boards and glue them together—five boards per panel. Trim the glued-up panels to 14" in width.

Next, glue up five 1 × 4 × 48"-long boards. From this panel, cut the side panels (B) and the divider (D).

Position the side panels between the top and bottom panel flush with the outside edges. Glue and nail the top and bottom panels to the sides with 4d finishing nails. Center the divider in the box and secure with glue and 4d nails driven through the top and bottom panels.

Cut the back panels (C) to size next. Align them with the outer edges of the partially assembled box. Make sure that the box is square. Then glue and nail the back panels to the box with 4d finishing nails.

Rip a 12'-long 1 × 4 to 3" in width. Glue and nail this board to the top edge of the box. Set the nails and fill the holes with wood putty.

Sand the box and finish it to match your kitchen cabinets. When the finish is dry, lift the box (or boxes) into position. Hide the gap between storage boxes and the ceiling with 1" mullion or batten molding (F). Cover the butt joints between boxes with 3/4" half-round or lattice molding. All molding pieces should be finished before installation.

MATERIALS LIST

1 × 4 × 12' (11) pine
1 × 4 × 4' (5)
3/4" × 4' × 8' AB plywood
1" pine molding (12')
4d finishing nails
Wood putty
Wood glue

CUTTING LIST

KEY	PIECES	SIZE/DESCRIPTION
A	2	3/4 × 14 × 144 top and bottom panels
B	2	3/4 × 14 × 15 side panels
C	2	3/4 × 16-1/2 × 72 back panels (plywood)
D	1	3/4 × 14 × 15 divider
E	1	3/4 × 3 × 144 face board
F	1	1 × 144 face board trim

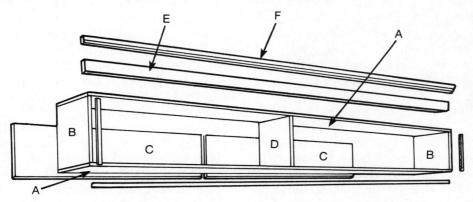

DINING ROOM DISPLAY SHELVES

These dining room display shelves offer a solution to the problem of display space. Their construction is simple and should not take long to complete. Their simplicity adds to their beauty and, topped with your favorite antique whatnots, these shelves create a country look that will complement any decor.

First, take the two 1 × 12s and rip each one to 9-1/2″ wide. Rip the cutoff strips to 1-1/2″ wide; these will be used for the back braces (B).

Next, cut the shelves to length from the 9-1/2″-wide pieces. Round the front corners of the shelves with a saber saw.

Lay out the shelf brackets on the 9-1/2″-wide cutoffs (see the illustrated grid pattern). Cut the brackets to shape with a saber saw.

Cut the back braces to length, and round the bottom corners.

Center each shelf over a brace so there is a 1″ overhang at each end. Center each shelf over a brace so that there is a 1″ overhang at each end. Drill and counterbore pilot holes through the shelves into the braces. Fasten the shelves to the braces, using glue and No. 8 × 1-1/2″ flathead wood screws. Then, fit a pair of brackets against the underside of each shelf and the front of the braces. Space them evenly from

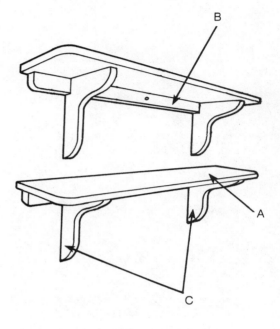

the ends of the shelves and fasten them with glue and No. 8 × 1-1/2" wood screws driven through the shelves. Be sure to counterbore the pilot holes. Fill all holes with wood putty.

Sand and finish the shelves before attaching them to the wall. When the shelves have dried, place them against the wall at the height you have chosen and check for level. While a helper holds the shelf level, drill counterbored holes into the back brace. Using No. 10 × 2-1/2" wood screws, screw the shelf to wall studs, or use 3/8" × 3" toggle bolts to mount the shelves to wallboard or paneling. Plug the holes with a contrasting color wood plug.

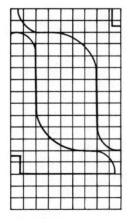

ONE SQUARE = 1"

MATERIALS LIST

1 × 12 × 8' #1 pine (2)
No. 10 × 2-1/2" wood screws
No. 8 × 1-1/2" wood screws
Toggle bolts (if necessary)
Wood plugs or buttons
Wood putty

CUTTING LIST

KEY	PIECES	SIZE/DESCRIPTION
A	2	3/4 × 9-1/2 × 72 shelves
B	2	3/4 × 1-1/2 × 70 back braces
C	4	3/4 × 8-1/2 × 12 brackets

CLOSET PANTRY

Any closet can be converted into a pantry by lining it with a plywood framework to hold shelves. The top shelf in the closet pantry shown was organized with vertical dividers on one side. The dividers keep cookie tins, party trays, and cutting boards at your fingertips. The remaining shelf space is ideal for storing appliances.

This project is designed as a freestanding insert with additional closet space on one or both sides. If a whole closet is utilized for pantry shelf space, eliminate the plywood sides and attach shelf cleats directly to the closet walls.

Begin by cutting the plywood panels to size. Measurements in the cutting list can be adjusted to fit a particular closet. The plywood sides can extend from floor to ceiling, or the framework can be built 18″ shorter than the total closet height so that the top panel also becomes a shelf.

Rout 1/4″ × 1/4″ dadoes in the top panel (A) and top shelf (C) to receive the 1/4″ plywood dividers (E). Also, rout a pair of 3/4″-wide × 1/4″-deep dadoes in the top and top shelf to receive the 3/4″ center divider (D). Using glue and No. 8 × 1-1/4″ flathead wood screws, attach plywood cleats (F) to the sides to support the shelves. Space them to use the area efficiently. Canned goods can be stacked double in an 8″ space. Larger items such as cereal boxes and soda bottles will need more room. The cleats for the top shelf must be 24-1/4″ from the top edge of the side panels.

Move the sides (B) into the closet and position the top panel flush with the outside edges of the sides. If room above the framework allows, secure the top to the sides using wood glue and 6d finishing nails. If the top panel is against the closet ceiling, glue it to the top edge of the side panels and drive several 6d finishing nails through it and into the ceiling to secure it.

Attach the shelves to the cleats, using wood glue and 4d finishing nails.

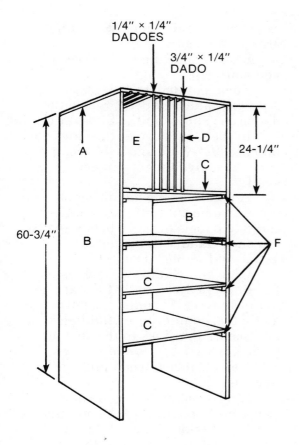

1/4″ × 1/4″
DADOES

3/4″ × 1/4″
DADO

E

D

A

C

24-1/4″

60-3/4″

B

B

B

C

C

F

MATERIALS LIST

3/4″ × 4′ × 8′ plywood sheets (4)
1/4″ × 4′ × 8′ plywood sheets (3)
No. 8 × 1-1/4″ wood screws
6d finishing nails
4d finishing nails
Wood glue

CUTTING LIST

KEY	PIECES	SIZE/DESCRIPTION
A	1	3/4 × 34 × 36 top panel
B	2	3/4 × 36 × 60 sides
C	4	3/4 × 32-1/2 × 36 shelves
D	1	3/4 × 24 × 36 center divider
E	7	1/4 × 24 × 36 dividers
F	8	3/4 × 3/4 × 36 cleats

   Spread glue in the dadoes in the top shelf and top panel and insert the dividers.
   Sand and paint the unit to match the room decor. Install shelf lining paper, if desired, and the pantry is ready to be stocked.

SPICE RACK

Add some zest to your kitchen decor with this impressive spice rack. The spice rack shown in the photograph is made of clear grade redwood, but feel free to substitute pine or a hardwood of your choice. It is wide enough to hold a round salt box, but the depth can be adjusted to any size. Take into consideration, too, the extras you want to display—plates, antique sugar bowls, dried flower arrangements, and so on. The dado and groove joinery adds to the appeal of the

rack and is easily done on a radial arm or table saw.

Start by cutting the shelves (A) and sides (B) to length.

Then, cut dadoes for the shelves 3/4" wide and 3/8" deep. Space the dadoes as shown in the illustration.

In the front edge of the sides cut notches 3/4" wide and 3/4" deep located 1" above the tops of each shelf.

A notch for the mounting bar must also be cut in the back edge of the side panels directly below the top shelf dado. Cut the notch 1-1/2" wide × 3/4" deep.

Glue and clamp the shelves to the sides, being sure that the assembly is square. If clamps are not available, counterbore pilot holes and secure the sides to the shelves with No. 6 × 1-1/4" wood screws. Fill the holes with wood plugs or buttons.

Rip five slats 3/4" wide and crosscut to length. Rip the mounting bar 1-1/2" wide and crosscut to length. Install the slats with glue and 2d finishing nails. Set the nails slightly below the surface and fill the hole with wood putty.

Install the mounting bar with glue and 4d finishing nails. Predrill before nailing to avoid splitting the bar.

After the glue sets up, round the corners and edges of the sides, shelves, and slats, using sandpaper or a router and a 1/4" corner rounding bit. Sand the unit thoroughly and finish as desired.

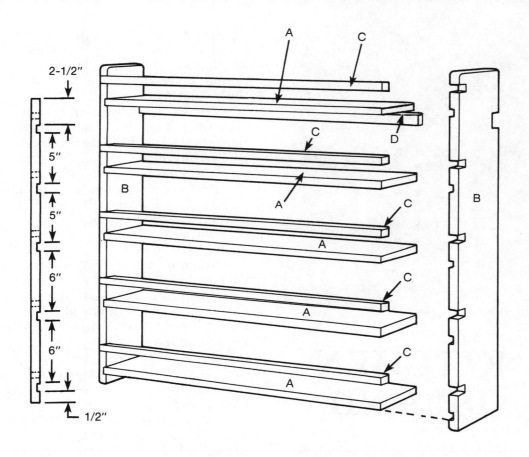

MATERIALS LIST
1 × 4 × 10′ clear all heart redwood (2)
No. 6 × 1-1/4″ wood screws (optional)
4d finishing nails
2d finishing nails
Wood plugs or buttons (optional)
Wood putty
Wood glue

CUTTING LIST		
KEY	**PIECES**	**SIZE/DESCRIPTION**
A	5	3/4 × 3-1/2 × 23-1/4 shelves
B	2	3/4 × 3-1/2 × 28-3/4 sides
C	5	3/4 × 3/4 × 24 retainer slats
D	1	3/4 × 1-1/2 × 24 mounting bar

KITCHEN ISLAND

If the addition of built-in storage and work space is not practical in your kitchen, consider building this movable cabinet. The high, deep shelves provide ample room for small appliances, and the drawers are long enough to hold large cooking and serving utensils. Dowel-supported side shelves hold jars of condiments and baking supplies securely and provide a place for materials needed close at hand to oven or mixing bowl.

The top of the island cabinet (thick enough to support clamped appliances) is constructed of double-layered particleboard faced with plastic laminate.

Finally, the casters allow for easy relocation, and the 34" height permits the whole cabinet to be tucked out of the way under a standard 36" countertop.

Begin construction of the kitchen island by building the side storage units. Cut the uprights (A), top and bottom pieces (B), and the shelves (C) to size.

Machine a 3/4" × 3/8" rabbet on each end of the uprights. Lay out and machine a 3/4" × 3/8" dado in each upright to hold one shelf per side. (The shelf position can be varied.) Machine a 3/8" × 1/2" rabbet along the back edge of the uprights and the top and bottom pieces of each side storage unit to accept the back panel.

Cut the dowels for the holding bars (D). Lay out and drill 1/2"-diameter holes 3/8" deep in the uprights to receive the ends of the bars.

Assemble the two side storage units, securing all joints with glue and finishing nails. Be sure to keep the front edges of the shelves flush with the front edges of the uprights to make room for adding the backs later. Cut the backs (E) of the side storage units to size. Lay out and drill parallel rows of 1/4"-diameter holes located 1-3/8" and 7-7/8" in from the rear edge of each panel back to accept the shelf supports for the adjustable shelf. Space the holes 2" apart on center. With glue and 2d finishing nails, fasten the backs to the side storage units.

Next, construct the bottom shelf and the middle shelf for the front side. Cut the front and back edge

MATERIALS LIST

1 × 6 × 10' #2 pine
1 × 6 × 8' #2 pine (3)
1 × 2 × 8' #2 pine (2)
3/4" × 4' × 4' particleboard
1/2" × 4' × 8' AC plywood
1/4" × 4' × 4' AC plywood
1/2"-dia. hardwood dowel (10')
30" × 34" plastic laminate
6d finishing nails
2d finishing nails
Contact cement
1" underlayment nails
No. 8 × 1-3/4" wood screws
No. 8 × 1-1/4" wood screws
1/4"-dia. shelf supports (4)
14" side-mounted drawer slides (2)
2-1/2" surface-mounted casters (4)
Wood glue

CUTTING LIST

KEY	PIECES	SIZE/DESCRIPTION
A	4	3/4 × 5-1/2 × 30 side storage uprights
B	4	3/4 × 5-1/2 × 23-1/4 side storage tops and bottoms
C	2	3/4 × 5 × 23-1/4 side storage shelves
D	4	1/2-dia. × 23-1/4 holding bars

CUTTING LIST (continued)

KEY	PIECES	SIZE/DESCRIPTION
E	2	1/2 × 23-1/4 × 29-1/4 side storage backs (plywood)
F	2	3/4 × 1-1/2 × 19 middle shelf front and back edge bands
G	2	3/4 × 1-1/2 × 13-3/4 middle shelf side edge bands
H	1	1/2 × 18-1/4 × 13-3/4 middle shelf panel (plywood)
J	2	3/4 × 1-1/2 × 19 bottom shelf front and back edge bands
K	2	3/4 × 1-1/2 × 23-1/4 bottom shelf side edge bands
L	1	1/2 × 18-1/4 × 23-1/4 bottom shelf panel (plywood)
M	1	1/2 × 19 × 28-1/2 middle partition (plywood)
N	1	1/2 × 8-3/4 × 18-7/8 adjustable shelf (plywood)
P	1	3/4 × 1-1/2 × 18-7/8 adjustable shelf edge band
Q	2	3/4 × 5-3/8 × 18-7/8 drawer fronts
R	4	3/4 × 5-3/8 × 14 drawer sides
S	2	3/4 × 4-7/8 × 16-3/8 drawer backs
T	2	1/4 × 17-1/8 × 14 drawer bottoms (plywood)
U	2	3/4 × 24 × 30 top

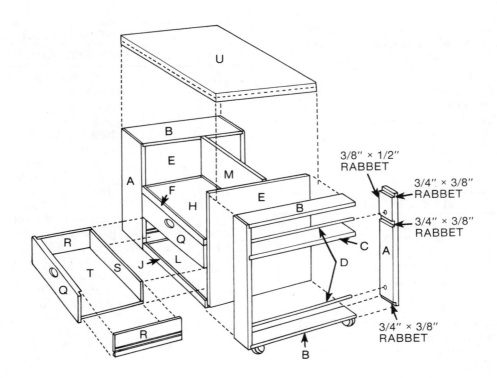

3/8" × 1/2"
RABBET

3/4" × 3/8"
RABBET

3/4" × 3/8"
RABBET

3/4" × 3/8"
RABBET

bands (F, J) to size. Machine a 3/4" × 3/8" rabbet on each end of the edge bands. Cut the side edge bands (G, K) to size. Machine a 3/8"-deep × 1/2"-wide rabbet along the top edge of all the shelf edge band pieces to accept the shelf panels (H, L). Cut the shelf panels to size.

Assemble the shelves, using glue and 6d finishing nails to fasten the edge bands to the panels.

Cut the middle partition (M) to size.

Position the bottom shelf flush with the sides and bottoms of the side units. Drill and countersink pilot holes through the back panels of the side units and into the bottom

shelf. Fasten the bottom shelf to the side units using wood glue and No. 8 × 1-1/4" flathead wood screws.

Position the center shelf 11" from the bottom shelf and flush with the sides of the side units. Drill and countersink pilot holes through the back panels of the side units and into the shelf. Fasten the shelf to the side units using wood glue and No. 8 × 1-1/4" flathead wood screws.

Position the middle partition against the back side of the center shelf and square it with the bottom shelf. Drill and countersink pilot holes through the back panel of the side units and into the edge of the partition. Secure it in place with wood glue and No. 8 × 1/4″ flathead wood screws.

Next, cut the adjustable shelf (N) to size. (More shelves can be added, if desired.) Cut the adjustable shelf edge band (P) to size. Lay out and machine a 3/8″ × 1/2″ groove down the center of the backside of the edge band to accept the shelf. Glue and nail the shelf and edge band together. Attach shelf supports to the shelf, positioned to match the 1/4″ holes previously drilled.

Cut the drawer fronts (Q), sides (R), and backs (S) to size. Machine a 3/8″ × 1-1/4″ rabbet on each end of the drawer fronts to accept the sides. Lay out and machine a 1/4″ × 3/8″ groove in the drawer sides and front to accept the bottom. Locate the groove 1/4″ above the bottom edge of the front and sides.

Cut the drawer bottoms (T) to size. Lay out and drill a 1″-diameter hole in each drawer front for a finger pull. Rout a 1/4″ radius on the inside and outside edges of the finger holes. Glue and nail the drawers together.

Mount drawer slides to the drawers and cabinet and install the drawers. Mount casters on the bottom of the cabinet.

Sand all surfaces and finish as desired.

Cut the pieces of particleboard for the top (U) to size. Fasten particleboards together, using glue and underlayment nails. Cover the sides and upper surface of the top with plastic laminate (or another covering). Install the top on the cabinet, and screw it in place with No. 8 × 1-3/4″ flathead wood screws.

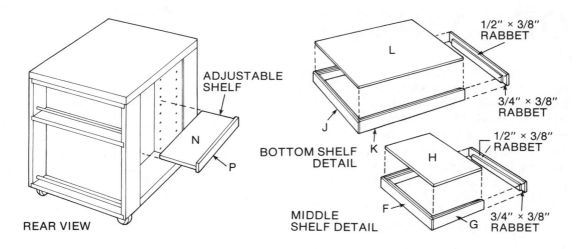

REAR VIEW

ADJUSTABLE SHELF

N

P

BOTTOM SHELF DETAIL

MIDDLE SHELF DETAIL

L

J

K

H

F

G

1/2″ × 3/8″ RABBET

3/4″ × 3/8″ RABBET

1/2″ × 3/8″ RABBET

3/4″ × 3/8″ RABBET

SPICE ORGANIZER

Your local hardware store is well stocked with materials that lend themselves to imaginative craftsmanship. For example, how many uses can you find for hardware cloth? To prime your idea file, here is a simple spice rack made of 2 × 4 pine boards, maple dowels, and 1/4" hardware cloth.

To make this freestanding project, first cut the rack sides (A) and support rods (B) to size. Mark the sides left and right.

Lay out and drill seven 1/2"-diameter holes through each rack side. (See the illustration for hole placement.) Back the sides with scrap wood while drilling to avoid splintering the wood.

Sand a 1/8" radius on all edges of both rack sides.

Lay out and cut three 1/16"-wide by 1/4"-deep crosscut slots across the inside of each rack side. Use a plywood blade to cut the narrow kerfs.

Lay out and cut one 1/16"-wide by 1/4"-deep groove along the inside rear edge of each rack side.

Cut a 1/16"-wide by 1/4"-deep groove down the length of four support rods. This groove will accept the edges of the hardware cloth shelves.

MATERIALS LIST

1 × 4 × 4' #2 white pine
1/2"-dia. maple dowels (8')
1/4" hardware cloth (3 square feet)
Wood glue

CUTTING LIST

KEY	PIECES	SIZE/DESCRIPTION
A	2	3/4 × 3-1/2 × 18 sides (white pine)
B	7	1/2 × 12 support rods
C	1	6-1/4 × 11-1/4 hardware cloth shelf
D	2	11-1/2 × 11-1/4 hardware cloth shelf
E	24	1/16 × 1/4 × 1/4 filler splines

Cut the hardware cloth shelves (C, D) to size. Bend 2-1/2" of the top and bottom edges of the middle and lower shelves at a 90-degree angle to fit into the proper slot in the support rods. Bend the bottom 2-1/2" of the top piece 90 degrees also.

Spray paint the shelves with your choice of spray enamel. Then, insert the shelves into the support rods and glue the support rods into the rack sides.

Cut the filler splines (E) from scrap stock. Insert a spline into both ends of every slot and groove in the sides and into both ends of the four grooved support rods. Trim the splines flush with the face of the rack sides.

Sand and finish the spice rack as desired.

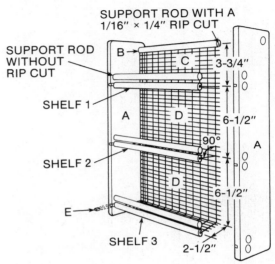

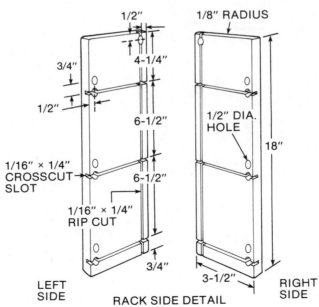

RACK SIDE DETAIL

PACK-IT-IN PANTRY

If your family is growing, then your need for food storage is growing also. A practical, permanent solution to a shortage of pantry space is the freestanding unit shown here. This compact pantry squeezes more than 22 square feet of shelving space inside approximately 5 square feet of floor space. There are shelves

on seven surfaces—on the back wall of the cabinet, on both sides of the swinging units, and on the inner surface of the two cabinet doors. And, although there are a lot of pieces to this pantry, the unit is constructed with butt joints. So, even someone with limited carpentry skills can build it.

Begin by cutting the cabinet sides (A) to size. Make a 5-1/4"-high × 2-1/2"-wide notch on the bottom front corner of each side to form the kick space. Cut the cabinet back (B), top and base (C), kick plate (J), upper shelves (F), divider/hinge carrier (H), and top and base cleats (D, E) to size.

Mark the positions of the top and base on the inner surface of each cabinet side. Using the pencil lines as reference, glue and screw the top and base cleats in place. Glue and screw the top and base onto the support strips.

Glue and screw the cabinet back and kick plate in place. Rip the 1 × 4 pine boards in half and from the resulting narrow boards, crosscut the face frame stiles (K) and rails (L).

Position the face frame stiles flush with the outside edges of the cabinet sides, and the top of the bottom rail flush with the top edge of the bottom panel. Drill and countersink pilot holes through the frame and into the edges of the cabinet panels. Install the frame with glue and No. 8 × 1-1/4" flathead wood screws.

Draw a vertical line down the center of the inner surface of the cabinet back. Draw a second vertical line 3/8" to the right of the center line as a guide for centering the di-

MATERIALS LIST

3/4" × 4' × 8' AC interior plywood (2 sheets)
1/2" × 4' × 8' AC interior plywood (2 sheets)
1/4" × 4' × 8' AC interior plywood
1 × 4 × 10' select pine (2)
6d finishing nails
No. 8 × 1-1/4" wood screws
No. 6 × 1" wood screws
2" piano hinge, 60" long (2)
2" piano hinge, 48" long (2)
Steel L-brackets (16)
Doorknobs
Magnetic latches
Wood glue

CUTTING LIST

KEY	PIECES	SIZE/DESCRIPTION
A	2	3/4 × 23-1/4 × 84 cabinet sides
B	1	1/4 × 31 × 84 cabinet back
C	2	1/2 × 23-1/4 × 29-1/2 cabinet top and base
D	2	3/4 × 3/4 × 23 cabinet top cleats
E	2	3/4 × 3/4 × 20-1/2 cabinet base cleats
F	2	1/2 × 15-1/4 × 29-1/2 upper shelves
G	4	3/4 × 3/4 × 15-1/4 upper shelf cleats
H	1	3/4 × 13 × 56 cabinet divider

CUTTING LIST (continued)

KEY	PIECES	SIZE/DESCRIPTION
J	1	1/4 × 5-1/4 × 31 kick plate
K	2	3/4 × 1-11/16 × 80 cabinet face stiles
L	2	3/4 × 1-11/16 × 27-1/2 cabinet face rails
M	4	3/4 × 3/4 × 3 face frame reinforcing strips
N	8	1/2 × 3-1/2 × 14-3/8 lower shelves
P	16	3/4 × 3/4 × 3-1/2 lower shelf cleats
Q	4	1/2 × 8-1/2 × 54 swinging unit sides
R	2	1/2 × 8-1/2 × 8-1/2 swinging unit tops
S	2	1/2 × 8 × 8-1/2 swinging unit bottoms
T	24	1/2 × 3-3/4 × 8-1/2 swinging unit shelves
U	28	1/4 × 1 × 8-1/2 swinging unit shelf lips
V	2	1/2 × 8-1/2 × 53 vertical shelf dividers
W	2	3/4 × 13-5/8 × 76-1/4 cabinet doors
X	4	1/2 × 4-1/2 × 71 door unit sides
Y	2	1/2 × 4-1/4 × 9-1/2 door unit tops
Z	18	1/2 × 4 × 9-1/2 door unit bottom and shelves
AA	18	1/4 × 1 × 9-1/2 door unit shelf lips

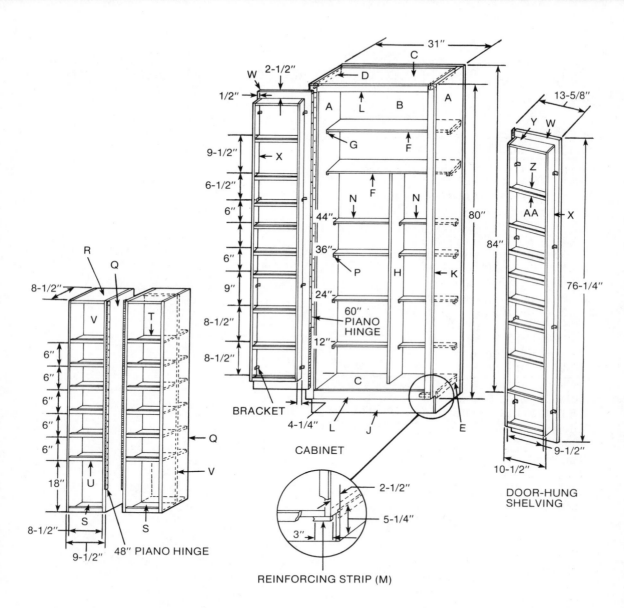

31"

C

W 2-1/2"

1/2"

D

A L B A

9-1/2" X

G F

6-1/2"

6"

N F N

6" 44"

36"

P H K

9" 24"

8-1/2" 60"
PIANO
HINGE

8-1/2" 12"

80"

84"

BRACKET C

4-1/4" L J E

CABINET

R

Q

8-1/2"

V T

6"

6"

6" Q

6"

6" V

18" U

S

S

8-1/2"

9-1/2" 48" PIANO HINGE

2-1/2"

5-1/4"

3"

REINFORCING STRIP (M)

13-5/8"

Y W

Z

AA X

76-1/4"

9-1/2"

10-1/2"

DOOR-HUNG
SHELVING

vider/hinge carrier. Extend both lines horizontally onto the base. Drill pilot holes through the center (first) line on the back and base. Spread glue on the bottom and rear edge of the divider/hinge carrier. Place it in position and screw it to the back and base.

Cut the upper shelf cleats (G) to size. Position the shelf support strips for the large shelves on the cabinet sides. Glue and screw them in place. Glue and screw the two large upper shelves to the shelf cleats and the back.

NOTE: *For increased flexibility in shelf spacing, adjustable supporting hardware can be substituted for the stationary cleats. Additional shelves can also be added as shown in the photograph.*

Cut the lower shelves (N) and their cleats (P) to size. Beginning at the cabinet base, establish points of 12", 24", 36", and 44" on each side of the cabinet and on each side of the divider/hinge carrier. Draw horizontal lines through these points. Position the tops of the cleats flush with these lines, and glue and screw the cleats to the side panels. Position the shelves on the shelf supports. (Note: These shelves can also be installed with adjustable supporting hardware.)

Now, build the swinging shelf units. Cut the top (R), bottom (S), sides (Q), and vertical shelf divider (V) for each shelf unit to size. Mark a top, front, and inside on each of the sides.

Starting from the inside bottom of each side, make a pencil mark at points 13", 19", 25", 31", 37", and 43". Draw a horizontal line at each of these points. These will be the

shelftop reference marks during assembly.

NOTE: *The number of shelves and/ or the spacing between the shelves can be altered to suit, as shown in the photograph.*

Draw a vertical centerline on the inner surface of each side. Draw a second vertical line 1/4" to the right of the centerline to help center double shelf divider. Drill pilot holes, 6" apart, along the center (first) line of each side. Drill three pilot holes 1/4" below each of the horizontal shelf-top lines. Glue and screw the double shelf divider to the sides using the previously drawn vertical lines as reference.

Glue and screw the top and bottom to the sides.

Cut the shelves (T) and shelf lips (U) to size. Using the horizontal reference lines, glue and screw the shelves in place. Glue and screw the shelf lips onto the shelf edges.

Install a piano hinge on the front upper right side of one unit and another hinge on the front upper left side of the other unit. The tops of the hinges should be flush with the unit top. Hang the units on the vertical divider/hinge carrier taking care that both units are centered to float freely. Finally, build the door hung shelving.

Cut the doors to size. (Note: Some width adjustments can be made later, if needed, when the door hinges are added and the door is hung. Paper shims can be placed between the stiles and hinges. Door tops or bottoms can be recut, planed, or sanded as necessary.) Mark each door to establish top, bottom front, back, and right and left side hinge locations.

Cut the sides (X), tops (Y), and bottoms (Z) to size. Mark the inside and bottom on each of the four sides.

Starting from the inside bottom of each side, make a pencil mark at points 8-1/2", 17", 26", 32", 38-1/2", 44-1/2", 51" and 60-1/2". Draw a horizontal reference line at each of these points. Drill three pilot holes 1/4" below each horizontal reference line. Glue and screw the sides, top, and bottom of each shelving unit in place.

Use brackets to mount a frame to the inner surface of each door.

Cut the shelves (Z) and shelf lips (AA) to size. Glue and nail the shelves and the shelf lips in place.

Fasten a piano hinge to each door's outside edge. The top of each hinge should begin 1/16" below the door's top edge. Position the doors in the cabinet face frame opening and fasten the hinges to the inside edges of the stiles.

Sand as needed. Apply at least two coats of oil-base paint to the exterior, sanding lightly between coats. The interior can be finished with one coat of sanding sealer or sanded and painted.

Install doorknobs and door fasteners.

KITCHEN NICHES

Another spill—quick, where are those paper towels? You will be better prepared to handle those all-too-frequent minor mishaps after you build this paper towel holder—no more searching under the sink or in the closet for paper towels.

The paper towel holder as well as the matching recipe holder and bookshelf are easy to make. All can be built from 1/2" plywood and painted to accent your kitchen decor. Or make them from standard pine boards for a more country look. The plans use dadoes to add rigidity to the construction, but simple butt joints nailed and glued can be used also. Make these kitchen niches as simple or as complex as you like.

Paper Towel Holder

Before building this project, measure your brand of paper towels to get the inside width dimension. Most standard rolls will turn freely in a space 12-1/2" wide. Also mea-

MATERIALS LIST

1/2″ × 4′ × 4′ AB or AC interior
  plywood
1″-dia. hardwood dowel (2′)
No. 6 × 5/8″ brass roundhead wood
  screw
2d finishing nails
3/4″ brads
1-1/2″-dia. hardboard discs (2)
Porcelain or brass knobs (2)
2″-dia. hardboard scraps (2)
Wood glue

CUTTING LIST (PAPER TOWEL HOLDER)

KEY	PIECES	SIZE/DESCRIPTION
A	1	1/2 × 12 × 13 top
B	1	1/2 × 12 × 13 shelf
C	2	1/2 × 9-1/2 × 12 sides
D	1	1-dia. × 13-1/4 dowel

CUTTING LIST (RECIPE AND COOKBOOK HOLDER)

KEY	PIECES	SIZE/DESCRIPTION
A	2	1/2 × 10-1/2 × 15 cabinet sides
B	1	1/2 × 13-1/2 × 15 cabinet back
C	1	1/2 × 10 × 13-1/2 shelf
D	1	1/2 × 4-1/2 × 10 divider
E	1	1/2 × 10-1/4 × 13-1/2 cabinet bottom
F1	2	1/2 × 3-7/8 × 6-1/8 drawer front
F2	4	1/2 × 3-7/8 × 9-1/2 drawer sides
F3	2	1/2 × 3-7/8 × 6-1/8 drawer back
F4	2	1/2 × 5-5/8 × 9-1/2 drawer bottom

sure the depth of your kitchen cabinets. The paper holder is designed to fit flush with the front of the cabinet. Adjust the cutting list to best accommodate your kitchen and particular paper products.

After verifying all dimensions, cut the pieces to size. Cut 1/2″-wide × 1/4″-deep rabbets along the inside top edges of the sides (C). Also rout a 1/2″ × 1/4″ dado 3″ from the top edge of each side. Then drill two 1-1/16″-diameter holes centered

3″ from the front edge and 2″ from the bottom edge of each side.

Spread carpenter's wood glue in the dadoes and rabbets, then assemble the unit and clamp until dry. The project can also be held together with 2d finishing nails until the glue sets up.

After the glue has set up, glue one hardboard cap over the outside of one of the holes. Attach the other disk to the other side using a No. 6 × 5/8″ brass roundhead screw.

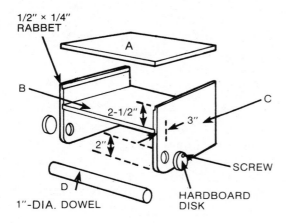

1/2″ × 1/4″ RABBET
A
B
2-1/2″
C
3″
2″
SCREW
D
HARDBOARD DISK
1″-DIA. DOWEL

Drive the screw through the top edge of the cap so that the cap can rotate away from the holes for removal of the dowel rod.

Recipe and Cookbook Holder

The recipe and cookbook holder is also easy to make. After verifying all dimensions, cut the individual pieces to size. Cut 1/2″ × 1/4″ rabbets on the back edges of the sides as well as the bottom edges of the sides and back. Also cut 1/2″ × 1/4″ dadoes in the center of the shelf and the bottom and 4-1/2″ from the bottom edges of the sides.

Assemble the project, using carpenter's wood glue in all the joints. Clamp the pieces together with bar clamps. The pieces can also be held together with 2d finishing nails while the glue sets up.

While the glue is drying, assemble the two recipe holder drawers. Butt joints, 3/4″ brads, and wood glue can be used to assemble the drawers, but they will last longer if rabbet joints are used. Cut 1/2″ × 1/4″ rabbets along the bottom edges of the front, sides, and back, and also along the sides of the front and back.

Assemble the drawers with brads and glue; clamp the pieces together until the glue sets up.

Paint, stain, or varnish the kitchen niches as desired. Then, screw the paper towel holder to the underside of a cabinet. Finally, attach drawer pulls to the recipe drawer fronts, and your work is done.

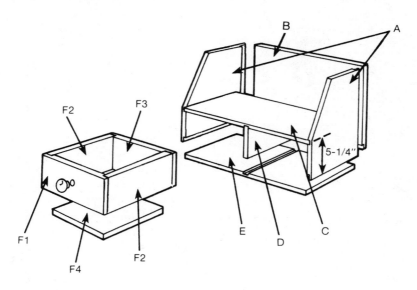

BROOM
CLOSET

This easy-to-build shelving system for a broom closet will also

work in a laundry area to provide a spot for storing an ironing board and cleaning supplies.

Adjust the height and width of the storage module as necessary to fit the available space. Leave at least 12″ between the top shelf and the closet ceiling and 6″ between the shelves and the closet door.

Begin construction of the broom closet by ripping a sheet of plywood into three pieces, each 15″ wide. From these three pieces, cut the storage module panels to length. (See the accompanying panel layout diagram.) Cut the lower cleat (F) to length from a scrap piece of 1 × 8.

The shelves (E) are supported by metal standards and clips. So, rout grooves 2″ in from the long edges of the left side panel and the center support panel so that the standards can be mounted flush with the surface of the panels. The actual width and depth of the grooves will depend on the size of the standards. Also, rout a 3/4″ × 3/8″ dado across the underside of the top shelf (C), 14-1/2″ from the left side.

Sand the pieces of the storage module. Apply veneer tape to the front edges of the plywood panels, and paint the pieces to match the closet interior.

Attach the left side panel to the wall using No. 8 × 1-1/2″ wood screws. On the right side of the closet, attach the lower cleat to the wall so that the top edge is 66-5/8″ from the floor. Attach hooks to this

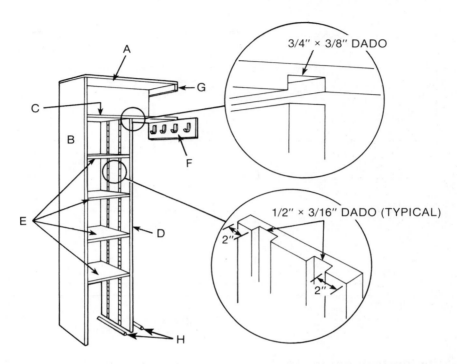

panel every 4″ to provide hangers for brooms, aprons, and other items. (A variety of hooks and clips is available at your local hardware store or home center.)

MATERIALS LIST

3/4″ × 4′ × 8′ CD plywood
1 × 8 × 2′ #2 pine
Standards with shelf supports (4)
L-brackets (2)
1/2″ quarter-round molding (3′)
No. 8 × 1-1/2″ wood screws
4d finishing nails
2d finishing nails
Hooks

CUTTING LIST

KEY	PIECES	SIZE/DESCRIPTION
A	1	3/4 × 15 × 36 top
B	1	3/4 × 15 × 78-1/4 left side panel
C	1	3/4 × 15 × 35-1/4 top shelf
D	1	3/4 × 15 × 67 center support panel
E	4	3/4 × 14-3/8 × 15 shelves
F	1	3/4 × 7-1/4 × 21 lower cleat
G	1	3/4 × 2-5/8 × 15 upper cleat
H	2	1/2 × 1/2 × 15 quarter-round molding

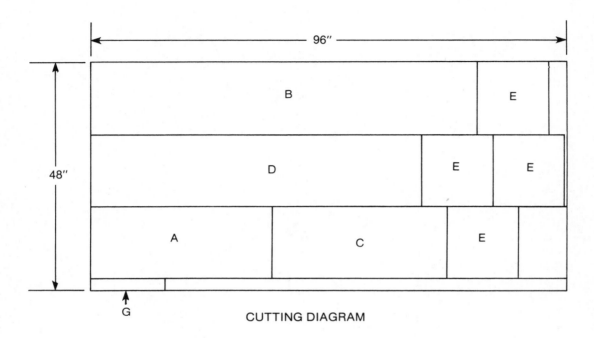

CUTTING DIAGRAM

Set the top shelf on the cleat. Attach it to the left side with two L brackets. Nail the shelf to the cleat with 4d finishing nails.

Fit the center support into the dado in the underside of the top shelf, and secure it with 4d finishing nails. Plumb the center support and, using 2d finishing nails, nail 1/2" quarter-round molding to the floor on both sides of the support.

Position the shelves on the shelf clips however your storage items will be best accommodated.

Using No. 8 × 1-1/2" flathead wood screws, screw the top cleat to the right wall so that the top of the cleat is 10-7/8" above the top shelf. Position the top of the storage module on the cleat and the top of the left side panel. Secure it with 4d finishing nails.

WOODEN POT RACK

A pot rack hung in a strategic spot in a kitchen will save time and footsteps for the cook. The pot rack shown is also an attractive way to utilize empty wall space. However, this rack works only for lids with a puckered lip. It will not work for lids with a flared lip.

The following instructions include measurements based on a cookware set that includes a 10″ frying pan with lid, a 1-quart sauce pan with lid, a 2-quart sauce pan with lid, and a 3-quart sauce pan with lid. Adjust all measurements to accommodate your individual cookware and your preferred arrangement of the cookware on the pot rack.

Begin by cutting the front board (A) to size. Then, lay out pots, pans, and lids on the grade A side of the front board, keeping the bottoms of the pots and pans facing up. Arrange the cookware as you would like it to hang on the finished pot rack. Trace the outlines of the cookware lightly onto the front

MATERIALS LIST

3/4" AC interior plywood
  (1/4 sheet)
1/4"-dia. × 2-1/2" dowel
4d finishing nails
No. 10 × 3" wood screws
Wood glue

CUTTING LIST

KEY	PIECES	SIZE/DESCRIPTION
A	1	3/4 × 7 × 48 front board (plywood)
B	1	3/4 × 7 × 48 backboard (plywood)
C	10	3/4 × 3 × 3 spacer blocks (plywood)

board. (These outlines will be used for reference only.)

Measure the outside diameter of each pot (not including the lip at the top) and draw a semicircle that size centered on the top edge of the board, within the light outline of each pot. You will cut along these semicircles.

Next, measure the inside diameter of each lid. Draw a semicircle that size within the semicircles drawn previously. These newly drawn semicircles will be cut out and used as lid hangers.

With your saber saw blade set at a 15-degree angle, cut out the lid

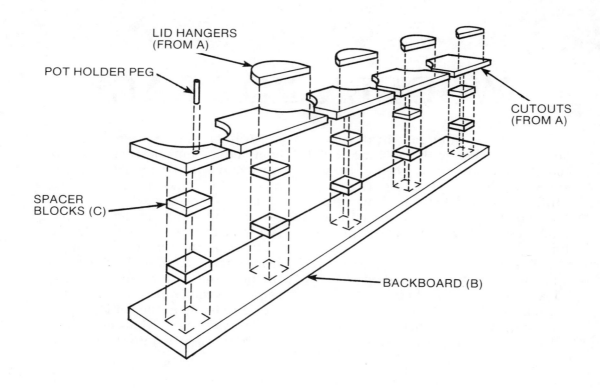

LID HANGERS (FROM A)

POT HOLDER PEG

CUTOUTS (FROM A)

SPACER BLOCKS (C)

BACKBOARD (B)

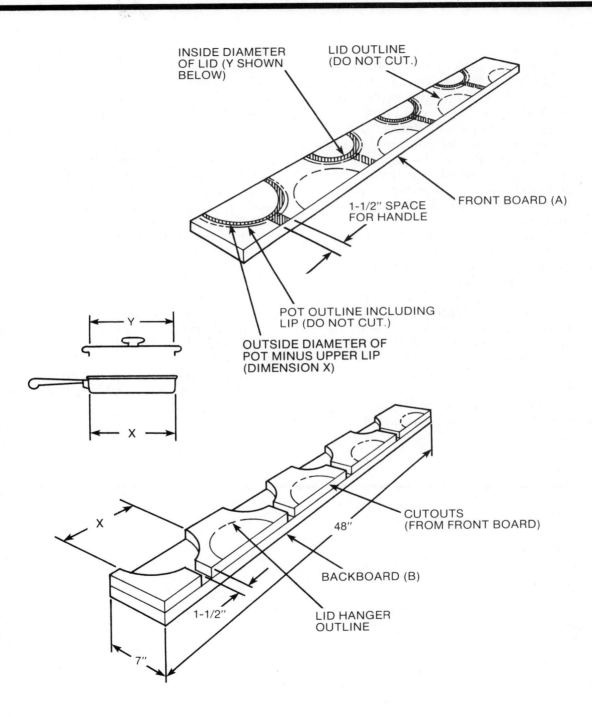

INSIDE DIAMETER
OF LID (Y SHOWN
BELOW)

LID OUTLINE
(DO NOT CUT.)

FRONT BOARD (A)

1-1/2" SPACE
FOR HANDLE

POT OUTLINE INCLUDING
LIP (DO NOT CUT.)

OUTSIDE DIAMETER OF
POT MINUS UPPER LIP
(DIMENSION X)

Y

X

X

48"

1-1/2"

7"

CUTOUTS
(FROM FRONT BOARD)

BACKBOARD (B)

LID HANGER
OUTLINE

hanger semicircles. (If you have a disc sander with an adjustable table, you can keep the saw blade vertical and create the beveled edges with the sander.) Lay out and draw 1-1/2"-wide spaces below each semicircle to accept the pot handles.

Cut out the handle spaces and cut along the semicircle lines drawn to match the pot diameters. Trim and sand all cutouts to the desired shapes.

Next, cut the backboard (B) to size. Lay out the cutouts on the grade A side of the backboard. Be sure to position the cutouts so that the pots and pans will fit properly between them. Trace the outlines of the cutouts onto the backboard and the outlines of the lid hangers onto the cutouts.

Cut the spacer blocks (C) to size.

Lay out and draw 3" × 3" squares on the backboard and on the backs of the cutouts to mark the locations of the spacer blocks. You might have to trim the spacer blocks on the left end of the pot rack to accommodate the large diameter of the frying pan.

Glue and nail two spacer blocks, one on top of the other, at each block location on the backboard. Then, glue and nail the cutouts onto the spacer blocks and the lid hangers onto the cutouts.

Drill two holes in the backboard to accept the mounting screws.

Drill a 1/4"-diameter hole in the cutout at the left end of the pot rack to accept the pot-holder peg. Apply glue and insert the peg.

Set all exposed nails and fill the holes. Sand the rack and paint it to match your kitchen's decor. Mount the rack using No. 10 × 3" wood screws inserted into wall studs or drywall anchors.

Section 3
Bedrooms and Playrooms

Bedroom storage needs vary with the age of the bedroom's occupants. During the day, a child's room becomes a playroom. After school, a teen's room becomes a study center. At the end of a busy day, an adult's bedroom is a place to read, listen to music, watch TV, write letters, and otherwise wind down before retiring. Each bedroom has its individual storage needs. This section responds to these needs with ten easy-to-build storage projects.

In a child's bedroom, storage for toys and clothing should be open, accessible, located at the child's level, and, above all else, sturdy. Consider finishing the child's storage units in bright pastels and primary colors to stimulate interest and activity.

For the teen developing his own individuality, provide a place to display collectibles and memorabilia, a quiet place to study or dream, and plenty of pegs to hang clothes. You never know, your teen just might straighten up the room without being told if given a special storage space.

As for you, try organizing your closet. You'll find lots of unused space there. A bed built on top of a platform of large drawers is another good idea for finding unused storage space. Design a system of wall shelves and drawer units to fill the empty wall around a headboard. The project plans in this section will show you how to do all of this and more.

HEADBOARD STORAGE

Organize your bedroom with this storage headboard. It's easy to make and will transform an otherwise blase wall. Use it as a display case for family portraits, house plants, or collectibles. Or keep your favorite novels and letter writing materials close at hand. Large drawers provide plenty of space for storing the clutter that so quickly accumulates in bedrooms. The headboard is designed to be built around a standard rolling steel bed frame, but there is enough room for a short headboard to fit under the bottom shelf.

Before beginning construction, measure your bed. The center shelving unit must be made 1-1/2" to 2" wider than the bed frame to allow for bedding and room while making the bed. The dimensions given in the cutting list apply to most regular full size mattresses but can be adjusted to fit any size bed or wall space. A queen size mattress is usually 60" × 80" and a king size mattress 76" × 80".

The following instructions describe the procedure for building one end unit, but material for two end units is included in the materials and cutting lists.

End Unit

Begin by cutting the 2 × 4 frame pieces to size. Assemble the frame with glue and 12d common nails.

Cut the side panels to size. Measure up 28-1/4″ from the bottom of each panel and square a line across the panels. Cut out the front of each panel from that line up so that the upper part measures 12-3/4″ across as shown in the drawing.

Cut a 3/4″-wide and 1/4″-deep rabbet along the rear inside edge of each side panel to make room for the back panel (C). Then, cut 3/4″ × 1/4″ dadoes across the inside face of each panel to receive the ends of the shelves (D) and the cabinet top (E). Locate the bottom of the dadoes at points 28-1/4″, 46-1/4″, and 64-1/4″ above the base of each panel so that they are spaced on 18″ centers.

Cut a notch in each of the lower front corners of each side panel. Cut the notches 2″ wide and 3-1/2″ high.

Cut the top shelf (B), cabinet top and shelves to size. Cut a notch 1/2″ deep and 12″ long in each side of the cabinet top as shown in the illustration.

Wood glue and No. 10 × 1-1/4″ flathead wood screws are used to assemble the end unit. Be sure to counterbore any screw holes that will be visible so that these holes can be later filled with putty. Begin by applying a thin layer of glue to the ends of the shelves and another thin layer in the dadoes. Fit the shelves between the sides and run screws through the sides and into the ends of the shelves.

Apply a thin layer of glue to the edges of the base and fit the base between the sides. Screw the sides to the base.

Apply glue to the edges of the back panel and in the rabbets. Position the back panel and screw the panel in place.

Glue and screw the kick plate to the front of the base.

Spread a thin layer of glue on the side and back edges of the top panel and along the top edges of the side and back panels. Position the top panel and fasten it to the sides and back.

After the cabinet and shelf unit is assembled, cut and assemble the cabinet face frame. The stiles and rails (J, K) are cut from 1 × 2s and fastened together with dowels. Space the rails 6-1/4″ apart. Fasten the face frame boards to the cabinet using 4d finishing nails and glue. Adding glue blocks between the face frame and cabinet sides will strengthen the unit considerably.

Make the drawer fronts 7-1/4″ high × 28″ wide so that they will overlap the face frame 1/2″ on each side around the drawer openings. Purchase commercial drawer guides

MATERIALS LIST

3″/4″ AB plywood (7 sheets)
2 × 4 × 8′ (2)
1 × 4 × 6′ select pine
1 × 2 × 10′ select pine (3)
3/8″-dia. dowel pins
1/4-round molding (optional)
No. 10 × 1-1/4″ wood screws
Adjustable shelf standards and
    brackets (optional)
12d common nails
4d finishing nails
Wood putty
Wood glue

CUTTING LIST (END UNIT)

KEY	PIECES	SIZE/DESCRIPTION
A	4	3/4 × 20 × 82-1/4 side panels (plywood)
B	2	3/4 × 12-3/4 × 30 top shelf (plywood)
C	2	3/4 × 29 × 82-1/4 back panel (plywood)
D	4	3/4 × 12 × 29 shelves (plywood)
E	2	3/4 × 21-1/2 × 30 cabinet top (plywood)
F	2	3/4 × 3-1/2 × 30 kick plate (plywood)
G	4	1-1/2 × 3-1/2 × 14-1/4 base frame
H	4	1-1/2 × 3-1/2 × 28-1/2 base frame
J	4	3/4 × 1-1/2 × 24-3/4 face frame stiles
K	8	3/4 × 1-1/2 × 27 face frame rails

CUTTING LIST (CENTER SHELVES)

KEY	PIECES	SIZE/DESCRIPTION
A	2	3/4 × 12 × 82-1/4 sides
B	1	3/4 × 12-3/4 × 57-1/2 top
C	2	3/4 × 12 × 56-3/4 shelves
D	1	3/4 × 46-5/8 × 57-1/2 lower back piece
E	1	3/4 × 35-5/8 × 57-1/2 upper back piece

before cutting and assembling the drawer sides, bottom, and back. Follow the drawer guide manufacturer's instructions to determine the amount of space needed between the sides of the drawer and the drawer openings in the frame.

Center Shelves

To build the center shelving unit, begin by cutting the plywood panels to size. The back of the unit is two pieces (D, E). The lower one is 46-5/8″ wide. The upper panel is 35-5/8″ wide. The butt joint between the two panels is hidden by the bottom shelf. To help support the long span of the shelves, nail quarter-round molding across the center panels, 18″ below the top of the upper panel and 3/8″ below the top of the lower panel. To increase the load-bearing capability of the shelves, two or three adjustable shelving standards can be screwed to the back panel and the center shelves (C) supported on brackets.

Rout 3/4″ × 3/8″ dadoes in the side panels to accept the ends of the shelves. Spread a thin bead of glue in each dado and fasten the sides to the shelves. Then, glue and screw the back to the sides. Finally, glue

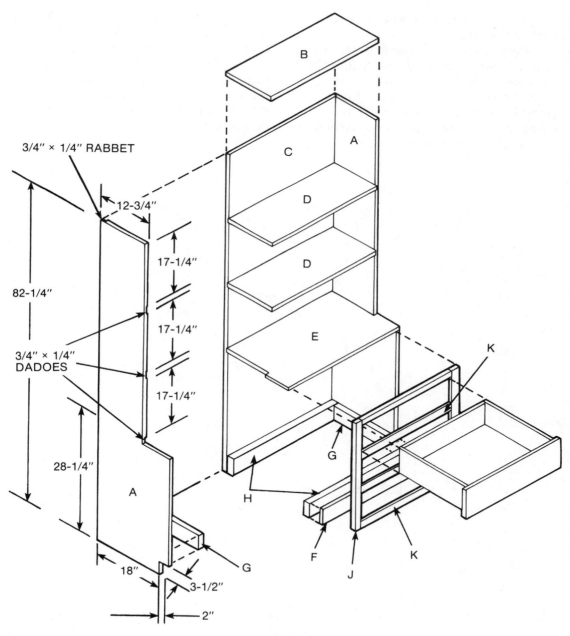

3/4" × 1/4" RABBET

12-3/4"

82-1/4"

17-1/4"

17-1/4"

17-1/4"

3/4" × 1/4"
DADOES

28-1/4"

18"

3-1/2"

2"

B

C

A

D

D

E

A

G

H

F

J

K

K

G

END UNIT

and screw the top panel to the sides and to the back.

Before screwing the center unit to the side units, sand and finish the shelves as desired. The units pictured were painted with a white semigloss latex. If you prefer to stain the shelves, trim the plywood edges with wood veneer tape.

Place the center unit in position along with the two end units. Drill and countersink pilot holes and screw the center unit side panels to the end units, using No. 10 × 1-1/4″ wood screws. Fill the holes with wood putty and touch up with paint or stain.

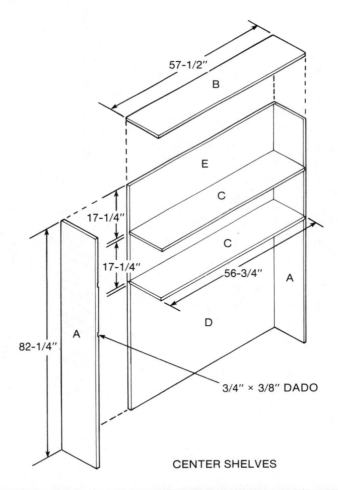

CENTER SHELVES

you have a bandsaw, stack the four blocks on top of each other, tape them firmly together, and cut them simultaneously.

Sand all the shelf brackets with sandpaper. If available, use a rotary sander to sand the curves.

The shelves are cut from an 8' length of common 2 × 8 lumber. You can simply cut the corners square, or you can round them off with a saber saw. Sand the end cuts smooth.

Spread glue on the tops of the brackets and position them 7-1/4" from the ends of the shelves. Keeping the brackets square with the backside of the shelves, drive 8d finishing nails down through the brackets into the shelves.

NOTE: Predrill to avoid splitting the brackets.

WALL SHELF

The simple wall shelf shown is a perfect way to display stuffed animals, plants, or photographs.

The shelf brackets (B) are made by cutting 5-1/2" squares from scrap 2 × 6. Measure 1-1/2" from the back edge of the squares, then measure and mark the same distance diagonally across the square from the top edge. Connect the two points with an arc using a compass or the bottom of a paint can as a guide. Cut out the arc with a saber saw or, if

MATERIALS LIST		
2 × 8 × 8'		
2 × 6 × 2'		
8d finishing nails		
No. 14 ×3" flathead wood screws		

CUTTING LIST		
KEY	**PIECES**	**SIZE/DESCRIPTION**
A	2	1-1/2 × 7-1/4 × 47-15/16 shelf
B	4	1-1/2 × 5-1/2 × 5-1/2 brackets

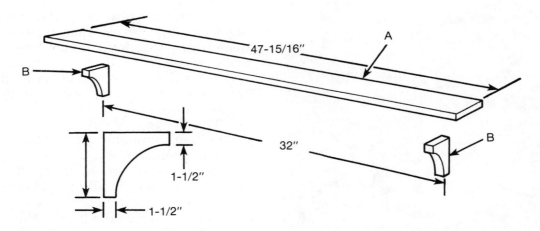

Drill pilot holes through the curved portion of the brackets to accept No. 14 × 3" flathead wood screws. Counterbore the holes so the screw heads sink below the wood surface.

Use a nail set to drive the heads of the nails below the surface of the boards and fill the holes with wood putty. Paint or finish the shelves and brackets as desired.

Attach the shelves to the wall by driving No. 14 × 3" flathead wood screws through the holes drilled in the brackets into the wall studs. Fill the holes with wood plugs or putty.

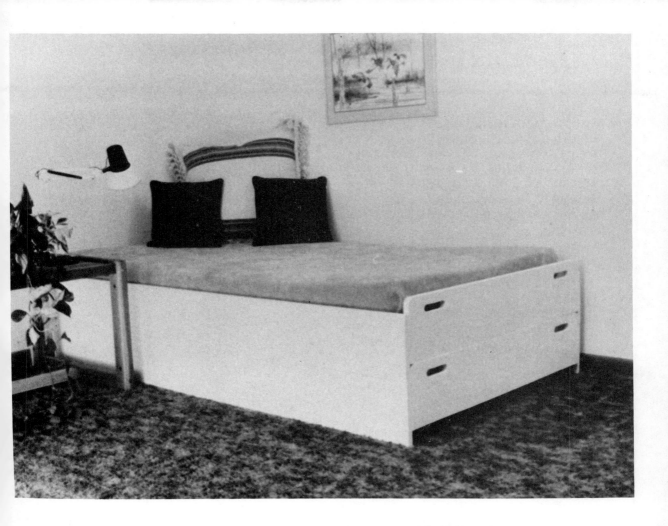

STACKABLE BEDS

Your guest room can do double duty with these stackable beds. Modern in appearance and simple in construction, these beds can be built before your weekend guests arrive, if you start now.

The design and cutting list are for a standard single bed mattress but the dimensions can be adjusted to accommodate any size mattress. Just make sure that you allow 1/2"

clearance between the mattress and the frame all around.

Begin by cutting the plywood panels to size. Use a table saw, if one is available, to rip and crosscut the sides and ends to size.

Carefully lay out the tenons and notches to be made on the bed's sides (A) and ends (B) as shown. Then, make the cuts with a saber saw. Make the handle slots by first drilling two 1″-diameter holes. Draw a line connecting the outside diameters of the holes. Finish cutting the slot with a saber saw. Use the saber saw to ease the corners of the end panels as shown in the detail drawing.

To support the mattress, cut 2 × 2 cleats (D, E) to fit the length of each side as shown. Fasten the cleats to the side and end panels with glue and 6d finishing nails.

Sand the cut edges of the plywood panels. Nail and glue them to-

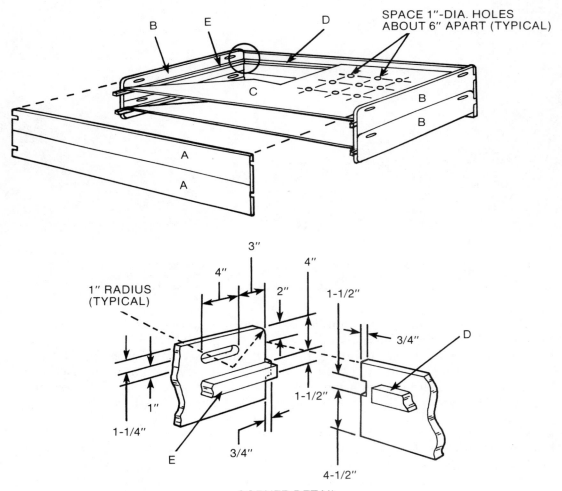

CORNER DETAIL

MATERIALS LIST

3/4" × 4' × 8' AB interior
  plywood (1-1/2 sheets)
5/8" × 4' × 8' AC interior
  plywood (2 sheets)
2 × 2 × 10' (4 boards)
6d finishing nails
4d finishing nails
Wood putty
Wood glue

CUTTING LIST

KEY	PIECES	SIZE/DESCRIPTION
A	4	3/4 × 8 × 77-1/2 sides
B	4	3/4 × 8 × 41-1/2 ends
C	2	5/8 × 40 × 74-1/2 bottom
D	4	1-1/2 × 1-1/2 × 74-1/2 side cleats
E	4	1-1/2 × 1-1/2 × 40 end cleats

gether. Use 4d finishing nails and wood glue. Set the nails and fill the holes with wood putty.

Spread some glue onto the top edge of the cleats and insert the 5/8" plywood bottom (C). Nail the plywood in place with 4d finishing nails. Set all nails with a nail set. Fill in the nail holes as well as the flaws in the plywood with wood putty.

Drill 1"-diameter holes spaced approximately 6" apart into the plywood bottom. The holes will help air the mattress.

Sand the entire unit and then paint it. Once the paint is dry you are ready to put on the mattresses, stack the beds, and get ready for company.

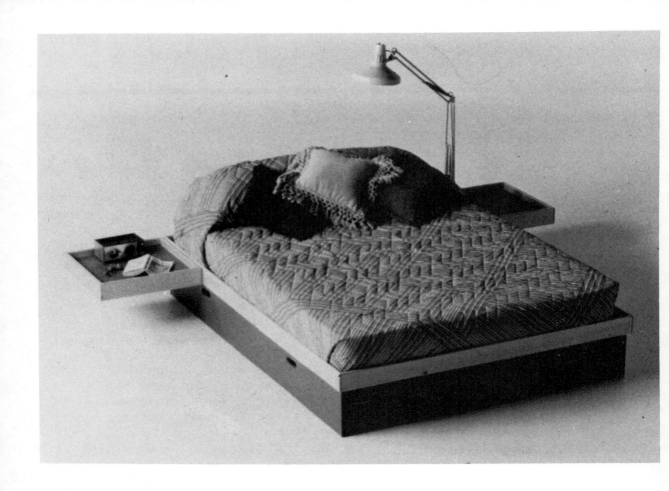

PLATFORM BED

This bed does double—even triple—duty. It is a contemporary-style platform bed with two attached nightstands. The platform, or box frame, is also a four-drawer storage unit. The four large drawers are ideal for storing extra linen and blankets, seasonal clothing, and other items that tend to take up closet space. The frame's dimensions can be modified to suit your mattress; just be sure to leave 1/2" clearance between mattress and base to allow tuck-in room for sheets, blankets, and cover.

Cut the side and end platform edge band members (A, B) to size. Rout a 3/4"-wide × 3/8"-deep rabbet on each end of the side edge band members. Rout another 3/4" × 3/8" groove 1-1/4" from the bottom edge of all edge band members. Cut the platform base panels (C) to size. Fasten the platform together using wood glue and 6d finishing nails.

Cut the end, middle, and center platform supports (D, E) to size. Lay out and cut an edge cross lap on the center and middle platform supports. (See cross lap detail.) Cut the

MATERIALS LIST

1 × 8 × 8' #2 pine (4)
1 × 8 × 6' (2)
1 × 4 × 10' #2 pine (2)
1 × 4 × 8' #2 pine (2)
1 × 2 × 8' #2 pine (2)
3/4" × 4' × 8' AD interior plywood
    (2 sheets)
1/4" × 4' × 4' AC interior plywood
6d finishing nails
4d finishing nails
No. 8 × 1-1/4" wood screws
1/2"-dia. × 12" steel dowels (4)
24" drawer glides (4 sets)
Wood glue

CUTTING LIST

KEY	PIECES	SIZE/DESCRIPTION
A	2	3/4 × 3-1/2 × 77-1/2 platform edge bands
B	2	3/4 × 3-1/2 × 55-3/4 platform edge bands
C	2	3/4 × 27-7/8 × 76-3/4 platform base panels (plywood)
D	3	3/4 × 9-7/8 × 53-1/2 end and middle supports (plywood)
E	1	3/4 × 9-7/8 × 74-1/2 center support (plywood)
F	2	3/4 × 9-7/8 × 26-3/8 center fillers (plywood)
G	2	3/4 × 1-1/2 × 76 bottom rails
H	4	3/8 × 3/4 × 8-3/8 end caps
J	2	3/8 × 1-1/2 × 8-3/8 end caps
K	4	3/4 × 7 × 38 drawer fronts
L	8	3/4 × 7 × 24 drawer sides
M	4	3/4 × 6-1/2 × 34 drawer backs
N	4	1/4 × 24 × 34-3/4 drawer bottoms (plywood)
P	4	3/4 × 3-1/2 × 19-1/4 table edge bands
Q	4	3/4 × 3-1/2 × 20 table edge bands
R	2	3/4 × 19-1/4 × 19-1/4 tabletops (plywood)
S	16	1/2 × 2-1/4 × 5-1/2 support blocking
T	8	1/2 × 5 × 5-1/2 support blocking
U	8	3/4 × 1 × 5 support blocking

bottom rails (G) of the platform support to size. Glue and nail the platform supports together.

Cut the center fillers (F) to size. Position the fillers against the headboard side of the middle support (D) and butt them against the long center support (E). Fasten the filler panels to the middle support, using glue and 4d finishing nails.

Fasten the platform to the platform support structure using No. 8 × 1-1/4" wood screws. Cut the end caps (H, J) for the middle and end cross members of the platform support to size. Glue and nail the end caps in place.

Cut the drawer fronts (K), sides (L), backs (M), and bottoms (N) to size. Cut a 2"-wide × 3/8"-deep rabbet on each end of the drawer fronts. Rout a 1/4" × 3/8"-deep groove, 1/4" up from the bottom edge on the drawer front and side pieces. Lay out and cut a 3/4"-wide × 2-1/2"-long finger hole

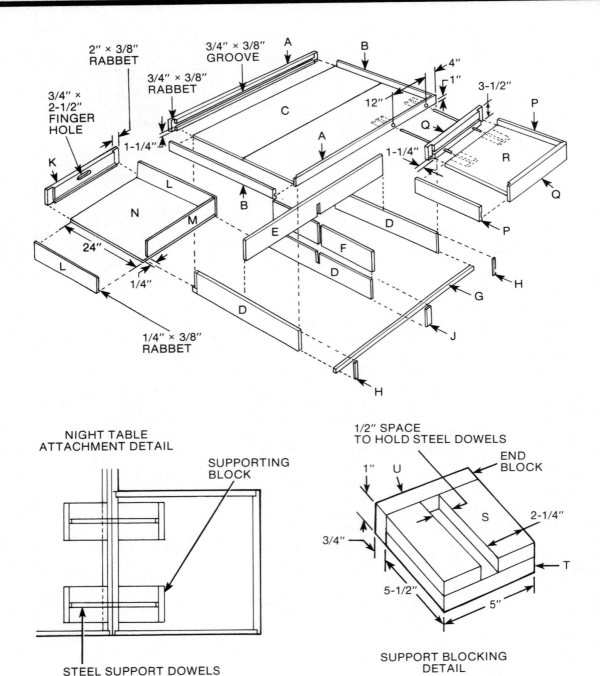

2" × 3/8" RABBET

3/4" × 3/8" GROOVE

3/4" × 3/8" RABBET

3/4" × 2-1/2" FINGER HOLE

1-1/4"

A

B

4"

1"

3-1/2"

P

12"

C

A

Q

R

B

K

L

L

N

M

B

E

F

D

D

Q

P

H

G

J

24"

1/4"

D

1/4" × 3/8" RABBET

H

1-1/4"

NIGHT TABLE ATTACHMENT DETAIL

SUPPORTING BLOCK

STEEL SUPPORT DOWELS

1/2" SPACE TO HOLD STEEL DOWELS

END BLOCK

1"   U

S

2-1/4"

3/4"

T

5-1/2"

5"

SUPPORT BLOCKING DETAIL

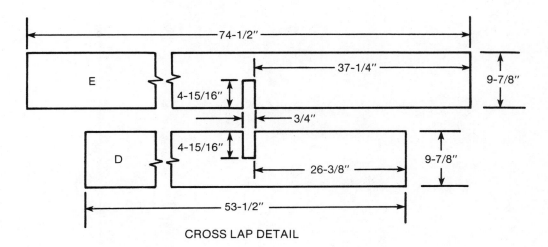

CROSS LAP DETAIL

in each drawer front. Assemble the drawers using glue and 4d finishing nails. Install the drawers using side-mounted drawer glides.

Cut the edge bands (P, Q) of the night tables to size. Machine a 3/4" × 3/8"-deep rabbet on each end of the 20" pieces. Lay out and machine a 13/16" × 3/8" groove 1-1/4" from the bottom edge of all edge band pieces. Cut the night tabletops (R) to size. Cover one side of the plywood tops with a plastic laminate (color of your choice). Glue and nail the night tables together.

Lay out and drill 1/2" corresponding holes in the edge bands of both platform and night table to accept the night table steel support dowels.

Rout a 1/4" radius on the top and bottom corners of both the plat-

form and night table edge bands, both sides of the finger holes in the drawer fronts, and in the 1/2"-diameter holes in the edge bands.

Cut the blocking pieces (S, T, U) to size from lumber scraps and nail and glue them together. Install blocking to the underside of the platform and the center of the night table to form pockets for the support dowels.

Finish sand all wood surfaces. Apply two coats of brushing lacquer to the platform, the platform edge band, and the edge bands of the night tables. Paint the platform support frame and the drawers to match the color of the plastic laminate on the tabletops. Install the drawers. Attach the night tables to the bed using the steel support dowels.

MODULAR CLOSET
ORGANIZER

Does your home need extra storage space? You might find the additional room in a closet. Most closets have a lot of unused space that could be put to work with a little organization. Here is a plan to help you squeeze more space from any closet in your house.

The modular closet consists of individual storage units that can be stacked on top of each other. Each module is 23-1/4" deep. The width and height of each module will vary depending on the articles being stored. The modules are made from 3/4" plywood, except for the back panels, which are made from 1/4" plywood. The cup hooks, shelf clips, hinges, and drawer slides are standard hardware store items. The cup hooks are used instead of a closet bar because they take up less vertical space. Each module should be sanded and finished as it is completed.

NOTE: *The rough edges of the plywood can be covered with veneer tape, adhesive-backed strips made especially for 3/4"-thick plywood. The veneer edging is applied using an ordinary clothes iron. After the "hot glue" sets, the edges of the veneer can be sanded flush with the edges of each board.*

Shelf/Drawer Module

Begin construction of the closet module by building the shelf/drawer module. Cut the sides (A), top and bottom (B), back (C), and partition (E) to size. Drill 1/4"-diameter holes, for shelf support pins, 3/8" deep, in the inside of the left side panel and the left side of the partition. Space

the holes 1-1/2" from the front and back edges and 2" apart.

Rout a 1/4"-deep × 3/8"-wide rabbet in the inside back edges of the sides, top, and bottom. Then using wood glue and 6d finishing nails, assemble the module by gluing and nailing the top and bottom to the sides. Install the back panel in the rabbets with glue and 3/4" brads. Position the divider and nail through the top and bottom with 6d nails. Install the shelf.

Next, cut the bottom rail (D) and the stile (G) to size. Using glue and 6d nails, fasten the rail flush with the bottom edge of the module. Then, glue and nail the stile to the top and side panels flush with the left side. Also, nail through the bottom rail and into the stile.

Cut the door (F) to size. Cut a 1"-wide × 4"-long finger hole in the top of the door 1-1/4" from the top. Attach the offset hinges to the door and stile and install the door.

Finally, cut the drawer sides (H), ends (J), bottoms (K), and fronts (L) to size. Machine a 1/4" × 3/8"-deep groove in the sides and ends to accept the bottom panels. Space the groove 1/4" from the bottom edge of each piece. Assemble the drawers with 3d finishing nails and glue. Position the drawer fronts flush with the bottom edge of the drawer and with equal overlaps on each side. Glue and screw the fronts to the ends using No. 8 × 1-1/4" wood screws. Counterbore the pilot holes and fill them with wood putty. Install the 20" drawer slides and install the drawers.

Shelf Module

Next, build the shelf module. Cut the sides (M), top and bottom (N), and back (P) to size. Drill parallel sets of 1/4″-dia. × 3/8″-deep holes where shelves are wanted. Glue and nail the top and bottom to the sides and rout a 1/4″ × 3/8″ rabbet along the inside edges of the sides, top, and bottom to accept the back. Glue and nail the back in place.

Cut the shelves (R), front stile (Q), and door (S) to size. Mount the shelves in the unit, then glue and nail the stile to the left side and to the top and bottom. Cut a 1″-wide × 4″-long finger hole and install the door with three 3/4″ offset hinges. Install two magnetic hinges to the top and bottom of the right side.

Shirt Module

Construct the shirt module next. Cut the sides (T), top and bottom (U), shelf (V), and back (W) to size.

Rout a 1/4″ × 3/8″ rabbet in the inside back edges of the sides, top, and bottom to accept the back panel. Glue and nail the top and bottom to the sides. Install the back with glue and 3/4″ brads.

Position the shelf 41-5/8″ from the bottom of the module. Secure in place with glue and 6d nails inserted through the sides and back. Install the cup hooks in the top. Position them in the center of the top, spaced equal distances apart.

Shoe Module

Construct the shoe module next. Begin by building the drawer casing. Cut the sides (X), top and bottom (Y), back (Z), and bottom rail (AA) to size. Rout a 1/4″ × 3/8″ rabbet along the inside back edges of the sides, top, and bottom to accept the back panel. Glue and nail the top and bottom to the sides. Install the back panel. Glue and nail the bottom rail to the front of the module.

Next, cut the shoe drawer ends (BB), bottom (CC), side rails (DD), and the drawer front (FF) to size. Also, cut twelve lengths of 3/8″-diameter dowel (EE) 22-1/4″ long.

Measure down 3-7/8″ and 11-7/8″ from the top of the long side

---

MATERIALS LIST

3/4″ × 4′ × 8′ AB interior plywood (5 sheets)
1/4″ × 4′ × 8′ AC interior plywood (2 sheets)
6d finishing nails
3/4″ wire brads
No. 8 × 1-1/4″ wood screws (12)
1/4″—20 × 2″ carriage bolts (4)
1/4″-dia. flat washers (8)
1/4″—20 wing nuts (4)
1″ cup hooks (42)
20″ drawer slides (4)
1/4″ metal shelf clips (20)
3/4″ offset hinges (5)
22″ drawer slide (1)
Magnetic latches (3)
Birch veneer tape
Wood putty
Wood glue

KEY	PIECES	SIZE/DESCRIPTION
CUTTING LIST		
A	2	3/4 × 22-1/2 × 28-1/2 sides
B	2	3/4 × 22-1/2 × 36 top and bottom
C	1	1/4 × 29-1/4 × 35-1/2 back
D	1	3/4 × 1-1/2 × 36 bottom rail
E	1	3/4 × 22-1/2 × 28-1/2 partition
F	1	3/4 × 10-3/4 × 28-1/4 door
G	1	3/4 × 7 × 28-1/2 stile
H	8	3/4 × 5-1/2 × 20-1/2 drawer sides
J	8	3/4 × 5-1/2 × 15-3/4 drawer ends
K	4	1/4 × 15 × 21-1/4 drawer bottoms
L	4	3/4 × 7 × 17-7/8 drawer fronts
M	2	3/4 × 22-1/2 × 52-1/2 sides
N	2	3/4 × 18 × 22-1/2 top and bottom
P	1	1/4 × 17-1/4 × 53-1/4 back
Q	1	3/4 × 7 × 54 front stile
R	4	3/4 × 16-1/4 × 21-1/2 shelves
S	1	3/4 × 10-3/4 × 53-7/8 door
T	2	3/4 × 23-1/4 × 82-1/2 sides
U	2	3/4 × 18 × 23-1/4 top and bottom
V	1	3/4 × 16-1/2 × 23 shelf
W	1	1/4 × 17-1/4 × 83-1/4 back
X	2	3/4 × 22-1/2 × 28-1/2 sides

CUTTING LIST (continued)

KEY	PIECES	SIZE/DESCRIPTION
Y	2	3/4 × 14 × 22-1/2 top and bottom
Z	1	1/4 × 13-1/4 × 29-1/4 back
AA	1	3/4 × 1-1/2 × 14 bottom rail
BB	2	3/4 × 11-1/2 × 23 drawer ends
CC	1	3/4 × 11-1/2 × 22-1/4 drawer bottom
DD	4	3/4 × 3 × 20-3/4 side rails
EE	12	3/8-dia. × 22-1/4 support rods (dowel)
FF	1	3/4 × 14 × 28-1/2 drawer front
GG	1	3/4 × 12 × 36 top
HH	2	3/4 × 3 × 11-1/4 sides
JJ	1	3/4 × 3 × 36 back

Shoe Module

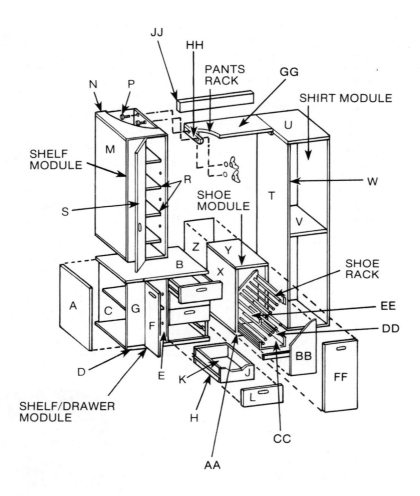

of the front, and scribe lines across the face of the front from these points at a 45-degree angle. Drill six holes centered on each of these lines and spaced equal distances apart.

Apply wood glue to the ends of the dowels and insert them in the drilled holes. Next, position the bottom side rails flush with the bottom edge of the front and back. Glue and

nail the rails in place. Then, position the top side rails 1″ from the top of the front and back and glue and nail in place.

Glue and nail the bottom to the front and back and to the bottom side rails.

Set the drawer unit on its back and position the front face on the subassembly with a 1-3/4″ overhang on the bottom and a 1-1/4″ overhang on each side. Drill and countersink pilot holes, then glue and screw the face to the unit using four No. 8 × 1-1/4″ wood screws.

Attach drawer slides to the bottom of the shoe drawer and to the sides of the case. Insert the drawer and position the unit in the closet module.

Pants Rack

The pants rack is made to fit between the shirt module and the shelf module. Each side piece of the pants rack is fastened to the sides of the shirt module and the shelf module with carriage bolts.

Begin by cutting the top (GG), sides (HH), and back (JJ). Glue and nail the top to the back and the sides to the top and back. Drill two 1/4″-diameter holes through each side piece. Center the holes 8″ apart.

Place the shelf and drawer module, the tall shelf module, and the shirt module in the closet. Position the pants rack between the shelf rack and the shirt rack, and mark the position of the holes on the sides of the two units. Drill the 1/4″-diameter holes and mount the pants rack between the units. Install the cup hooks centered in the rack top and spaced equal distances apart.

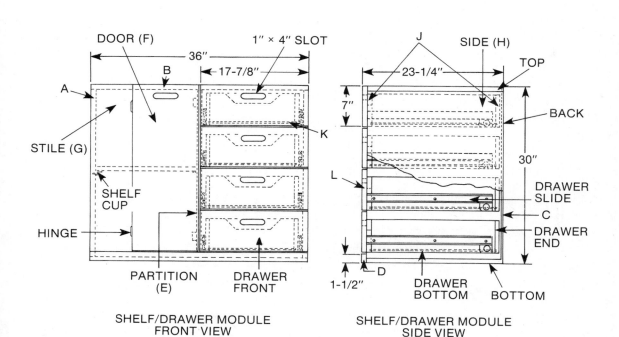

SHELF/DRAWER MODULE
FRONT VIEW

SHELF/DRAWER MODULE
SIDE VIEW

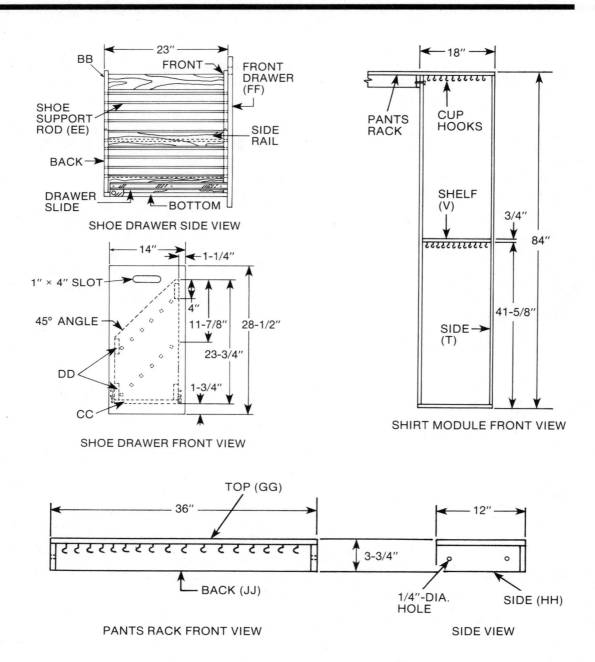

BB

FRONT

23"

FRONT DRAWER (FF)

SHOE SUPPORT ROD (EE)

SIDE RAIL

BACK

DRAWER SLIDE

BOTTOM

SHOE DRAWER SIDE VIEW

14"

1-1/4"

1" × 4" SLOT

45° ANGLE

4"

11-7/8"

28-1/2"

23-3/4"

DD

1-3/4"

CC

SHOE DRAWER FRONT VIEW

18"

PANTS RACK

CUP HOOKS

SHELF (V)

3/4"

84"

SIDE (T)

41-5/8"

SHIRT MODULE FRONT VIEW

TOP (GG)

36"

12"

3-3/4"

BACK (JJ)

1/4"-DIA. HOLE

SIDE (HH)

PANTS RACK FRONT VIEW

SIDE VIEW

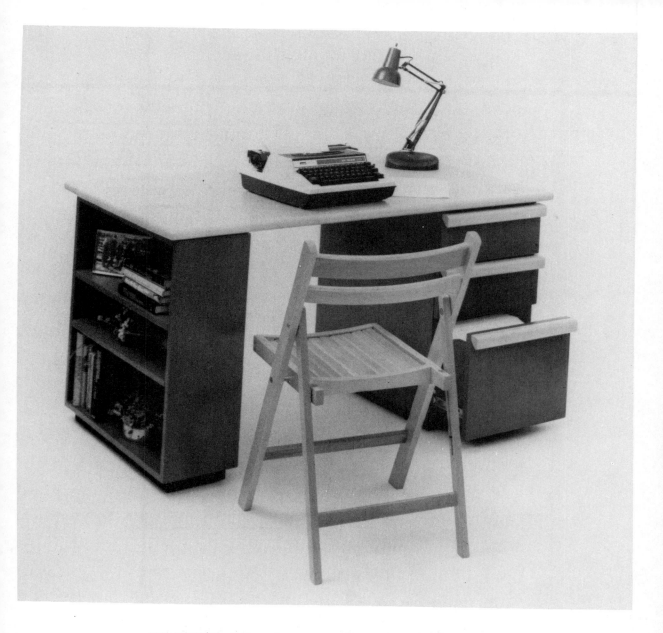

BEDROOM DESK

Here is a desk that offers you a tremendous amount of storage area, yet takes up less space than the average desk. At one end are drawers to hold scissors, tape, envelopes, and so forth. The bottom drawer is conveniently sized to hold files. At the other end are bookcases with ad-

MATERIALS LIST

3/4" × 4' × 8' AC interior plywood
1/2" × 4' × 4' AC interior plywood
1/4" × 4' × 4' AC interior plywood
5/4 × 6 × 6' select pine (5)
6d finishing nails
4d finishing nails
1" brads
No. 12 × 1-3/4" roundhead wood
No. 12 × 1" roundhead wood screws
No. 10 × 1-1/4" wood screws
  screws
Drawer glides (3 pairs)
Wood glue

CUTTING LIST

KEY	PIECES	SIZE/DESCRIPTION
A	2	3/4 × 23-3/4 × 25-3/4 cabinet sides
B	2	3/4 × 14-1/2 × 23-3/4 cabinet top and bottom
C	4	3/4 × 2-1/2 × 14-1/2 dividers
D	2	3/4 × 1-1/2 × 13-1/4 short plinth members
E	2	3/4 × 1-1/2 × 21 long plinth members
F	1	1/4 × 15-1/4 × 25 back panel
G	1	1/4 × 15-1/2 × 23-1/4 spacer
H	2	1/2 × 10 × 22-1/2 bottom drawer sides
J	1	1/2 × 10 × 12-1/2 bottom drawer front
K	1	1/2 × 6 × 12-1/2 bottom drawer back
L	1	3/4 × 12-1/2 × 16 bottom drawer face
M	4	1/2 × 5 × 22-1/2 upper drawer sides

CUTTING LIST (continued)

KEY	PIECES	SIZE/DESCRIPTION
N	2	1/2 × 5 × 12-1/2 upper drawer fronts
P	2	1/2 × 4-1/2 × 12-1/2 upper drawer backs
Q	3	1/2 × 12-1/2 × 22 drawer bottoms
R	2	3/4 × 6-3/8 × 16 upper drawer faces
S	3	1-1/8 × 1-1/2 × 16 drawer pulls
T	2	3/4 × 9 × 25-3/4 bookcase sides
U	2	3/4 × 9 × 23 bookcase top and bottom
V	2	3/4 × 1-1/2 × 6-1/4 short plinth members
W	2	3/4 × 1-1/2 × 21-3/4 long plinth members
X	2	3/4 × 8-3/4 × 22-5/8 shelves
Y	1	1/4 × 23-3/4 × 25 back panel
Z	1	1/4 × 8-1/2 × 24 spacer
AA	1	1-1/8 × 27 × 54 desktop

justable shelves to hold all of those books and repair manuals that do not fit anywhere else. Attractive and versatile, the desk makes a wonderful addition to a bedroom or any room of your home.

Cut the drawer cabinet sides (A), top and bottom (B), dividers (C), and short and long plinths (D, E) to size. (See cutting diagram for the correct layout of all desk parts.) Attach the drawer cabinet's sides to

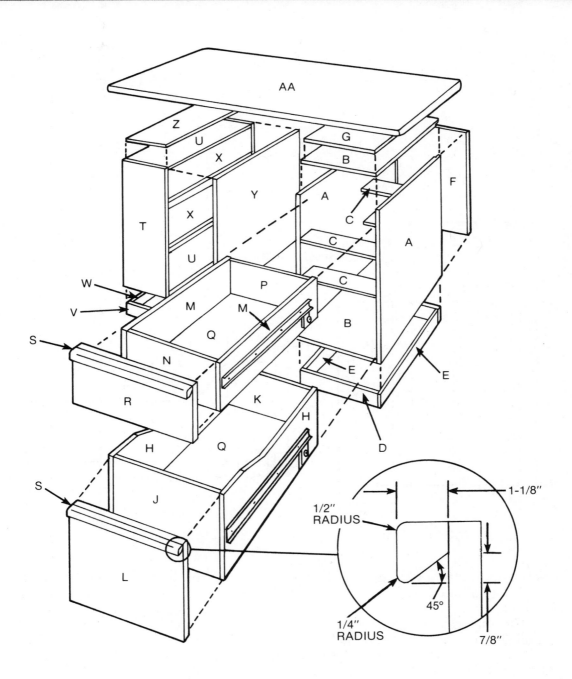

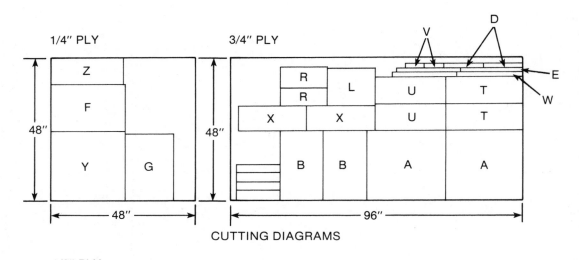

1/4" PLY   3/4" PLY

CUTTING DIAGRAMS

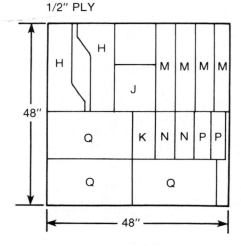

1/2" PLY

CUTTING DIAGRAM

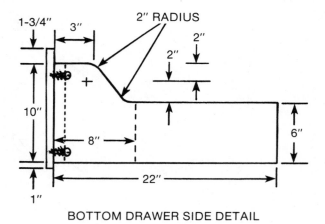

BOTTOM DRAWER SIDE DETAIL

its top and bottom with glue and 6d finishing nails to form the drawer cabinet frame.

Cut the drawer cabinet's back panel (F) to size. Insert this back panel into the rabbet at the back end of the drawer cabinet frame. Fasten with 1" brads.

Machine a 1/4"-deep × 3/8"-wide rabbet along the inside back edge of the drawer cabinet frame to accept the drawer cabinet's back panel (F). Locate the four dividers between the sides at the front and back of the drawer cabinet frame 12-1/4" and 18-3/4" from the bottom edge of the

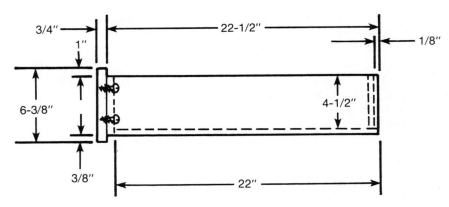

TOP AND MIDDLE DRAWER DETAIL

cabinet sides. Fasten the dividers to the sides using glue and 6d nails.

Fasten the long and short plinth members together (with the ends chasing each other) using glue and 6d nails. Center this plinth assembly on the drawer cabinet bottom and fasten it with glue and nails.

Cut the bottom drawer sides (H), bottom (Q), back (K), front (J), and face (L) to size. (See cutting diagram.) Lay out and cut the bottom drawer sides to the required shape. (See bottom drawer side detail.) Assemble the bottom drawer using glue and 4d finishing nails.

Drill four 5/16"-diameter holes in the four corners of the drawer front. Position the drawer face on the drawer front and mark the locations of the holes. At these locations, drill 3/16"-diameter pilot holes. Do not drill through the face. Fasten the drawer face to the drawer front with No. 12 × 1" roundhead wood screws and washers. The oversized holes in the drawer front will allow the drawer face to be adjusted.

Cut the sides (M), front (N), backs (P), bottoms (Q), and faces (R) of the middle and top drawers to size. Assemble the middle and top drawer front, back, bottom, and sides using glue and 4d finishing nails. Fasten drawer faces to the middle and top drawers following the procedure described for the bottom drawer.

Cut the drawer pulls (S) to size. Chamfer a 7/8" × 45-degree angle on each drawer pull. Rout a 1/2" radius along the top front of each drawer pull and a 1/4" radius along the bottom front of each drawer pull. Drill pilot holes through the back side of the drawer faces and loosely fasten a drawer pull to each drawer face with No. 10 × 1-1/4" flathead wood screws. The drawer handles will be removed later for finishing.

When installed the upper edge of the top drawer should be 1/8" below the cabinet top. Successive drawer fronts should be 1/8″ apart, leaving a 1/8″ space between the bottom edge of the bottom drawer and the lower edge of the cabinet bottom. Install the drawer slides in the drawer cabinet and on the top, middle, and bottom drawers. Be sure the drawer slides are properly aligned. Follow the manufacturer's installation instructions carefully.

Cut the sides (T), top and bottom (U), and shelves (X) of the bookcase to size. Drill ten 1/4″-diameter holes, 3/8″ deep, in each bookcase side to accept the bookcase shelf supports. Machine a 1/4″-deep × 3/8″-wide rabbet in the inside edges of the sides, top, and bottom to accept the back panel.

Fasten the bookcase sides to its top and bottom with glue and 6d nails, forming the bookcase frame.

Cut the back panel (Y) to size. Fasten the back panel to the bookcase frame with glue and 4d nails. Cut the bookcase frame's short and long plinth members (V, W) to size. Fasten these plinth members together (with the ends chasing each other) using glue and 6d nails. Glue and nail this plinth assembly to the bottom of the bookcase frame.

Cut the spacers (G, Z) to size. Center them on the tops of the cabinet and bookshelf respectively and fasten them with glue and 1″ brads.

Glue up enough #2 pine to form a 1-1/8″ × 27″ × 54″ desktop (AA). Rout a 1/2″ radius along all the edges of the desktop piece.

Sand all the desk parts. Apply two coats of clear finish to the desktop and the drawer pulls. (The drawer pulls should be removed during the finishing and painting.) Paint all plywood parts as desired. The plinths and the spacers could be painted black.

Drill 5/16″-diameter clearance holes in the underside of the cabinet and shelf top panels for the wood screws. (The clearance holes will allow for variations in expansion and contraction between the plywood cabinet and solid wood top.) Fasten the desktop to the bookcase and drawer cabinet with twelve No. 12 × 1-3/4″ roundhead wood screws with washers.

Install the drawers and book shelves. You might have to adjust the drawer faces for proper alignment.

TOY CHEST

Where to store toys is a major consideration in any home with children, and this project will give your offspring a beautiful chest to keep their belongings. Be sure to install a support to prevent the lid from dropping on little fingers. Also consider adding a false bottom so that your toddler can reach all the toys. The overflow can be stored underneath and periodically rotated with other toys for variety.

This chest can also be adapted for a variety of storage uses around the house. Use it for storing firewood, line it with cedar and store sweaters and scarfs, or build it with redwood and set it outside to store pool or deck equipment.

Some of the measurements for this project depend on the thickness of the wood used. Since you might encounter variations in thicknesses if stock from several mill sources gets mixed, be sure you measure and fit as you go.

Begin by crosscutting 24 pieces of 1 × 6 tongue and groove boards into 23" lengths. Dry assemble four of the boards for each end panel and eight of the boards for both the front panel and the back panel. Cut off the exposed tongue on each panel.

Cut the rails and stiles for the end panel frames next. Subtract the combined width of the stiles from the width of the panel to determine the exact width of the rails. Butt the frame pieces together and glue and clamp them, making sure that the frame is square. After the glue dries, fasten the tongue and groove side panel to the frame, using glue and No. 6 × 1-1/4" wood screws. Drill through the panel into the frame—two screws through each interior board and four screws spaced evenly apart and arranged in a staggered row through each end board.

Follow the same procedure to build the front and back of the chest. The only difference in construction is that the frames and the assembled tongue and groove panels should not be flush on each end. In-stead, the frame should be made approximately 3" longer than the panel so that the frame laps the side panels. Measure the thickness of the sides to determine the exact amount of overlap needed.

Cut the bottom braces (F, G) to size. The front and back braces should be cut flush with the edges of the tongue and groove panels. The side braces should be set back 1/2" from the edges of the side panels to provide clearance for the front and rear braces. Glue and screw the

MATERIALS LIST

1 × 6 × 8' tongue and groove (10)
1 × 3 × 8' (5)
2 × 2 × 12'
No. 6 × 2" wood screws
No. 6 × 1-1/4" wood screws
4d finishing nails
Wood plugs or buttons
Piano hinge
Lid support
Chest handles (2)
Wood glue

CUTTING LIST

KEY	PIECES	SIZE/DESCRIPTION
A	4	3/4 × 2-1/2 × 23-3/4 front and back stiles
B	4	3/4 × 2-1/2 × 40 front and back rails
C	4	3/4 × 2-1/2 × 23-3/4 end stiles
D	4	3/4 × 2-1/2 × 16 end rails
E	24	3/4 × 5-1/4 × 23 front, back, end panels (T&G)
F	2	1-1/2 × 1-1/2 × 42 bottom braces
G	2	1-1/2 × 1-1/2 × 16-1/2 bottom braces
H	8	3/4 × 5-1/4 × 19-3/8 bottom (T&G)
J	2	3/4 × 2-1/2 × 45 top stiles
K	2	3/4 × 2-1/2 × 17-1/2 top rails
L	4	3/4 × 5-1/4 × 43-3/8 top panels (T&G)

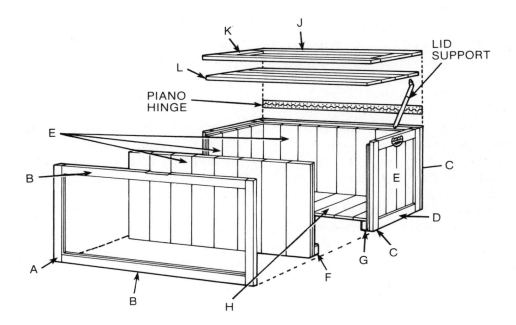

braces flush with the bottom of the panels with No. 6 × 2″ wood screws.

Assemble the four sides of the box chest. Drill and counterbore four pilot holes per side through the front and back stiles (A) into the side frames. Fasten the frames together using glue and No. 6 × 1-1/4″ wood screws. Fill the holes with plugs or buttons.

Crosscut to length the eight tongue and groove boards for the bottom panel. Lay the boards in the box on the supports. Work the boards up into an accordian shape to fit the last few boards in place; then push them all down flat against the nailers. You can also trim the

last board a bit to allow sufficient clearance for fitting the panel together. The boards can then be spaced equal distances apart before fastening them to the supports with 4d finishing nails.

Construct the top frame (J, K) to fit flush with the outside edges of the chest. Crosscut four 1 × 6 tongue and groove boards (L) to length for the top panel. Dry assemble the boards in place between the chest frames, sitting on the lip created by the chest panels. It will be necessary to rip the tongue (and possibly a bit more of the width) from the last board to get the top to fit. If necessary, also trim the boards to fit lengthwise. Keep in mind that a small amount of clearance must be provided between the top panel and the chest frames to allow the top to open and close without rubbing or binding.

After the boards for the top panel have been properly trimmed to fit the chest opening, reassemble the panel on the top frame, set back 3/4″ from all sides. Predrill and countersink pilot holes for No. 6 × 1-1/4″ wood screws. With

glue and screws, fasten the panel to the frame.

Rout an opening 1/2″ deep and 4″ wide in the top front rail for finger space needed to open the top.

Cut a piano hinge to length and attach it to the top and rear top rail. If the top panel rubs against the chest frames, relieve the edges of the panel with a sanding block or hand plane. Sand and finish the chest. Then, install the lid support and chest handles.

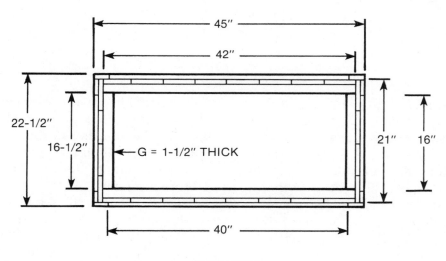

TOP VIEW

BOOK RACK

Organize your reading material with this attractive little book rack. Build several, in fact. One would be ideal on top of a nightstand by your bed to hold your current library selections. Place one on the children's bureau to hold their favorite bedtime stories. Build another for your desk so that often-used reference books will be always within reach. In the kitchen, build one to show off your collection of cookbooks. The possibilities are many, and the dimensions can be adjusted to closely match the "literary collection" each is designed to hold.

Begin by cutting the shelf (A), back (B), and sides (C) to length. Round the top and facing edges of the sides, as well as the corners. Round the top facing edge of the back piece and the front edges of the shelf.

Bevel the bottom end of the sides by measuring up 1/2" from the bottom rear edge and drawing a line from that point to the lower front edge. Cut along this line.

Butt the lower edge of the back against the face of the shelf, making their rear edges flush, as shown in the drawing. Drill and countersink pilot holes through the underside of the shelf and fasten the pieces together using glue and No. 6 × 1-1/4″ wood screws.

Fit the shelf assembly between the sides, making their rear edges flush. Drill and counterbore pilot holes through the sides into the shelf assembly and fasten it with glue and No. 6 × 1-1/4″ wood screws. Fill the holes with wood plugs.

Sand the assembly and finish as desired.

MATERIALS LIST

1 × 6 × 5′ #2 pine
No. 6 × 1-1/4″ wood screws
Wood plugs
Wood glue

CUTTING LIST

KEY	PIECES	SIZE/DESCRIPTION
A	1	3/4 × 5-1/2 × 16 shelf
B	1	3/4 × 5-1/2 × 16 back
C	2	3/4 × 5-1/2 × 8 sides

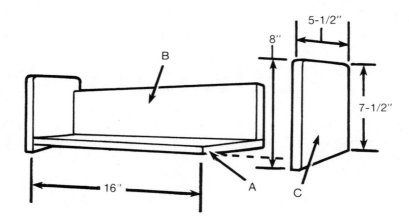

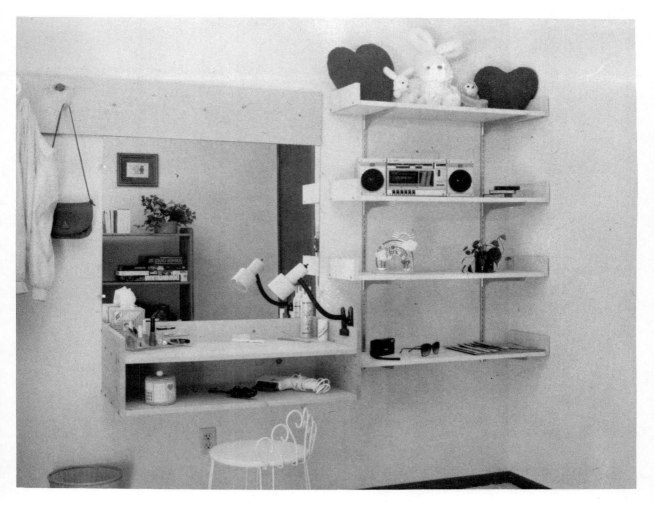

VANITY

Pamper your daughter with her own bedroom vanity. Not only will it free up the bathroom for the rest of the family, but it will also create storage space for all the personal treasures girls tend to collect. The vanity has plenty of shelf space for cosmetics and lotions. Four large wall shelves provide space for stuffed toys, school books, or any other of her favorite things. The overhead board holds dowels for hanging clothes, hats, and purses.

Begin construction by cutting the vanity sides (A), top and bottom (B), back (C), overhead board (D), and the shelves (E), and shelf sides (F) to size from 3/4" plywood. Sand the edges and finish as desired. Apply edging tape to the exposed plywood edges for a neater look.

Position the shelf ends flush with the front and bottom edges of the shelves. Position the sides of the vanity flush with the front edge of the top and bottom, and fit the rear edges of the top and bottom. Drill pilot holes through the sides in both the shelf and the vanity units. Assemble the units using wood glue and No. 10 × 1-1/2″ brass oval-head screws. Use two screws per wall shelf side panel and eight screws per vanity side.

Drill a pair of 1/2″-diameter holes, spaced 6″ apart and centered on the width of the overhead board to receive the dowels. Drill the first hole 6″ from the left edge of the board. Drill the holes at an upward angle to increase their holding ability. Cut the 12″ length of dowel in half. Place glue on one end of each peg and insert the pegs into the holes in the overhead board.

NOTE: *Additional pegs can be added as desired.*

Determine the height of the vanity from the floor. The bottom of the vanity should be about 2″ above the child's knees when sitting. Attach the vanity to the wall with eight No. 10 × 3″ brass screws and grommets. Screw through the back of the assembly and into the wall studs.

Mount the mirror above the vanity, using plastic mirror brackets.

Fasten the overhead board above the mirror and flush with the right side of the vanity. Secure in place with No. 10 × 3″ brass screws. Screw into wall studs or use some type of hollow wall anchor.

Install the shelving system by screwing two shelf standards into the wall studs or into wall anchors with No. 10 × 2″ brass screws. Use a level to make sure that the shelf standards are vertical, and measure the distance from the bottom of each standard to the floor to make sure they are evenly aligned. Install the shelf brackets and insert the shelves.

MATERIALS LIST

3/4″ × 4′ × 8′ AB interior plywood (1-1/2 sheets)
1/2″-dia. hardwood dowel (12″)
No. 10 × 3″ brass oval-head
No. 10 × 2″ brass wood screws
  wood screws
4′ shelf standards (2)
12″ shelf brackets (8)
30″ × 36″ mirror
Mirror hanging hardware
Plywood edge tape
Wood glue

CUTTING LIST

KEY	PIECES	SIZE/DESCRIPTION
A	2	3/4 × 12 × 20 sides
B	2	3/4 × 19-1/4 × 34-1/2 top and bottom
C	1	3/4 × 12 × 34-1/2 back
D	1	3/4 × 8 × 72 overhead board
E	4	3/4 × 12 × 34-1/2 shelves
F	8	3/4 × 3-1/2 × 12 shelf sides

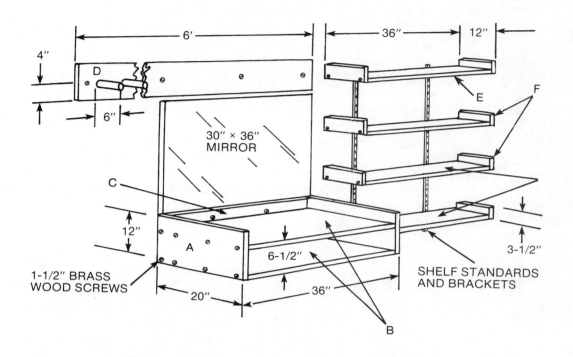

4"

6'

D

6"

30" × 36"
MIRROR

36"

12"

E

F

C

12"

A

6-1/2"

3-1/2"

1-1/2" BRASS
WOOD SCREWS

20"

36"

B

SHELF STANDARDS
AND BRACKETS

Section 4
Bath, Laundry, and Sewing Rooms

Bathrooms, laundry rooms, and sewing rooms have little, if anything, in common. However, each does have its special storage needs. For example, the bathroom typically has a medicine cabinet, a linen closet, and shelves for shaving creams, deodorants, and other personal toiletry items. If you are cramped for storage space in one or more of these areas, the projects in this section will provide a welcome relief. Many of them are built with moisture-resistant woods such as redwood or cedar. It is also advisable to use a waterproof adhesive when building projects for a steamy bathroom.

The laundry room needs space for detergents, bleaches, measuring cups, and other washing and ironing supplies. Consider hanging a storage cabinet above the washer and dryer so that the necessary supplies are always within reach. You will find plans for this storage unit and others in this section.

For the seamstress in the family, consider creating a sewing center. You provide the room; we provide the plans. The sewing center in this section has more than enough shelves, drawers, and pigeonholes to satisfy the most productive of home fashion designers. The center is great for other craft and hobby storage needs, as well.

BATHROOM STORAGE CABINET

Most bathrooms are full of items that should be stored out of sight and out of the reach of child-ren. But bathroom storage does not have to be purely utilitarian. It can also be beautiful. The bathroom cabinet shown here is made from clear all heart redwood. The moisture resistance and dimensional stability of redwood make it ideal for the bathroom's steamy environment. This cabinet has not only a roomy storage cabinet but also several display shelves and a towel rod. It is easy to construct, too, because it uses standard size boards available at any lumberyard and simple butt joints. A waterproof resorcinol glue is used to withstand the humidity of the bathroom.

Before beginning construction, remove the floor molding from the wall against which the cabinet will sit. The molding will be cut to fit and replaced after the cabinet is complete.

Begin construction of the unit by building two cabinet support boxes. Cut the box pieces (E, F, G) from 1 × 4s and assemble them with 6d galvanized finishing nails and waterproof resorcinol wood glue.

Next, cut the two side panels (A) to length. Length can vary, depending on ceiling height.

Attach the cabinet support boxes to the top and bottom of the side panels. Use resorcinol glue and No. 6 × 1-1/4″ wood screws. Counterbore the screw holes and fill them with redwood plugs. Make sure that the backs of the boxes and the rear edges of the side panels are flush and that the boxes are square with the side panels.

MATERIALS LIST
1 × 8 × 10′
1 × 8 × 8′ (3)
1 × 4 × 10′(3)
1 × 4 × 8′
1 × 2 × 5′
No. 10 × 3″ roundhead wood screws
No. 6 × 1-1/4″ wood screws
6d galvanized finishing nails
1-1/2″-dia. hardwood dowel (3′)
1-1/2″ decorative hinges (4)
Redwood plugs
Magnetic latches
Doorknobs
Plug type shelf supports (optional)
Resorcinol wood glue

CUTTING LIST		
KEY	PIECES	SIZE/DESCRIPTION
A	2	3/4 × 7-1/4 × 84 -1/2 side panels
B	3	3/4 × 7-1/4 × 28-1/4 shelves
C	2	3/4 × 6-1/2 × 28-1/4 cabinet top and bottom
D	2	3/4 × 6-1/2 × 28-1/4 cabinet shelves
E	4	3/4 × 3-1/2 × 28-1/4 support box front and back rails
F	2	3/4 × 3-1/2 × 5 top support box sides
G	2	3/4 × 3-1/2 × 3-1/2 bottom support box sides
H	2	3/4 × 3-1/2 × 8 towel rod holders
J	8	3/4 × 3-1/2 × 36 door panels
K	4	3/4 × 1-1/2 × 13 door braces
L	1	1-1/2-dia. × 28-1/8 towel rod

Stand the unit in place and plumb it. Fasten the unit to the wall with No. 10 × 3″ roundhead wood screws or other appropriate wall fasteners. Drive the fasteners through the backs of the support boxes and use washers between the screw heads and the boxes.

Glue and nail a 1 × 8 shelf (B) on top of the bottom support box. Note that the shelf must be flush with the sides and back of the box.

Cut two 28-1/4″-long pieces out of 1 × 8; then rip each to a width of 6-1/2″ to form the cabinet top and bottom (C). Fasten the cabinet top to the top support box with glue and 6d finishing nails.

Fasten the cabinet bottom shelf between the side panels, locating its upper face 37-1/2″ below the upper edges of the side panels. Carefully mark the location of the shelf. Fasten cleats to the side panels below the shelf locations. Sit the bottom shelf on the cleats and secure the shelf to the cleats with glue and No. 6 × 1-1/4″ flathead wood screws. Counterbore the holes and fill them with redwood plugs.

Cut two 8″ lengths of 1 × 4; drill a 1-1/2″-dia. hole in both as shown in the detail drawing of the towel rod holder (H). Cut the radius on the lower end of both holders. Cut the towel rod (L) to length, place the rod

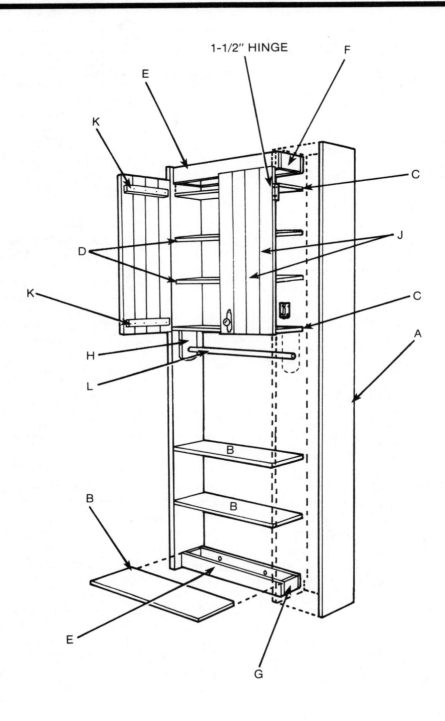

1-1/2" HINGE

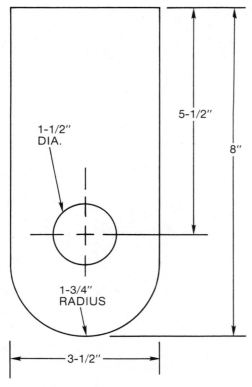

**1-1/2"
DIA.**

5-1/2"

8"

**1-3/4"
RADIUS**

3-1/2"

TOWEL ROD HOLDER DETAIL

bore the pilot holes and fill the holes with redwood plugs.

Determine the location of the other shelves (B) and fasten support cleats to the sides at each point. Fasten the shelves to the cleats. Or drill 1/4"-diameter holes 2" apart and 1-1/2" from the edges of the side panels and support the shelves on shelf support pins. Allow at least 24" from the towel rod to the top shelf.

Next, build the cabinet doors. For the door panels (J), use 1 × 4s, making the sides with the best grain face out. Butt four 1 × 4s edge to edge and attach 1 × 2 braces (K) across each door 1-1/2" from the top and bottom. Counterbore the pilot holes; glue and screw with No. 6 × 1-1/4" wood screws, two per 1 × 4 board. Fill the holes with redwood plugs.

Hang the cabinet doors with two 1-1/2" decorative hinges per door. The doors fit flush with the side panels and have a 1/8" gap between them and a 1/16" gap on each side. They should be centered vertically over the opening. Install magnetic latches and doorknobs as desired. Cut the floor molding to fit and replace it.

in the holes, and center the towel rod holders under the bottom cabinet shelf. Glue and screw the holders to the panel sides. Counter-

LAUNDRY ROOM CABINET

Detergents for light colored clothing, detergents for dark colors, detergents for cold water, detergents for hot, detergents for delicate knits; then there are bleaches, fabric softeners, stain removers—where can a person store them all? The laundry room cabinet unit shown here provides plenty of space, even for bulk quantities. And it can be handily anchored to the wall above the washer and dryer.

Begin by cutting the 3/4″-plywood pieces to width and length. As you can see in the detail drawings, the top (A) and bottom (B) are rabbeted and dadoed to accept the side panels (C) and partitions (E, F). The cabinet right side and the center and right side partitions are dadoed to accept the shelves (G, H). Cut the rabbets and dadoes with a radial arm saw or table saw equipped with a dado blade attachment. Make all dadoes and rabbets 1/4″ deep × 3/4″ wide.

Also, notch the two left side shelves (H) so they clear the center face board (K) when it is installed. Note that the center partition is 3/4″ narrower than the other partitions to make room for the center face board.

Lay out the corners of the doors (J) and the handholds with a compass and cut out with a saber saw.

After the rabbets, dadoes, and notches have been cut, assemble the cabinet sides, top, bottom, and partitions with wood glue and 6d finishing nails. Turn the cabinet on its face and square it with a carpenter's square. Nail and glue the back (D) in place.

Next, squeeze a bead of glue into the shelf dadoes and insert the shelves (G). Then, glue and nail the center face board to the center partition. Use 6d finishing nails and set them below the surface. Fill the holes with wood putty.

Use a wood chisel to notch out the hinge-mortises in the side panels and center face board. Locate the hinge-mortises 3″ from the top and bottom of the cabinet. Chisel to the depth of a folded hinge.

Sand and paint the cabinet and doors. Then mount the cabinet on the wall over your washer and dryer. Make sure that it is level before screwing it to the wall. Use No. 10 × 3″ wood screws and drive them into the wall studs.

Now you are ready to hang the doors. Separate the hinge leaves and screw half of each hinge in the mortises. Hold one door in place and mark the hinge positions on the

MATERIALS LIST

3/4″ × 4′ × 8′ AC interior plywood (2 sheets)
2″ loose-pin hinges (8)
No. 10 × 3″ wood screws
6d finishing nails
Magnetic latches (4)
90-degree door stops (2)
Wood putty
Wood glue

CUTTING LIST

KEY	PIECES	SIZE/DESCRIPTION
A	1	3/4 × 12-3/4 × 60 top
B	1	3/4 × 12-3/4 × 60 bottom
C	2	3/4 × 12-3/4 × 23 sides
D	1	3/4 × 24 × 60 back
E	2	3/4 × 12-3/4 × 23 inner partitions
F	1	3/4 × 12 × 23 center partition
G	2	3/4 × 12-3/4 × 14 right side shelves
H	2	3/4 × 12-3/4 × 15-1/8 left side shelves
J	4	3/4 × 14-3/8 × 30 doors
K	1	3/4 × 3-1/4 × 22-1/2 face board

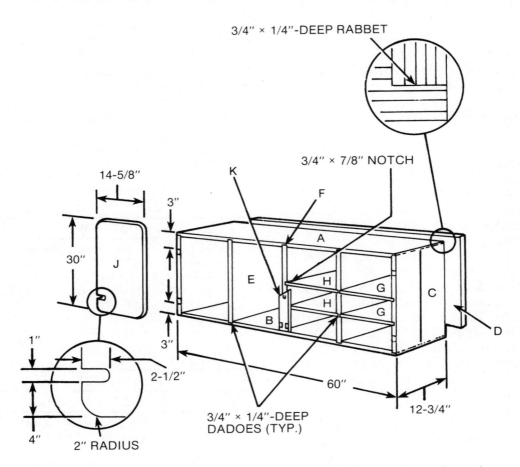

3/4" × 1/4"-DEEP RABBET

3/4" × 7/8" NOTCH

14-5/8"

3"

30"

J

K

F

A

E

H

H

G

G

C

B

D

1"

2-1/2"

3"

60"

12-3/4"

4"

2" RADIUS

3/4" × 1/4"-DEEP DADOES (TYP.)

back side of the door. Screw the other hinge halves to the door and hang it in place. Hold the second door in position, align it with the door already hung, and mark the hinge position. Continue in this fash-

ion until all four doors have been hung. When the doors are hung, install magnetic latches. Also install two 90-degree door stops to the two center doors to prevent them from opening more than 90 degrees.

SEWING CENTER

Are your dress patterns stowed in a box in the hall closet? Is your dining room table the site for laying out and cutting patterns? Do you often resort to setting up a card table for your portable sewing machine?

If you dream of your own private sewing room, complete with mirror, ironing board, and cutting table, this sewing center can make that dream come true.

The actual sewing center is enclosed in two floor-to-ceiling units that measure 9'5-1/2" in total length and are enclosed by three doors. The center features storage for patterns, fabrics, and yarns, and includes additional drawers and cubby holes for many craft and hobby needs. A compact sewing table can be stowed beneath the pigeonholes and your sewing machine stands ready for emergency clothing repairs.

This project incorporates a full-length mirror for checking your "outfit-to-be," and a fold-down ironing board that saves space and is ready whenever you need it.

MATERIALS LIST

3/4" × 4' × 8' AB interior plywood
  (12 sheets)
1/2" × 4' × 8' AB interior plywood
1/8" × 4' × 8' tempered hardwood
  (1-1/2 sheets)
2 × 2 × 6' #2 pine
1 × 6 × 10' select pine
1 × 6 × 8' select pine (3)
1 × 4 × 8' #2 pine
1 × 2 × 8' #2 pine (5)
1/2" × 3" × 8' select pine (14)
No. 10 × 2" wood screws
No. 10 × 1-1/4" wood screws
No. 8 × 1-1/4" wood screws
No. 6 × 1-1/4" wood screws
4d finishing nails
3d finishing nails
2d finishing nails
3/4" wire brads
3/8"-dia. dowels
Drawer knobs (13)
4" brass butt hinges (15)
L-brackets (4)
2" casters (4)
Wooden table slides 2" high,
  62" exterior (1 set)
Table leaf pins
Fold-down ironing board
Framed mirror 30" × 30"
3/16"-dia. hardwood plugs
Wood glue
Magnetic door latches (3)

	CUTTING LIST	
KEY	**PIECES**	**SIZE/DESCRIPTION**
A	4	3/4 × 23-15/16 × 96 case sides (plywood)
B	3	3/4 × 4 × 96 face frame stiles
C	1	3/4 × 4 × 67-5/8 face frame rail
D	1	3/4 × 4 × 33-7/8 face frame rail
E	2	3/4 × 20 × 25-5/8 shelf module sides (plywood)
F	2	3/4 × 20 × 73 shelf module top and bottom (plywood)
G	3	3/4 × 20 × 71-3/4 shelves (plywood)
H	3	3/4 × 7-1/4 × 20 upper shelf dividers (plywood)
J	9	3/4 × 5-5/8 × 20 lower shelf dividers (plywood)
K	1	1/4 × 26-7/8 × 73 shelf module back (plywood)
L	2	3/4 × 20 × 52-3/4 pigeonhole module top and bottom panels (plywood)
M	2	3/4 × 20 × 24-1/2 side panels (plywood)
N	1	3/4 × 20 × 23-1/4 support panel (plywood)
P	4	3/4 × 20 × 47 shelves (plywood)
Q	35	3/4 × 20 × 4-1/4 shelf dividers (plywood)
R	1	1/4 × 24-1/2 × 54 back (plywood)
S	1	3/4 × 5 × 23 face panel (plywood)

KEY	PIECES	SIZE/DESCRIPTION
CUTTING LIST (continued)		
T	10	1/2 × 3-7/8 × 8-5/8 pigeonhole drawer faces (plywood)
U	20	1/2 × 3-7/8 × 19 drawer sides (plywood)
V	10	1/2 × 3-7/8 × 8-5/8 drawer backs (plywood)
W	10	1/8 × 8-1/8 × 19 drawer bottoms (hardboard)
X	2	3/4 × 20 × 69-5/8 drawer module side panels (plywood)
Y	14	3/4 × 13-1/2 × 20 drawer supports (plywood)
Z	1	3/4 × 7-1/8 × 13-1/4 kickplate (plywood)
AA	1	1/4 × 14-3/4 × 69-5/8 back (plywood)
BB	13	3/4 × 3-7/8 × 13-1/8 drawer faces (plywood)
CC	13	3/4 × 3-7/8 × 13-1/8 drawer backs (plywood)
DD	26	1/2 × 3-7/8 × 19 drawer sides (plywood)
EE	13	1/8 × 12-5/8 × 19 drawer bottoms (hardboard)
FF	2	3/4 × 1-1/2 × 69-1/2 cleats (#2 pine)
GG	1	3/4 × 4-1/4 × 69-5/8 spacer panel (plywood)
HH	1	3/4 × 3-1/2 × 54 pigeonhole module cleat (#2 pine)

KEY	PIECES	SIZE/DESCRIPTION
CUTTING LIST (continued)		
JJ	2	3/4 × 12-1/2 × 20 storage cubicle sides (plywood)
KK	1	3/4 × 12-1/2 × 20 center divider (plywood)
LL	2	3/4 × 20 × 37-1/2 cubicle top and bottom (plywood)
MM	1	1/4 × 13-3/4 × 37-1/2 cubicle back (plywood)
NN	2	3/4 × 1-1/2 × 20 cleats (#2 pine)
PP	4	3/4 × 16-1/8 × 32 table leaves (plywood)
QQ	2	1-1/2 × 1-1/2 × 33-1/4 table legs (#2 pine)
RR	1	3/4 × 2 × 31 table skirt (#2 pine)
SS	1	3/4 × 3 × 32 false front (#2 pine)
TT	3	3/4 × 32-3/8 × 91-3/4 door panels (plywood)
UU	6	3/4 × 5/8 × 91-3/4 door edge bands
VV	6	1/2 × 3 × 62 door trim pieces
WW	6	1/2 × 3 × 27-1/2 door trim pieces
XX	12	1/2 × 2 × 25-3/8 door trim pieces
YY	3	1/2 × 2 × 31-1/2 door trim pieces
ZZ	3	1/2 × 2-1/8 × 91-3/4 door trim pieces
AAA	3	3/4 × 1-1/2 × 94-1/2 reinforcement strips

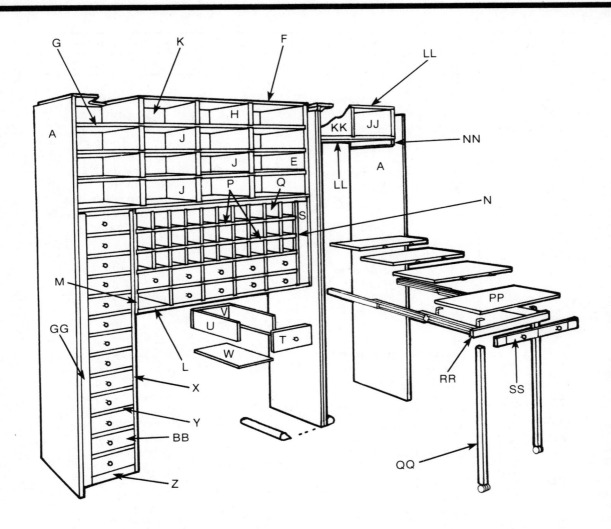

Sewing can be made simple with the right size table for laying out and cutting fabrics and patterns. The sewing center includes a table that can be extended to 62″ long. When you are finished using the table, the drawer leaves can be easily removed and stacked for storage. The clothing rod above the table lets you hang in-progress projects and a pair of oversized cubicles add to your storage space.

Storage Case

This sewing center is designed for a room with an 8′1/2″ ceiling. If you build the sewing center in a room with a ceiling height less than

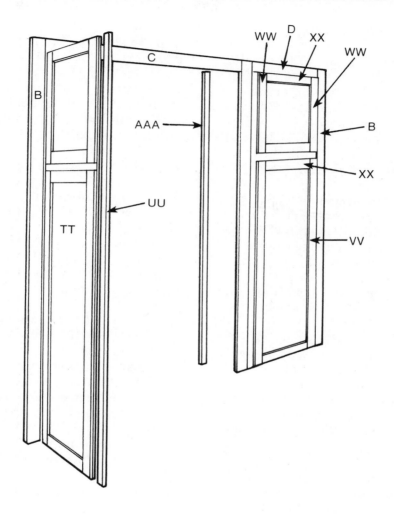

8'1/2", cut the case sides 1/2" shorter than the ceiling height to allow clearance for the panels to be stood up. The center is made up of two units. A unit 74-1/2" wide contains a shelving module, pigeonhole module, and drawer module. The second unit, measuring 39" wide, contains a fold-down table.

The storage case consists of four side panels (A) and a face frame (B, C, D). The sides of the case are erected as the upper shelving modules are installed in the left and right units. The face frame is attached after the case sides and the various storage modules have been installed.

Shelf Module

Begin construction of the shelf module by cutting the sides (E), top and bottom (F), shelves (G) and shelf dividers (H, J) to size. Machine 3/4" × 1/8" dadoes across the side panels of the shelf module. The first dado is located 7-1/8" from the top. The other two are spaced 5-3/8" apart below the first dado.

Next cut a series of 3/4" × 1/8" dadoes across the inner face of each module top and bottom panel along with a rabbet of the same dimensions across each end. Measuring from either end, leave 17-1/8" of space between the rabbet and the first dado, then 17" of space between successive dadoes.

Use the module top and bottom panels as patterns for locating parallel dadoes on the three module shelves. Just remember that the shelves are 1-1/4" shorter than the top and bottom panels, so they must be centered along the length of those panels for proper marking. Once the layout is done, cut back-to-back 3/4" × 1/8" dadoes on each of the shelves so the dividers will fit between them as shown in the drawing.

Spread glue in the rabbets and dadoes and on the edges of the shelves, dividers, and sides. Loosely clamp the top, bottom, sides, and shelves together. With a block and hammer, tap the dividers into place. Then, drive No. 8 × 1-1/4" wood screws through the top and bottom into the sides and through the sides into the shelves. Maintain the clamping action until the glue dries.

Cut the back panel (K) to size. Smear glue on the back edges of the module, position the back panel flush with the edges of the module, and tack the panel in place with 2d finishing nails.

While the glue is drying on this module, rip two sheets of 3/4" plywood down the middle to create the four case sides (A). Then have a couple of helpers hold the module in place while you fasten it to the wall. Mark the locations of studs in advance to help you place screws properly and use No. 10 × 2" wood screws.

Note that our design presumes the module will fit against an 8'1/2"-high ceiling. To make the upper shelf more accessible, lower the height of the module several inches and compensate by shortening the drawer module at its lower end.

Ask your helpers to continue supporting the module while you enclose it with a pair of the case side panels. Raise and plumb the case sides and fasten them to the module using No. 10 × 1-1/4" wood screws. Countersink the screws to make them flush with the panels. If there is more than a few inches of space between the left end of the unit and a side wall, you may want to run the screws through the left module side into the case side to make them less visible. On the other hand, if that end of the unit is next to a wall you may wish to fasten it directly to the wall. In that case, you can eliminate the left case side to save on materials.

Pigeonhole Module

The pigeonhole unit is constructed with ten drawers and thirty pigeonholes. Begin by cutting the top and bottom panels (L), the side panels (M), the support panel (N), the four shelves (P), and the thirty-five shelf dividers (Q) to size.

Then lay out and machine the 3/4" × 1/8" rabbets and dadoes used to join the pieces together. The inner faces of the side panels get rabbets at either end to receive the ends of the top and bottom. The support panel is shorter than the sides and fits between the top and bottom. However, since the shelves stretch from the left side panel to the support panel (N), those two panels get the dadoes for receiving the shelf ends. On the side panel the first dado is spaced 4" from an end rabbet. On the support panel it must be spaced 4-1/8" from one end to allow for the way that piece is installed. On both pieces, the dadoes are then spaced 4" apart.

The top panel gets twice as many dadoes as the bottom panel. In both cases, the layout must be made from the left end, because the space at the right end is atypical. Begin by allowing 1/8" for the ends fitting into the side panel. From that point on, lay out the dadoes at 4" intervals

on the top panel and 8-3/4" intervals on the bottom panel. Then use the top panel as a pattern to lay out dadoes on both faces of the top two shelves and the upper face of the third shelf. Use the bottom panel as a pattern for locating the dadoes on the underside of the third shelf and both faces of the fourth shelf. Before marking the shelves, make sure their left ends are flush with the left ends of the top and bottom panels.

Dry fit the parts of the module to make sure everything is properly cut, then begin the final assembly using wood glue and No. 8 × 1-1/4" screws. Since you may find it difficult to handle all the parts at once, you may wish to start by loosely joining the top, bottom, shelves, and sides, holding them together with clamps while driving the dividers into place, then drawing everything tightly together and inserting screws at several joints.

An optional approach is to build the module up, tier by tier, beginning with the bottom, the bottom row of dividers, and the support panel, moving up shelf by shelf to the top, then adding the side panels last. In either case, use clamps to pull everything square before the glue hardens. A slow-setting glue would be a good choice to use here.

Line the opening between the right support panel and the right side panel with 3/4" cleats. Cut a face panel (S) to fit snugly in the opening and fasten it to the cleats with glue and 3d finishing nails.

Cut a back panel (R) from 1/4" plywood. Smear glue on the back-side of the module and position the panel flush with the edges. Tack the panel to the module with 3/4" wire brads.

Cut the drawer faces (T), sides (U), backs (V), and bottoms (W) to size. Machine 1/2" × 1/4" rabbets along the ends of the faces and backs. Machine a 1/8" × 1/4" groove 1/4" above the bottom edge of each piece.

Assemble each drawer with carpenter's wood glue. Do not glue the bottoms. Check to make certain the frame is square. Then, clamp the unit until the glue sets up.

While the glue is drying, set the pigeonhole module aside and construct the drawer module.

Drawer Module

Begin construction of the drawer module by cutting the two side panels (X), the drawer supports (Y), and the kickplate (Z) to size. Note that the sides of this module should be cut to fit between the shelf module and the floor. If the ceiling height is more or less than 8'1/2", the height of the module sides as given in the cutting list must be altered.

Next, machine a 3/4" × 1/8" rabbet on the top inside edges of the side panels. Then, machine thirteen dadoes 3/4" wide and 1/8" deep spaced 4" apart, measuring down from the rabbet at the top.

Apply glue to the edges of the drawer supports and slide them into place. Drive No. 8 × 1-1/4" wood screws through the sides to anchor the supports.

Use screws and glue to fasten the kickplate between the sides beneath the bottom shelf support.

Cut the back panel (AA) to size. Square the unit and fasten the back to the module with glue and 3/4" wire brads.

Cut the drawer parts (BB, CC, DD, EE) to size. Then, machine a 1/2" × 1/4" rabbet across the ends of the drawer faces and backs. Also, machine a 1/8" × 1/4" groove 1/4" above the bottom of the front, backs, and sides to accept the bottom panel.

Glue the drawer frames together, making sure they are square, and clamp them securely.

Now that both the pigeonhole module and drawer module have been constructed, have someone hold the pigeonhole module in place against the right case side flush with the front edge of the shelf module. Fasten the module side to the case side by driving No. 10 × 1-1/4" wood screws through the case side. Countersink the pilot holes so that the wood screws seat flush with the panel.

Then, position the drawer module beside the pigeonhole module. Make sure that the front edges of the modules are flush. Then drive screws through the drawer module into the side of the pigeonhole module. Countersink the pilot holes so that the screws seat flush with the panel.

Measure and cut two cleats (FF) to fit between the shelf module and the floor. These will act as nailers for the spacer panel (GG). Fasten one cleat to the case side and the other cleat to the side of the shelf module. Locate the cleats so that when the panel is placed over them it will be flush with the front of the drawer module.

Cut the spacer panel to fit snugly in the available space and fasten it to the cleats with glue and 3d finishing nails.

Cut a 1 × 4 cleat (HH) to length. Position it against the underside of the pigeonhole module and screw it to the wall. Be sure to screw into wall studs.

Overhead Storage Cubicle

Because not every sewing project can be completed in a day, a roomy overhead storage cubicle and clothes rod are included in the right side compartment. Sewing projects in the cutting stage can be kept in the cubicles where they are easily accessible. Works-in-progress can be hung from the bar. The bar is also a handy place to hang freshly ironed clothes.

Make the overhead storage unit by cutting the top and bottom (LL), sides (JJ), and center divider (KK) to size. Machine 3/4" × 1/8" rabbets in the ends of the top and bottom panels and a 3/4" × 1/8" dado in the center of each panel. Glue and screw the unit together.

Cut the back (MM) to size from 1/4" plywood. Fasten the back to the module with glue and 3/4" wire brads.

Place the left case side of this unit against the right side of the unit already installed. Make sure their front edges are flush, then fasten the two panels together using No. 10 × 1-1/4" wood screws. Countersink the screws so their heads are flush with the surface of the panels.

Now have a helper hold the storage cubicle in place while you mark the location of its bottom edge on the case side. Cut the cubicle cleats (NN) to size and fasten one to the left case side using countersunk No. 10 × 1-1/4" wood screws. Fasten the other cleat to the remaining case side in a parallel location.

Raise the right case side into position parallel with the other case side and set the storage cubicle on the cleats. Fasten the cubicle to the two case sides using No. 10 × 1-1/4" wood screws. Then center and fasten the clothes rod to the underside of the cubicle.

Pullout Table

By adding leaves you can make this pullout table more than 5' long, perfect for almost any sewing project. And when you don't need it, simply slide the table sides back into place and stack your leaves on top.

The table unit is composed of a series of four leaves (PP) that fit on commercially built table slides. Purchase slides that measure at least 2" high with a maximum opening of 62".

Fasten the table slides to the case sides, setting the tops of the slides approximately 36" above the floor. (That height should be about the same as the height of the table legs once the casters have been installed.) Block out the wall on the right side as needed to allow the slide to clear the door and use screws at least 3/4" longer than the thickness of the slides.

Cut the skirt (RR) to size and screw it to the ends of the slides.

Cut the false front (SS) to size. Score its face with kerfs 1/8" wide × 1/16" deep and attach knobs so that the panel appears to be the front of two drawers.

Cut the two legs (QQ) to length. Fit them between the slides and fasten them to the back of the false front using two No. 10 wood screws for each leg.

The false front fits across the skirt with a 1/2" overlap on both sides. Clamp it in position. Drill and countersink two pilot holes through the skirt. Drive No. 8 × 1-1/4" wood screws through the skirt into the back of the false front to hold it in place.

Cut the table leaves to size and mark them 1, 2, 3, and 4. Lay out the panels in order, butt them together, and align their edges. Measure 10" from each side and square a line across the panel joints at these points. Using a doweling jig, drill 3/8"-diameter holes 1" deep in the center of each panel edge where marked.

Drive table pins into the holes in leaf number 4 and into the holes on the outside edges of leaves 2 and 3.

Leaf number 1 is the only leaf that is permanently attached. Cover leaf number 1 with plastic laminate. Center it on the drawer slides so that it extends out over the false front by 2-1/4". Attach leaf number 1 with L-brackets to the slides.

Before covering the rest of the leaves with the plastic laminate, fit them together to see if they will fit easily into the opening. If the joints are tight and difficult to fit, leaf number 4 can be trimmed from the back edge.

When the leaves fit properly, cover them with the laminate.

Facings and Doors

Cut the face frame stiles and rails (C, D, E) to size. Note that the length of the stiles must be adjusted if the ceiling height is more or less than 8'1/2". Dowel the rails, which fit across the top of the case, to the stiles, which will cover the sides.

Fit the face frame over the front of the sewing center, making its outer edges flush with those of the outer case sides. Push it up against the ceiling if you like, then fasten it to the case sides using glue and 6d finishing nails. Set the nails and putty the holes.

The three doors are constructed of plywood sheets trimmed with 1/2" pine moldings so that they appear to be double frame and panel doors.

Begin construction of the sewing center doors by cutting the three door panels (TT) to size. Then, cut six edge bands (UU) to length from rail and stile rippings and fasten them to the long edges of the panels with glue and 4d finishing nails.

The raised panel look on the doors is created by fastening 1/2"-thick pine boards to the front face of the plywood panels. The double-door look is created by leaving 1/8" spaces between boards. Cut the door trim pieces (VV, WW, XX, YY, ZZ) to length and fasten them to the door panels using wood glue and 2d finishing nails. Arrange the trim pieces in the manner shown on the door trim detail drawing. Note that the thin vertical trim pieces (ZZ) go on the opposite side of each door from where the hinges are mounted.

Cut three reinforcement strips (AAA) for use in hanging the doors. Fit one strip behind each face frame stile, making its edge flush with the edge of the stile on which the hinges must be mounted. Fasten the strips to the backs of the stiles using wood glue and No. 6 × 1-1/4" wood screws. Then cut hinge mortises in the reinforced stile edges and in the edges of the doors. Install the hinges and hang the doors.

Cut small blocks from scrap lumber and fasten them either to the back of the face frame rails or to the floor to serve as doorstops. Attach magnetic latches to these blocks and to the backs of the three doors.

Next, attach the fold-down ironing board to the back of the door covering the pigeonhole module.

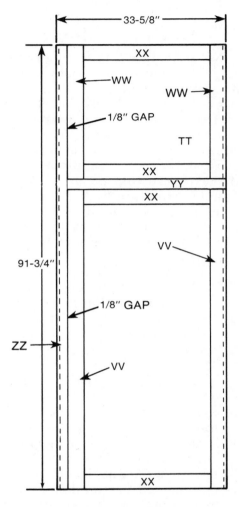

DOOR TRIM DETAIL
(RIGHT SIDE HINGED DOOR)

Make certain that the ironing board you purchase from your local building products dealer will fit into the space between the door and the front of the pigeonhole module.

Finally, attach a full-length mirror to the back of the door that closes over the drawer module.

Sewing Table

Not only does this sewing table easily fit behind closed doors, but your sewing machine can also stay in its ready-to-work position. The two drawers on each end are perfect for storing seam rippers, pins, spools of thread, and scissors.

The table legs are equipped with casters so you can easily move the table to any spot in the room or house. In fact, you might want to roll it close to the window so you catch a bit of sun while sewing new creations.

Cut the table parts to size and sand all parts before assembly.

If you wish, you can make the edges of the top (A) more attractive by nailing quarter-round, ogee, or other decorative moldings to them.

Cut the four legs (D) to size. Pick an inside edge for each leg. Measure from the top 8" down along that edge and mark that point for beginning tapered cuts on the two inside faces of the leg. Then go to the bottom and measure from the inside edge 1" across each adjacent face and mark those points for ending the tapered cuts. These cuts can most easily be made with a table saw and a taper-cutting jig, but you can use a bandsaw or jigsaw and touch up the cut surfaces with a hand plane or belt sander.

Arrange the legs the way they will go on the table and mark the inside faces of each so you will remember which ones will receive a side stretcher (B) and which ones

MATERIALS LIST (SEWING TABLE)

3/4" × 4' × 8' AB interior plywood (1/2 sheet)
1 × 4 × 8' #2 common pine
2-1/2" × 2-1/2" × 25" #2 common pine (4)
2 × 3 × 5' #2 pine
1/8" × 4' × 8' tempered hardboard (1/4 sheet)
6d finishing nails
Shaker drawer knobs (2)
16" drawer slides (2 sets)
2-1/4" stem casters (2 pair)
L-brackets (8)
Wood glue

CUTTING LIST

KEY	PIECES	SIZE/DESCRIPTION
A	1	3/4 × 17 × 42 top
B	2	3/4 × 3-1/2 × 34-1/2 side stretchers
C	2	3/4 × 3-1/2 × 12 end stretchers
D	4	2-1/2 × 2-1/2 × 25 legs
E	2	3/4 × 2-1/2 × 10-3/8 drawer faces
F	4	3/4 × 2-1/2 × 15 drawer sides
G	2	3/4 × 2-1/2 × 9-3/8 drawer backs
H	2	1/8 × 8-1/4 × 14-5/8 drawer bottoms
J	1	1-1/2 × 2-3/4 × 13-1/2 inside brace
K	4	1-1/2 × 2-1/2 × 14-1/4 packing

will receive an end stretcher (C). Then lay out and cut mortises for the ends of the stretchers. Locate all the mortises 1/4" from the outer edge of the face in which they are

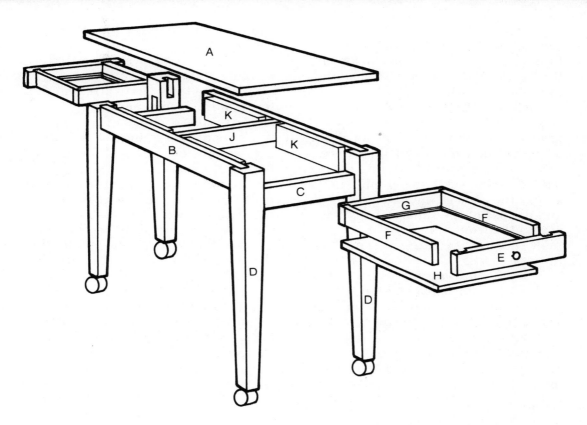

cut. Make them 3/4″ wide, 3/4″ deep, and 3-1/2″ long. Start the mortises for the side stretchers at the top of the legs so the stretchers will be flush with the tabletop, but begin the mortises for the end stretchers 2-9/16″ below the top so drawers can slide over the top of the stretchers.

After cutting the stretchers to size, dry fit the frame to make sure everything goes together properly and that the frame ends up square. Mark the centerpoint along the length of each side stretcher and measure the space between them at those points. Cut a brace (J) to fit that space. (If everything is properly cut and assembled that space should measure 13-1/2″.) If you like, you can make the brace out of two pieces of 3/4″ plywood glued together.

Once you are sure all frame parts are properly cut, glue up the frame and clamp it until the glue sets. Make sure the brace is properly centered and that its upper edge is flush with the upper edges of the side stretchers. You might want to reinforce the fastening of the brace with finishing nails driven through the stretchers into its ends or tiny glue blocks placed in the joints be-tween brace and stretchers. But, be-fore inserting glue blocks, make sure they will not interfere with the later installation of the drawers.

After cutting all drawer parts to size, cut 1/8"-wide and 1/4"-deep grooves 1/8" above the bottom edges of the backs, fronts, and sides to re-ceive the hardboard bottoms. Then cut 3/4"-wide × 3/8"-deep rabbets across the ends of the back pieces and dadoes of the same dimensions across the front pieces 1/2" from their ends for fastening the ends of the side pieces.

Dry fit the bottoms (H) into the 1/8"-wide slots. Then glue up the drawer sides and facings. Attach the knobs to the front of the drawers.

Cut the drawer packing (K) to size and fasten it to the side stretchers, using glue and 6d finish-ing nails. Hold the packing back 3/4"

from the legs to allow room for an L-bracket.

Attach the drawer slides to the packing and to the drawers.

Cut the tabletop to size and cen-ter it on the frame. Secure it to the side stretchers using eight L-brackets placed in the 3/4" spaces between the drawer packing and the legs and brace.

Turn the table upside down and drill 1/4"-diameter holes centered in the ends of each leg to accept the stem-type casters. The depth of the holes will depend on the length of the stem. Follow the manufacturer's instructions for installation.

Sand the table and drawers. Paint the table a color to comple-ment the sewing center. If a stain finish is desired, glue veneer tape to the exposed plywood edges of the top and drawer faces before finishing.

MIRRORED WALL CABINET

You don't have to be a master craftsman to build this simple but beautiful mirrored wall cabinet. Hung on a wall or set on a vanity, this unit will provide plenty of open shelf space for displaying knick-knacks and necessaries as well as a mirrored cabinet for keeping medicines and beauty aids out of sight.

You can adjust the shelves of this versatile redwood cabinet to whatever height you need. Use it in the bathroom, bedroom, kitchen, or wherever attractive, versatile storage space is needed.

Construction of this wall cabinet is simple. All pieces in the cabinet case are butted together and secured with carpenter's wood glue and No. 6 × 1-1/2" wood screws. Be sure to counterbore all pilot holes and fill the holes with wood plugs. The door frame is assembled with glue and dowels.

Begin construction by cutting the sides (A), top (B), bottom (C), and vertical dividers (D) to size. Mark and drill 1/4"-diameter holes 3/4" deep for the shelf supports in the sides and vertical dividers. Space the holes 3/4" from the edges of the boards and 1-1/2" to 2" apart.

Assemble the outer frame, using glue and two No. 6 × 1-1/2" wood screws per joint. Remember to countersink pilot holes and fill them with hardwood plugs.

Next, cut the side shelves (E) to size and use them to determine the position of the vertical dividers. Install the dividers using glue and two screws per joint.

Cut the mounting bars (K) to size and install them under the top in the side compartments, flush with the back. Use wood glue and two screws through the top and one screw through the sides.

Cut the center shelves (G) and the horizontal divider (F) to length. Install the divider so that its bottom edge is 23" from the top surface of the top. Use wood glue and two No. 6 wood screws per joint. Counterbore the screw holes so you can cover the screw heads with wood plugs.

Cut the door rails (H) and stiles (J) to size. Assemble the door frame using glue and two dowel pins per joint.

MATERIALS LIST

1 × 6 × 8' clear all heart redwood (3)
1 × 3 × 8' clear all heart redwood
1/8" × 1' × 2' tempered hardboard
No. 6 × 1-1/2" wood screws
1/2" brads
1/4"-dia. hardwood dowels (2')
3/16" × 11-3/4" × 18-3/4" mirror
1-1/2" concealed hinge (2)
Magnetic catch
Door pull
Wood plugs
Wood glue

CUTTING LIST

KEY	PIECES	SIZE/DESCRIPTION
A	2	3/4 × 5-1/2 × 30 sides
B	1	3/4 × 5-1/2 × 38-1/2 top
C	1	3/4 × 5-1/2 × 38-1/2 bottom
D	2	3/4 × 5-1/2 × 28-1/2 vertical dividers
E	6	3/4 × 5-1/2 × 11-1/4 side shelves
F	1	3/4 × 5-1/2 × 14-1/2 horizontal divider
G	2	3/4 × 5-1/2 × 14-1/2 center shelves
H	2	3/4 × 2-1/2 × 11 door rails
J	2	3/4 × 2-1/2 × 23 door stiles
K	2	3/4 × 2-1/2 × 11-1/4 mounting bars
L	1	1/8 × 11-3/4 × 18-3/4 hardboard mirror backing

Machine a 3/8" × 3/8" rabbet on the back inside edges of the door frame for the mirror.

Attach the door to the cabinet

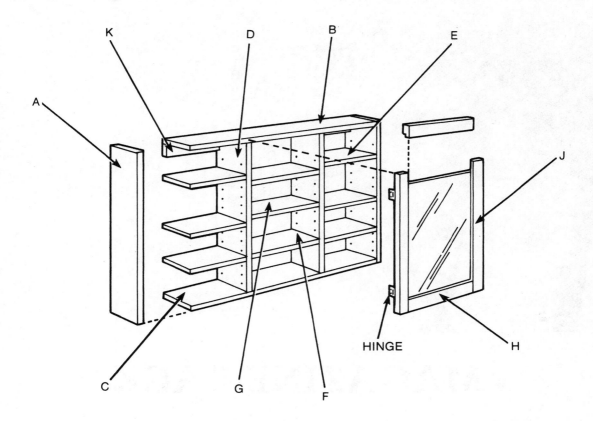

with 1-1/2" concealed hinges designed for overlapping doors.

Cut the shelf supports from 1/4"-diameter hardwood dowels. Cut each one 3/4" in length and insert them in the desired shelf support holes.

Sand and finish the cabinet and shelves as desired. Then attach the magnetic catch and door pull. Install the mirror and hardboard backing in the door frame. Hold them in place with 1/2" brads.

MAGAZINE RACK

Magazines have a way of collecting in corners and hiding under couches and chairs. To keep your reading material organized, build this simple magazine rack. Then, attach it to the wall in a room where you and others in the family often spend time reading. It will look great in a bedroom, a family room, even in a bathroom.

Begin by cutting the back (A), sides (B), shelf facings (C), and shelf bottoms (D) to size from an 8' length of 1 ×12. Transfer the pattern given in the illustration to the sides, and cut the curves with a bandsaw, a jigsaw, or a saber saw.

NOTE: *If you tape the sides together, you can cut the curves in both pieces simultaneously.*

Rip a 70-degree bevel on the back edge of the shelf bottoms.
Position the square side edges of the shelf bottoms against the back of the facings 1/2″ above their

MATERIALS LIST

1 × 12 × 8′ pine
3d finishing nails
No. 6 ×1-1/2″ flathead wood screws
  (2)
Plastic screw anchors (2)
Wood glue

CUTTING LIST

KEY	PIECES	SIZE/DESCRIPTION
A	1	3/4 × 10 × 23 back
B	2	3/4 × 7-1/2 × 23 sides
C	2	3/4 × 8-1/2 × 10 shelf facings
D	2	3/4 × 2-1/2 × 10 shelf bottoms

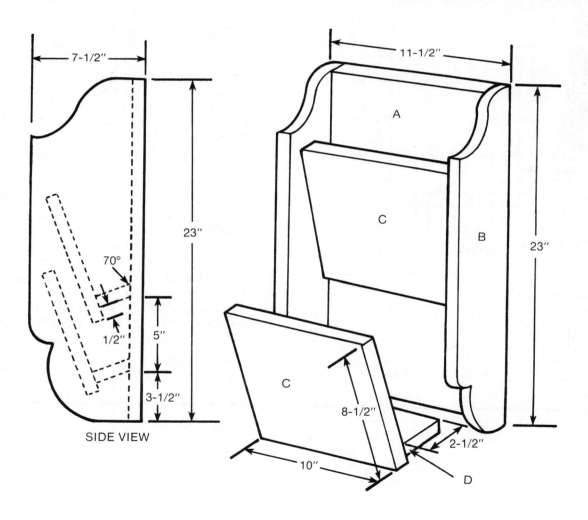

SIDE VIEW

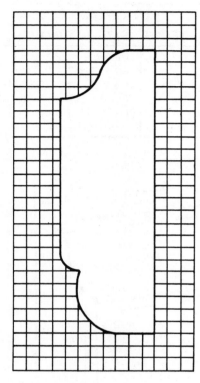

PATTERN FOR SIDES

lower edges as shown in the side view drawing. Fasten the facings to the bottoms using glue and 3d finishing nails.

Using a pencil and combination square, draw lines across the face of the back panel 3-1/2" and 8-1/2" above the bottom of the panel. Position the bottom edges of the shelf bottoms against these lines and fasten the back to the shelves with glue and 3d nails. When inserting the nails, start them no more than 3/8" above the lines on the back and drive them straight or angled slightly down to avoid penetrating the sloping surface of the shelf bottoms.

Position the side panels flush with the top and back edges of the back panel. Secure the sides to the back and to the shelves with glue and 3d nails.

Drill and countersink a pair of pilot holes for No. 6 screws through the back panel just above the upper shelf for mounting the rack to the wall. Sand and paint the rack to match the room decor.

Attach the rack to the wall, using two No. 6 ×1-1/2" flathead wood screws and plastic screw anchors.

the top and bottom edges of the back give the cabinet a country look.

Begin by gluing up sufficient 1 × 4 pine stock to make the sides (A), back (B), shelves (C, D), and door panels (G).

NOTE: *Arrange the boards so that the growth rings on adjacent boards run in alternate directions. This will help to minimize cupping.*

MATERIALS LIST

1 × 4 × 8' #2 pine (6)
1 × 4 × 6' #2 pine
1 × 2 × 10' #2 pine
3/4"-dia. dowel (4')
Semiconcealed hinges (4)
Magnetic catches (2)
3/8"-dia. dowel pins (16)
1/4"-dia. shelf pins (4)
Wood glue

CUTTING LIST

KEY	PIECES	SIZE/DESCRIPTION
A	2	3/4 × 8 × 36 sides
B	1	3/4 × 19 × 36 back
C	3	3/4 × 7-1/4 × 19 fixed shelves
D	1	3/4 × 7-1/4 × 18-1/4 adjustable shelves
E	4	3/4 × 1-1/2 × 6-7/16 door rails
F	4	3/4 × 1-1/2 × 20 door stiles
G	2	3/4 × 6-7/8 × 17-7/16 door panels
H	2	3/4-dia. × 19 dowels

WALL-HUNG LINEN CABINET

Here's a project that is just right for a half bath or any bathroom that might not have sufficient closet space. The cabinet provides the extra space needed for storing linen, beauty aids, and other bathroom necessities. The construction is simple: the sides are dadoed, rabbeted, and bored to accept the shelves, back, and dowels. Decorative curves on

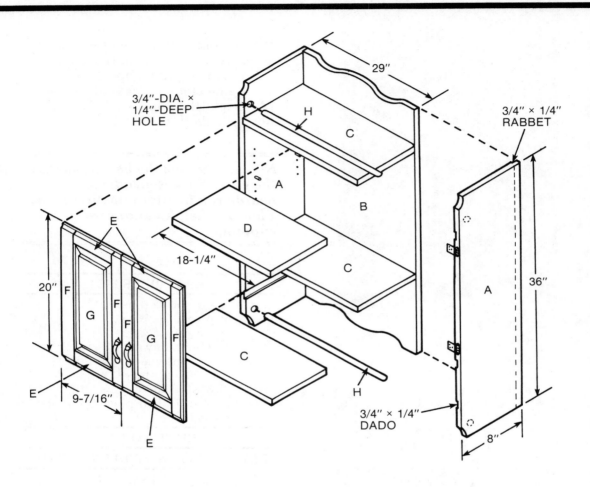

3/4"-DIA. ×
1/4"-DEEP
HOLE

29"

3/4" × 1/4"
RABBET

18-1/4"

20"

9-7/16"

36"

8"

3/4" × 1/4"
DADO

Rip and crosscut the panels to size. Cut the dowels (H) to length.

Machine a 3/4"-wide × 1/4"-deep rabbet along the inside rear edge of each side panel to receive the back panel.

Cut a series of three 3/4" × 1/4" dadoes across the inside face of each side panel to receive the ends of the fixed shelves. Locate one dado 4-1/2" down from the top of the panel, a second dado 4-1/2" above the bottom, and a third dado 6-1/4" above the second one, as shown in the side view drawing.

Drill a parallel pair of 3/4"-diameter holes 1/4" deep into the inside face of each side panel to receive the ends of the dowels, as shown in the exploded view drawing. Center the holes 1" from the front edge and 2-1/2" from the top and bottom ends of each panel as shown in the side view drawing.

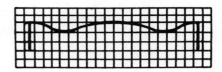

ONE SQUARE = 1"

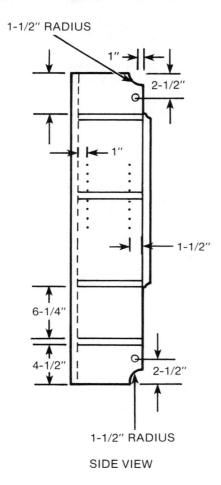

1-1/2" RADIUS

SIDE VIEW

drill them to the depth needed for the type of pins you purchase.

Cut a 1-1/2"-radius curved notch out of both front corners of each side panel, as shown in the side view drawing. Also, cut a decorative shape in the top and bottom edges of the back panel, using the grid pattern as your guide.

Dry assemble the cabinet to make sure that the pieces fit properly. Then, disassemble the unit and spread glue in the dadoes, rabbets, and the holes drilled for the dowels. Also, spread glue on the ends of the three fixed shelves and the dowels. Reassemble the unit and clamp until dry.

Sand and finish the cabinet as desired.

The frame and panel doors shown in the photograph overlap the side panels 1/4" and fit flush with the top edge of the top shelf and the bottom edge of the lower fixed shelf.

Cut the door rails (E) and stiles (F) to length. Drill pairs of holes, 3/8"-dia. × 1-1/16"-deep, in the inside edges of the stiles and in the ends of the rails to accept 3/8"-dia. × 2"-long dowel pins.

Rout 1/4"-wide grooves in the inside edges of each piece to accept

Drill two parallel rows of 1/4"-diameter holes into the inside face of each side panel to accept pins for supporting the adjustable shelf. Begin the series of holes about 9" below the top and end about halfway down the panel, as shown in the drawings. Center the front row of holes 1-1/2" from the front edge of the panel and back row 1" inside the rabbet. Space the holes 1" apart and

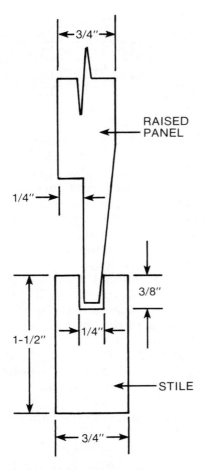

3/4"

RAISED
PANEL

1/4"

3/8"

1/4"

1-1/2"

STILE

3/4"

FRAME AND PANEL
DETAIL

the raised panels. Cut the grooves 3/8" deep in the rails and 1" deep in the stiles. Stop the grooves 1/2" from the ends of the stiles.

Bevel the front face and cut a shoulder in the rear face of the panels as shown in the detail drawing. Sand and finish the panels before assembling the doors.

Assemble the panels and frame members with dowels in each corner. Do not glue the raised panels in the grooves: allow them to "float" in the grooves so that they can expand and contract without stressing the frames.

Shape the outside edges of the doors with a 1/2"-radius cove bit. Sand the frames and finish them.

Install 1-1/2" hinges on the doors and fasten the doors to the cabinet. Install magnetic latches under the top shelf, then install door pulls.

SHAKER DESK

What's a sewing center without a place to plot and plan your next project? This attractively designed Shaker desk can be built in three phases: first the drop-down tabletop, then the hutch, and finally, the drawers.

The desk is a good place to keep sewing books and guides, pencils, tracing paper, and a file of creative ideas found in magazines. But you might want to use it for storing stationary, keeping a diary, or even collecting bills. It is a very comfortable table for writing, and when you're finished, just close up the tabletop and have that neat, simple look basic to Shaker design.

Table

Begin by cutting the table legs (A) and stretchers (B, C) to length. Taper two adjacent faces on each leg so that the leg is 1-1/2" square at the bottom. Begin each taper 2-1/2" from the top of the leg and run it in a straight line to the bottom. Once the tapers are made, consider the two tapered faces the "inside" faces of the leg. (See the illustration for detail.)

Cut a 3/4"-wide, 2-1/2"-long, and 3/4"-deep mortise on each inside face of each leg to receive an end of one of the stretchers. Begin each mortise at the top of the leg and set it 1/2" in from an outer edge of the piece.

Dry fit the stretchers and legs to make sure the frame is square. Then, disassemble the frame, put glue on all joints, reassemble it, and clamp until dry.

Cut the tabletop (D) to size. Place the top on the leg/stretcher assembly so that it is flush with the back edge and extends out 3/4" beyond the other three edges of the table. Make sure that the assembly is square; then, fasten the top in place by driving 6d finishing nails down through the top and into the stretchers.

Cut to size the pieces that make the frame of the slant-top writing

MATERIALS LIST

2-1/4″ × 2-1/4″ × 8′ #2 common pine
1 × 12 × 8′ #2 common pine (4)
3/4″ × 4′ × 4′ AB interior plywood
1/4″ × 2′ × 4′ AB interior plywood
1/8″ × 2′ × 4′ tempered hardboard
1-1/2″ × 33-1/2″ brass piano hinge (1)
1/4″-dia. hardwood dowels
No. 8 × 2-3/4″ wood screws
No. 8 × 2″ wood screws
No. 3 × 3/8″ wood screws
6d finishing nails
Shaker knobs (5)
3/4″-wide preglued pine edge
    banding
Wood glue

CUTTING LIST

KEY	PIECES	SIZE/DESCRIPTION
A	4	2-1/4 × 2-1/4 × 24-1/4 table legs
B	2	3/4 × 2-1/2 × 30-1/2 stretchers
C	2	3/4 × 2-1/2 × 18-3/4 stretchers
D	1	3/4 × 22-1/2 × 35 tabletop (plywood)
E	2	3/4 × 2-1/4 × 21 writing table frame sides
F	1	3/4 × 2-1/4 × 32 writing table frame back rail
G	1	3/4 × 1-9/16 × 33-1/2 writing table frame front rail
H	1	3/4 × 9-7/8 × 35 writing tabletop
J	2	3/4 × 12 × 21 hutch sides
K	1	3/4 × 13-1/4 × 35 hutch top
L	2	3/4 × 11 × 16-1/2 center dividers

CUTTING LIST (continued)

KEY	PIECES	SIZE/DESCRIPTION
M	2	3/4 × 9 × 11 drawer supports
N	2	3/4 × 11 × 13-1/4 drawer support
P	1	3/4 × 11 × 32-1/4 pigeonhole support
Q	6	3/4 × 4 × 11 pigeonhole dividers
R	1	1/4 × 21-1/4 × 32-1/2 hutch back (plywood)
S	1	3/4 × 12-3/4 × 35 hutch bottom
T	1	3/4 × 20-3/8 × 33-3/8 hutch door panel (plywood)
U	4	3/4 × 3-5/8 × 8-5/8 drawer fronts and backs
V	2	3/4 × 3-5/8 × 12-7/8 drawer front and back
W	2	3/4 × 3-5/8 × 9-3/8 drawer front and back
X	8	3/4 × 3-5/8 × 10-1/8 drawer sides
Y	1	1/8 × 8-3/8 × 9-7/8 drawer bottom
Z	1	1/8 × 9-7/8 × 11-7/8 drawer bottom
AA	2	1/8 × 7-5/8 × 9-7/8 drawer bottoms

portion of the desk. Rip a 5-degree bevel on the upper edge of the writing table frame front rail (G) with the saw fence set so that the front face of the piece will be 1-1/2″ in width.

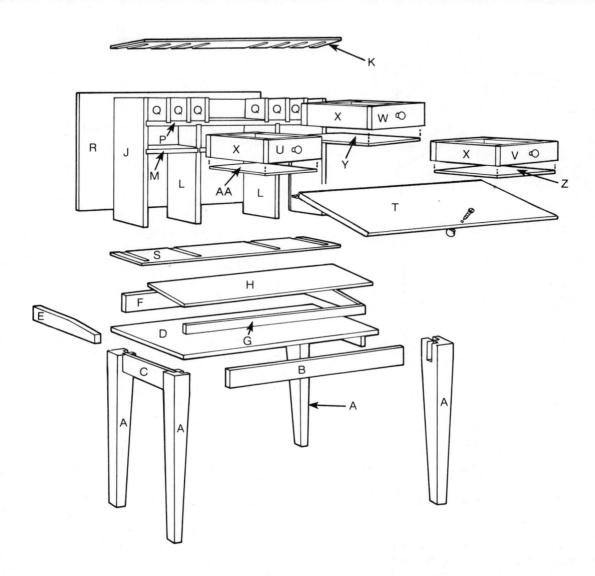

Taper the upper edge of each writing table frame side (E), beginning at a point 12-3/4" from the rear, so that its height is reduced to that of the front rail where the two intersect.

Join the sides to the front and rear rails with dowels. After positioning the frame flush with the back edge of the top and 3/4" from each side, fasten the writing table frame to the tabletop with wood

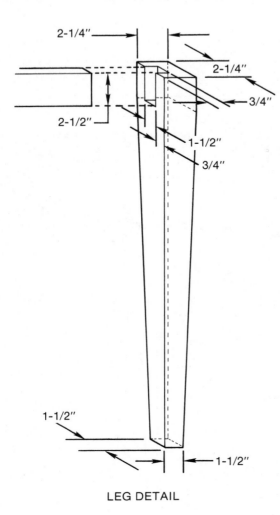

2-1/4"
2-1/4"
3/4"
2-1/2"
1-1/2"
3/4"
1-1/2"
1-1/2"

LEG DETAIL

Hutch

The hutch portion of the desk relies upon dado joints and glue to hold the case together. Begin by cutting the hutch pieces to size. You may choose whether you want to form the top, bottom, and sides from glued-up 1 × 12 stock, as we did, or to make them out of plywood. If you decide on plywood, subtract 1/16" from the listed dimensions for each edge you will later cover with preglued edge banding.

Rout 3/4"-wide and 1/8"-deep stopped dadoes in the upper face of the hutch bottom (S) and in the bottom face of the hutch top (K) to receive the hutch sides (J) and center dividers (L). Set the outer dadoes 3/4" in from the sides of the panels and set the inner dadoes 8-3/4" inside each outer one. Begin all dadoes at the rear edges of the panels. On the bottom panel, stop the outer dadoes 3/4" from the front edge and the inner dadoes 1-1/2" from the front edge of the hutch bottom. On the top panel, stop the outer dadoes 1-1/4" from the front edge and the inner dadoes 2" from the front edge. Clean out the corners at the front of each dado with a chisel.

After cutting the center dividers to size, rout 3/4" × 1/8" dadoes across both faces of each, 3-7/8" down from the upper edge, and an additional dado 8-5/8" down from the top on the inner face only. Cut a pair of dadoes of the same dimensions across the inside face of each

screws and glue. Drive No. 8 × 2" wood screws through the front rail and No. 8 × 2-3/4" wood screws through the rear rail. Be sure to predrill and counterbore pilot holes to avoid splitting the rails and to sink the screw heads below the surface of the wood.

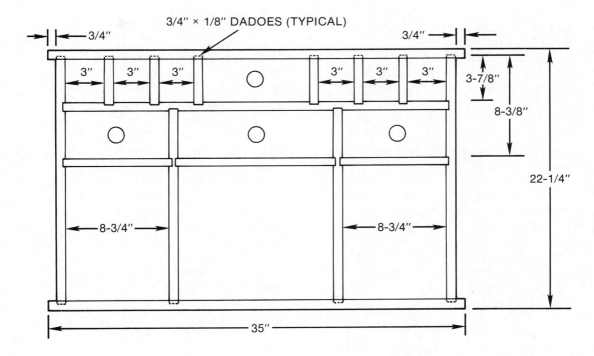

hutch side (J). Locate the first 3-7/8″ down and the second 8-3/8″ down from the upper edge of the piece.

The pigeonhole support (P) is cut with two 3/4″ × 1/8″ dadoes on its bottom side to hold the center divider. Space each dado 8-7/8″ from either end. On the top side of the pigeonhole support, machine six 3/4″ × 1/8″ dadoes to hold the pigeonhole dividers (Q). Space the outer dadoes 3-1/8″ from the sides of the support. Space the other dadoes 3″ apart.

The bottom surface of the hutch top (K) is cut with 3/4″ × 1/8″ stopped dadoes to match those in the pigeonhole support. Machine the

outer dadoes 3/4″ from the sides of the top, space the next dado on each side 3″ from the outer dadoes, and space the remaining dadoes 3″ apart. Stop the dadoes 1-1/4″ from the front edge of the top.

Cut a 1/4″ × 1/4″ rabbet along the inside back edges of the sides, top, and bottom to accommodate the back of the hutch unit.

Dry fit the hutch pieces together. Make sure that all interior panels are recessed 1/4″ from the rear to make room for the back panel. Then, using clamps and carpenter's wood glue, assemble the case. When the glue dries, attach the hutch back (R) with No. 3 × 3/8″ wood screws.

Check often to make certain the joints are square.

Cut the hutch door panel (T) to size, and cover its top and side edges with iron-on edge banding.

Attach a piano hinge to the front lip of the hutch bottom and to the bottom edge of the door. Install the Shaker doorknob and magnetic latches to door.

Cut the writing tabletop to size. Bevel the back edge of the tabletop 5 degrees. Extrude a bead of carpenter's wood glue along the top edge of the frame. Position the writing surface so that the top extends 3/4" beyond the frame sides and front. Clamp the writing surface to the frame until dry.

Drawers

All of the drawers are the same height and depth, but there are three different widths. Cut the fronts and backs (U, V, W), sides (X), and bottoms, (Y, Z, AA) to size. Then, machine 3/4" × 3/8" rabbets on the inside edges of the fronts and backs to receive the sides. Cut 1/8"-wide × 1/4"-deep grooves 1/8" above the bottom edge of the inside faces of the front, side, and back pieces to receive the drawer bottoms.

Dry assemble the drawers by fitting the sides between the fronts and backs and the bottoms in the grooves in the other pieces. Make sure that the bottoms do not prevent the other parts from fitting snugly. Then, reassemble the drawers with glue in all rabbet joints, but leave the bottoms free to respond to movement in the solid wood parts.

Sand the Shaker desk; finish as desired.

Section 5
Garages, Basements, and Attics

Remember when there used to be room in your garage to park a car? But somehow over the months and years, garden tools, sports equipment, Christmas decorations, and scrap lumber have accumulated, taking up every inch of space.

Why don't you build some of the projects in this section and organize your garage storage? Or build shelves in the basement and the attic for storing some excess baggage there. To help you dig out from under years of accumulated "wealth," this section contains all of the information you will need to make your garage, basement, and attic "storage-smart"—with room leftover for your car.

For the garage, a number of wall units and shelving systems show you how to put your walls to work. There is even a project to utilize the wasted space over your car's hood. When you've used all available wall space for storage, look up. Storage units can be suspended from ceiling joists as well. Be sure to keep fragile items, poisonous chemicals, flammable liquids, and cutting or piercing tools up high or behind locked doors to avoid injury to children.

Basements and attics have their own special storage challenges. Moisture is often a problem in a basement. The solution to perspiring walls and wet floors is suspended storage. If the joists for the floor above are exposed, simply fasten suspended storage units to them. However, avoid storing items that will rust or become affected with mildew in the basement. Those things are better off stored in the attic.

STACKABLE STORAGE

Roomy, sturdy storage units are easy to make when you use standard size lumber and simple reinforced butt joints. The three storage units pictured demonstrate the flexibility this simple design permits. The units can be built to any height and made either one, two, or even three boards deep. They can be open shelves or enclosed with cabinet doors. The secret is to design each unit so that maximum space is gained without ripping any boards to fit.

To do this, plan the height and width of each module equal to the cumulative width of the boards. For example, a unit 29" high will accommodate four 1 × 8 back panel boards without ripping. A unit 33" high can be made with six 1 × 6 back panel boards. Plan the width of the storage units around the width of the cabinet doors. Measure the total width of the doors, then add 1-7/8") (1-1/2" for the thickness of the side panels and 3/8" for door clearance) to determine the overall module width. Cut to this length the boards that make up the top, bottom, and back.

Basic Storage Module

The storage units pictured are all 30-7/8" wide and use 1 × 8 lumber for the major components. To make the basic modular unit (one board deep), cut the top and bottom (A) and sides (B) to length from 1 × 8s. (For a more attractive appearance, add 1-1/2" to the length of the side boards and miter the top and bottom.) Apply a bead of carpenter's wood glue where the boards meet at the corners, and secure the joint with 4d finishing nails or No. 6 × 1-1/4" flathead wood screws. Then, cut the back panel boards (C) to length and glue and nail them to the frame with 4d finishing nails and glue. Set all nails and fill the holes with wood putty for a more finished look.

Cut the shelves (D) and shelf cleats (E) to length. Fasten pairs of shelf cleats to the sides at the desired shelf locations with the back ends of the cleats flush against the back of the module. Cut the shelves to length and fasten them to the cleats with glue and 3d finishing nails.

Tall Storage Module

Storage modules two or more boards deep can be constructed by clinching 1 × 8 boards together with 1 × 1 or 1 × 2 cleats to create panels two boards wide. The tall storage module pictured is such an example. To make the 58" high × 15-1/4" deep unit, cut the side (B) and top and bottom (A) boards to length. Cut twelve 1 × 1 cleats (E) to length.

Divide the top, bottom, and side boards into two equal groups, and assemble each set into a rectangular frame. Then, butt the two frames edge to edge and use four of the cleats to tie them together at their four inside corners. Fasten each corner cleat to all the boards it touches using wood glue and 3d finishing nails. Position the cleats with their rear ends flush with the back edges of the module.

Cut the eight back panel boards (C) to length and fasten them to the back of the module using wood glue and 4d finishing nails. Then, fasten the remaining cleats to the module sides in parallel pairs at the heights desired for the shelves, using wood glue and either screws or finishing nails. After the glue has dried, cut the shelves (D) to length and set them in place. The shelves can either be left unfastened for later removal or attached to the cleats using 3d finishing nails. Set all nails and putty the holes.

Cabinet Module

The cabinet module can be built either one or two boards deep. If desired, shelves can be added as earlier described, except that 3/4″ must be ripped from the width of the shelves to allow for the doors.

Doors for the cabinet module are made from 1 × 8 boards, two per door butted side to side and secured with a pair of cleats. Crosscut the boards for the doors 1-3/4″ shorter than the total height of the module to allow the doors to fit between the top and bottom of the module. Cut each cleat 1/8″ shorter than the total width of the door. Center them across the width of the doors, positioned 2″ from the top and bottom edges. Fasten the cleats to the doors with glue and No. 6 × 1-1/4″ flathead wood screws. If the doors are more than 36″ high, use three cleats per door.

Mount two hinges on the outside edge of the door, 2″ from the upper and lower edges. Predrill

MATERIALS LIST

1 × 8 × 10′ #2 pine (15)
1 × 2 × 5′ #2 pine
1 × 1 square molding (21′)
4d finishing nails
3d finishing nails
No. 6 × 1-1/4″ wood screws
Door pulls (1 pair)
Magnetic latches (2 sets)
Wood putty
Wood glue

CUTTING LIST (BASIC STORAGE MODULE)

KEY	PIECES	SIZE/DESCRIPTION
A	2	3/4 × 7-1/4 × 30-7/8 top and bottom
B	2	3/4 × 7-1/4 × 27-1/2 sides
C	4	3/4 × 7-1/4 × 30-7/8 back panel boards
D	2	3/4 × 7-1/4 × 29-1/4 shelves
E	4	3/4 × 3/4 × 6-1/2 cleats

CUTTING LIST (TALL STORAGE MODULE)

KEY	PIECES	SIZE/DESCRIPTION
A	4	3/4 × 7-1/4 × 30-7/8 top and bottom
B	4	3/4 × 7-1/4 × 56-1/2 sides
C	8	3/4 × 7-1/4 × 30-7/8 back
D	4	3/4 × 7-1/4 × 29-3/8 shelves
E	12	3/4 × 3/4 × 13-3/4 cleats

CUTTING LIST (CABINET STORAGE MODULE)

KEY	PIECES	SIZE/DESCRIPTION
A	4	3/4 × 7-1/4 × 30-7/8 top and bottom
B	4	3/4 × 7-1/4 × 27-1/2 sides
C	4	3/4 × 7-1/4 × 30-7/8 back
D	4	3/4 × 3/4 × 13-3/4 cleats
E	4	3/4 × 7-1/4 × 27-1/4 doors
F	4	3/4 × 1-1/2 × 14-3/8 door cleats
G	1	3/4 × 3/4 × 2 doorstop

holes for the screws to avoid splitting the wood. If doors are more than 48″ high, use three hinges per door.

Cut a doorstop (G) from scrap material. Center it under the top between the sides and set back 3/4″ from the front edge. Fasten it to the top with glue and small finishing nails.

To install the doors, allow 1/8″ clearance top and bottom and along each side. Be sure that the doors are flush with the face of the unit before setting the screws.

Sand and finish the modules with clear polyurethane varnish to seal and protect the wood.

Install purchased door pulls and magnetic latches.

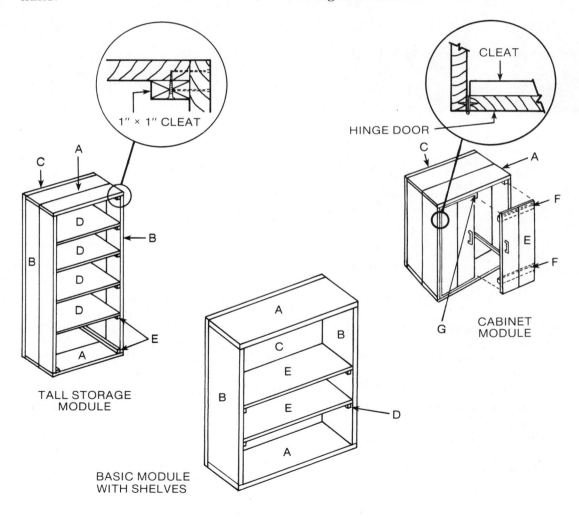

1″ × 1″ CLEAT

CLEAT

HINGE DOOR

TALL STORAGE MODULE

BASIC MODULE WITH SHELVES

CABINET MODULE

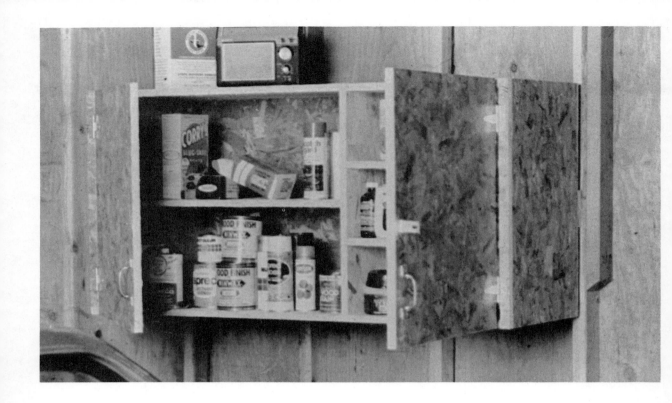

OVERHOOD
STORAGE

One of the wasted storage areas in many garages is the space above the car. The overhood cabinet pictured here is a simple solution to that problem. It is made of 3/4" waferboard and assembled with dado joints for rigidity. Build it with or without cabinet doors, and if you hang it on support strips as shown in the illustration, the cabinet can be removed when necessary.

Begin this project by cutting the waferboard panels to size. (See cutting diagrams.) Then, machine 3/4" × 3/8" dadoes in the center of the left side panel (A) and the left side of the center divider (D). Then, machine two 3/4" × 3/8" dadoes centered 7-7/8" and 15-3/8" from the bottom edge of the right side panel (A) and 7-1/2" and 15" from the bottom edge of the right side of the center divider. Finally, machine 3/4" × 3/8" dadoes 29-5/8" from the left end of the top and bottom panels (B).

Machine a 3/4" × 3/8" rabbet in the rear inside edge of the top, side, and bottom panels. The back panel (C) will sit in this rabbet. Also, cut a rabbet in the inside top and bottom edges of the side panels to accept the top and bottom panels.

Assemble the cabinet with wood glue and No. 6 × 1-1/4″ wood screws. Countersink all pilot holes. Begin by gluing and screwing the sides to the bottom. Make sure that all edges are flush. Place the center divider and shelves (E, F) in their proper dadoes. Then, set the top in place and glue and screw the sides to it. Place the back panel in position and secure with glue and screws through the side, top, and bottom panels.

Crosscut a 1 × 4 pine board into two pieces 47-7/8″ long. Rip one piece down the middle at a 45-degree angle to make the upper mounting strips. Fasten one strip to the cabinet and the other strip to the wall so that they interlock as shown in the drawing. Make sure that the wall section is level and placed at a convenient height.

Rip 2″ from the other 1 × 4 piece to form the lower mounting strips. Fasten the two strips together as shown in the drawing, using glue and 3d finishing nails.

Hang the cabinet on the top support strip and align the bottom support strip so that the cabinet rests in the rabbet formed by the two pieces. Mark the position of the bottom strip, remove the cabinet, and nail the strip to the wall studs with 10d nails.

If you want to put doors on the cabinet, cut two hinge posts (G) to size from the remainder of the 1 × 4 and glue and screw them to the front edges of the side panels. Cut two doors (H) to fit in the opening and secure them to the hinge posts with 4″ wraparound hinges.

Sand and finish the unit as desired. Install door pulls and hasp.

MATERIALS LIST

3/4″ × 4′ × 8′ waferboard
  (1-1/4 sheets)
1 × 4 × 10′ #2 pine
No. 6 × 1-1/4″ wood screws
10d finishing nails
3d finishing nails
4″ wraparound hinges (4)
Door pulls and hasp (2)
Wood glue

CUTTING LIST

KEY	PIECES	SIZE/DESCRIPTION
A	2	3/4 × 15-3/4 × 24 left and right side panels
B	2	3/4 × 15-3/4 × 48 top and bottom panels
C	1	3/4 × 23-1/4 × 48 back panel
D	1	3/4 × 15 × 23-1/4 center divider
E	1	3/4 × 15 × 30 left shelf
F	2	3/4 × 15 × 18 right shelves
G	2	3/4 × 1-1/2 × 24 hinge posts
H	2	3/4 × 22-3/4 × 24 doors
J	2	3/4 × 3-1/2 × 47-7/8 mounting strips

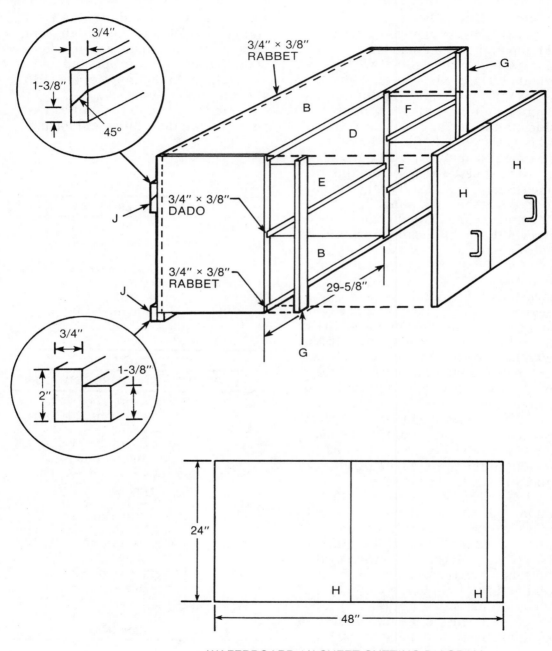

3/4″

1-3/8″

45°

3/4″ × 3/8″
RABBET

3/4″ × 3/8″
DADO

J

3/4″ × 3/8″
RABBET

J

3/4″

2″

1-3/8″

B

D

F

F

E

B

G

G

29-5/8″

H

H

H

24″

H   H

48″

WAFERBOARD 1/4 SHEET CUTTING DIAGRAM

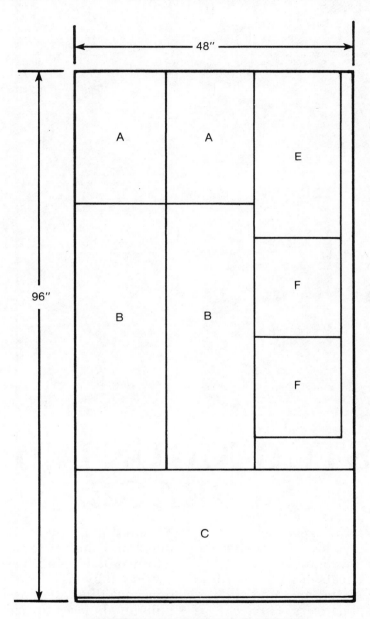

WAFERBOARD CUTTING DIAGRAM

STUD-MOUNTED STORAGE

Creating storage space in a garage does not have to be expensive. This project shows how you can turn two 4 × 8 sheets of waferboard into a system of stud-mounted shelves and tool hangers. Three 8' shelves are suspended by stud-mounted shelf brackets. Corner shelves are supported by cleats.

This design is obviously very flexible. Build shelves to the length and width suited to your needs.

Begin by laying out the cutting diagrams illustrated here. Cut the individual pieces to size.

Cut the corner shelf blanks (C) to size and cut each blank in half diagonally.

Cut the shelf bracket blanks (B) to size. From one end of each blank measure down 13". Then, from the opposite end and on the opposite side, measure down 13" again. Draw a line connecting the two points and cut diagonally across each blank to make the shelf brackets.

Drill out the 2"-diameter holes in the tool hangers (F) with a hole saw.

To install the wall shelves (A), use a line level and a chalk line to snap a level line at the desired height of each shelf. Using an adjustable carpenter's square, draw a line across the face of each stud square to the shelf line. Nail the top of the shelf brackets flush with this

MATERIALS LIST

3/4" × 4' × 8' waferboard panels (2)
6d common nails
4d finishing nails

CUTTING LIST

KEY	PIECES	SIZE/DESCRIPTION
A	3	3/4 × 9-7/8 × 96 shelves
B	6	3/4 × 8-7/8 × 21-7/8 shelf bracket blanks
C	3	3/4 × 29-7/8 × 29-7/8 corner shelf blanks
D	12	3/4 × 2-7/8 × 29-7/8 cleats
E	1	3/4 × 5-7/8 × 35-7/8 kick plate
F	32	3/4 × 5-7/8 × 5-7/8 tool hangers

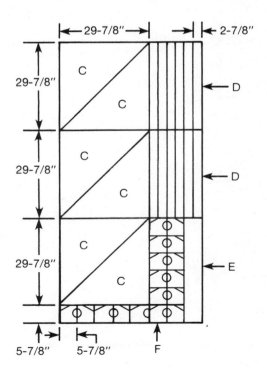

line, using four 6d nails per bracket. Tack the shelves to the brackets with 4d finishing nails.

To install the corner shelves (C), first determine the desired height of the shelves and, using a 24″ level, draw a line at each point across the edge of the wall studs. Nail the shelf cleats to the studs level with this line, and tack the shelves to the cleats (D) with 4d finishing nails. Tack the kick plate (E) to the underside of the front shelf.

The tool hangers are installed in much the same way. Snap a level line at the desired height of the hangers. Square a line across the faces of the studs, and nail the hangers flush with these lines.

The shelves and tool hangers can be left unfinished, but several coats of polyurethane varnish will seal them against moisture and dirt.

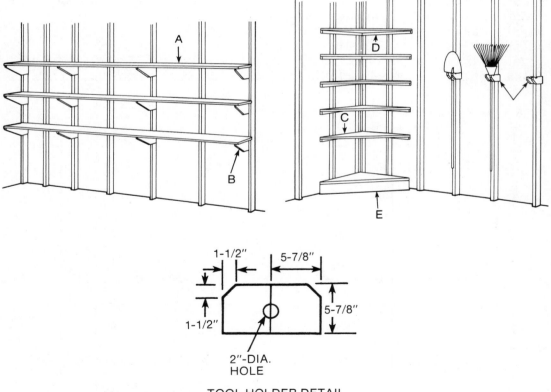

TOOL HOLDER DETAIL

SPORTS EQUIPMENT STORAGE

Sports equipment for the active family is a major storage category—one with its own particular needs. For example, if skiing, hockey, or fishing are your hobbies, you need room to hang up wet clothing and extra-long cubby holes to store your hockey sticks, skis, and/or fishing tackle. This sports storage center provides space for this equipment and more. There is plenty of shelf and cabinet space to keep bats, balls, skates, tennis rackets, golf clubs—whatever your recreation requires. Feel free to modify the plans given here to best handle your storage needs.

Begin construction of the sports storage center by cutting the sides (A), backs (B), tops (C), and shelves (D, E) to size. Divide the panels into three groups. Set aside three of the wider shelves (D) and one narrower shelf (E) for each of the units that will have doors. The remaining two larger shelves will be used in the clothes rack unit.

To avoid confusion when laying out and cutting rabbets and dadoes, mark the upper end, inside face, and rear edge on each side panel, and whether it will fit on the left or right side of its unit. Also, mark an upper end and an inside face on each back panel.

Machine a 3/4" × 3/8" rabbet along the inside edge at the upper end of each side and back panel to receive the top panel. Also, cut rabbets of the same dimensions along the rear edges on all side panels to receive the edges of the back panels.

Drill a 1-1/2"-diameter hole 1/2" deep into the inside face on each side panel in the clothes rack group to accept the end of a clothespole. Center these holes 4" from the top and 4" from the front edge on each of these two panels. Then cut a piece of 1-1/2"-diameter dowel to 24-7/8"

in length to serve as the clothespole.

Machine 3/4" × 3/8" dadoes across the inside faces on all six side panels to hold the ends of the shelves. Place the dadoes for the bottom shelf 4" above the lower ends on each pair of panels. On the four panels that will be used for units with doors, locate the dadoes for

MATERIALS LIST

3/4" × 4' × 8' waferboard
  (3-1/2 sheets)
1 × 8 × 2' #2 pine
1 × 4 × 2' #2 pine
No. 8 × 1-1/4" wood screws
1/2" T-hinges (8)
Magnetic catches (4)
Door pulls (4)
1-1/2"-dia. × 3' hardwood dowel
Wood glue

CUTTING LIST

KEY	PIECES	SIZE/DESCRIPTION
A	6	3/4 × 15-7/8 × 72 sides
B	3	3/4 × 24-3/4 × 72 backs
C	3	3/4 × 15-1/2 × 24-3/4 tops
D	8	3/4 × 15-1/8 × 24-3/4 exterior shelves
E	2	3/4 × 14-3/8 × 24-3/4 interior shelves
F	4	3/4 × 11-7/8 × 29-7/8 doors
G	2	3/4 × 7-1/4 × 10 lower spacers
H	2	3/4 × 3-1/2 × 10 top spacers
J	1	1-1/2-dia. × 24-7/8 clothespole

the middle shelves according to where the doors will be placed. If the door will fit on the upper half of the unit, locate the dadoes for the middle shelf 30" below the rabbets for the top panel. On the unit with doors below, place the dadoes for the middle shelf 30" above those for the bottom shelf. On all three pairs of panels, the dadoes for the remaining shelves can be placed wherever you wish.

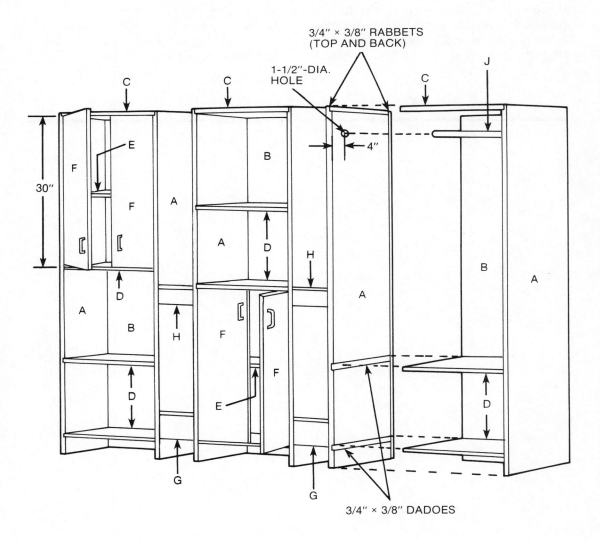

3/4" × 3/8" RABBETS (TOP AND BACK)

1-1/2"-DIA. HOLE

3/4" × 3/8" DADOES

Assemble the three storage cabinets using glue and No. 8 × 1-1/4" wood screws. Be sure to place the smaller shelves in those areas that will be covered by doors, since they are sized specifically to allow the doors to close.

When you have completed the three cabinet units, cut the door panels (F) to size. Sand the cabinets and the doors and finish as desired, then mount the doors so that when they are closed their fronts are flush with the front edges of the cabinets. Install door pulls and magnetic latches.

Cut two pairs of 10"-long spacers, one pair from 1 × 8 stock (G) and the other from 1 × 4 stock (H). Sand and finish the spacers to match the storage units, then fit them between the units to create additional storage space as shown in the drawing and photo.

GARDEN STORAGE CENTER AND TOOL RACK

For the avid gardener, storage space is a must. Seeds, fertilizers, soil conditioners, insecticides—all supplies that must be stored high and dry. Then, there are garden implements—shovels, rakes, cultivators, hand trowels, clippers—not to mention seed flats, peat pots, stakes, twine, hoses, and so on. To keep everything in order, why not build this garden storage center? The materials are inexpensive, construction is simple, and the results are more than satisfying.

Begin by laying out the cutting patterns as shown in the illustrations. Cut the individual pieces to size and make the finger space cutouts on the drawer fronts. Machine 3/8"-deep dadoes and rabbets in the sides (A) to accept the top (B), bottom (B), and shelves (C, J). Note that the dimensions given on the project drawing locate all dadoes working from the floor up.

Dry assemble the storage center with the back edges of the sides, top, bottom, and shelves flush. If every panel fits properly, disassemble the unit, smear glue in the rabbets and dadoes, on the ends of the shelves, and on the top and bottom. Reassemble the unit, using bar clamps to hold the panels together while fastening the sides to the top and bottom and the shelves with 6d finishing nails.

Next, assemble the bins. Using glue and 6d finishing nails, fasten the sides to the bottoms, the fronts to the sides and bottoms (flush with the bottom edges), and the sides and bottoms to the backs. The bins can be strengthened by adding glue blocks between the fronts and sides.

Hang the doors (H) between the upper two wide shelves (C). Use 4" strap hinges, two per door. Add magnetic latches to the lower cabinet shelf.

Finish the unit as desired. In the storage center pictured, the panel faces are finished with clear polyurethane varnish. The door and bin front, as well as the edges of the unit, are painted.

Tool Rack

Large garden implements can be hung outside of the storage center. A

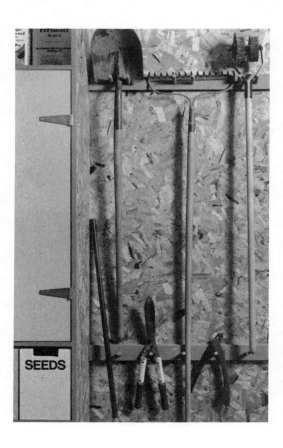

MATERIALS LIST (GARDEN STORAGE CENTER)
3/4" × 4' × 8' waferboard panel (2-1/2 sheets)
6d finishing nails
4" strap hinge (4)
Door pulls (2)
Door latches (2)
Doorstop
Wood glue

CUTTING LIST (GARDEN STORAGE CENTER)

KEY	PIECES	SIZE/DESCRIPTION
A	2	3/4 × 11-7/8 × 96 sides
B	2	3/4 × 11-7/8 × 47-1/4 top and bottom
C	4	3/4 × 11-7/8 × 47-1/4 shelves
D	3	3/4 × 15-1/8 × 15-3/8 bin fronts
E	3	3/4 × 13-7/8 × 14 bin backs
F	6	3/4 × 11 × 14-3/4 bin sides
G	3	3/4 × 11 × 13-7/8 bin bottoms
H	2	3/4 × 23-1/8 × 39 doors
J	2	3/4 × 11-1/8 × 47-1/4 cabinet shelves

MATERIALS LIST (TOOL RACK)

1 × 4 × 8' #2 pine
5/8"-dia. hardwood dowel (6')
6d finishing nails
Wood glue

CUTTING LIST (TOOL RACK)

KEY	PIECES	SIZE/DESCRIPTION
A	2	3/4 × 3-1/2 × 47-15/16 upper and lower racks

simple tool organizer is shown here. Made of 1 × 4 pine and 5/8"-diameter dowels, the upper rack is designed to hold long-handle tools. The lower rack is designed for small pruning tools.

Cut the 1 × 4s to length. Drill 5/8"-diameter holes through the strips, spaced as shown in the illustration. Glue 5" lengths of 5/8"-diameter dowel in the holes. Nail the strips to the wall with 6d finishing nails. Finish as desired.

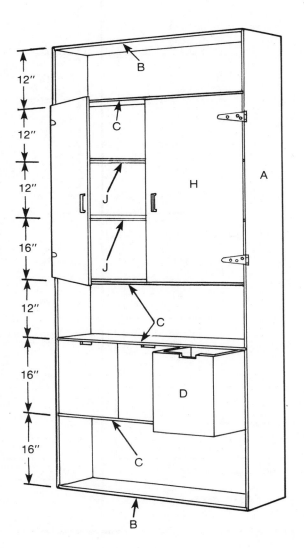

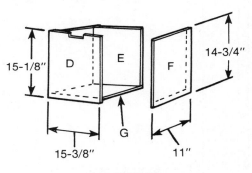

BIN DETAIL

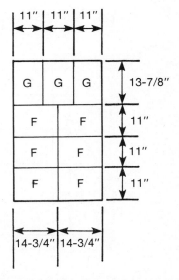

HALF-SHEET CUTTING DIAGRAM

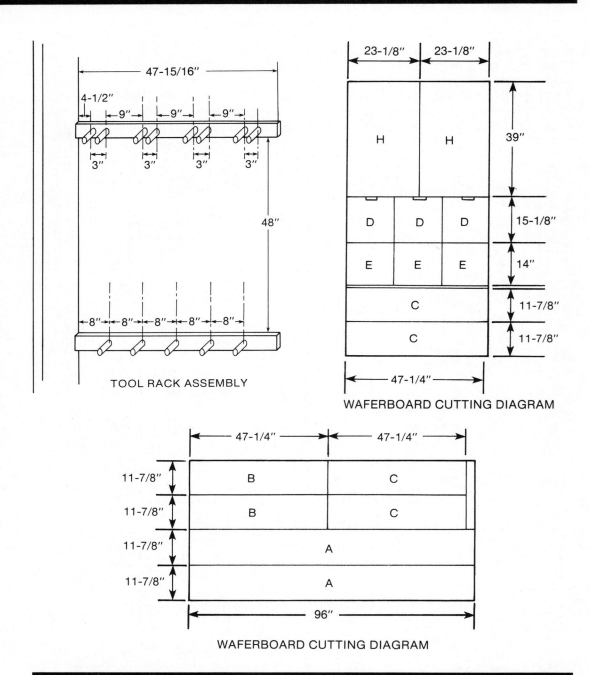

TOOL RACK ASSEMBLY

WAFERBOARD CUTTING DIAGRAM

WAFERBOARD CUTTING DIAGRAM

HOME
RECYCLING CENTER

Many communities require or at least encourage separation of home garbage into recyclable components. Aluminum cans, steel cans, newspapers, glass, even plastics can be reused.

But where can this garbage be stored between pickups or drop-offs at the local recycling center? Most homes are not set up for handling three or four categories of garbage. Storage for recycling usually means piles of newspapers in one corner of the basement and bags of cans and bottles toppling over in another. To eliminate that, build this home recycling center.

Attractive, convenient, and easy to build, the recycling center provides one central location for storing last week's residues. Cans are crushed with a press and then hidden away in receptacles. Paper ties keep newspapers in a compact pile, and two spacious drawers for glass keep bottles out of sight, protected from accidental breakage. For mobility, the recycling center is mounted on casters.

Begin by building the frame. Cut the upper frame sides (A) to size. Lay out and machine 3/4"-deep × 1-1/2"-wide dadoes and rabbets on each of the upper frame sides to accept the vertical members (F). Locate these cuts as shown in the upper frame detail drawing.

Cut the upper frame cross members (B) to size. Lay out and machine a 3/4"-deep × 1-3/4"-wide rabbet lengthwise on three of the four upper frame cross members to accept the vertical and end panels (G, J).

Lay the upper frame sides on edge, back to back, with the dadoes facing out.

Fit the cross members (B) between the sides as shown in the upper frame detail. Note that the unrabbeted cross member goes at the can end of the frame. The two middle cross members are aligned with the dadoes in the frame sides and are placed with their rabbeted

MATERIALS LIST

3/4" × 4' × 8' AC interior plywood
1/4" × 4' × 8' AC exterior plywood
  (1-1/4 sheets)
2 × 4 × 8' construction grade
  pine (4)
1 × 2 × 10' #2 pine (7)
No. 14 × 2-1/2" wood screws (2)
No. 12 × 1" wood screws (16)
1-1/4" underlayment nails
8d finishing nails
6d finishing nails
18-gauge 1" wire nails
1" screw eyes (5)
3" casters (4)
Standard wall-mounted can opener
  with magnetic lid holder
Semigloss latex paint
Wood filler
#24 twine
Wood glue

edges facing down and toward the outside. Make sure the upper edges of all the frame members are flush and that everything is square, then fasten the frame together using wood glue and 8d finishing nails.

After cutting the lower frame sides (C) to length, machine a 3/4"-deep and 1-3/4"-wide rabbet along the inside edge of the upper face of each to accept the bottom panel (E). Also, cut 3/4"-deep × 1-1/2"-wide rabbets and dadoes across the outer edges of both pieces to match those cut in the upper frame sides.

After cutting the lower frame ends (D) to length, machine 3/4" × 1-3/4" rabbets across the underside of their ends so that they will fit into the rabbets on the sides

CUTTING LIST		
KEY	**PIECES**	**SIZE/DESCRIPTION**
A	2	1-1/2 × 3-1/2 × 48 upper frame sides
B	4	1-1/2 × 3-1/2 × 21 upper frame cross members
C	2	1-1/2 × 3-1/2 × 48 lower frame sides
D	2	1-1/2 × 3-1/2 × 20-1/2 lower frame ends
E	1	3/4 × 20-1/2 × 44-1/2 bottom panel (plywood)
F	8	3/4 × 1-1/2 × 26 vertical members
G	2	3/4 × 22-1/2 × 22-5/8 vertical panels (plywood)
H	1	3/4 × 21-1/4 × 22-1/2 bottle shelf (plywood)
J	1	3/4 × 7 × 22-1/2 end panel (plywood)
K	1	3/4 × 12-7/8 × 22-1/2 paper shelf (plywood)
L	2	3/4 × 1-1/2 × 21 can press base side cleats
M	2	3/4 × 1-1/2 × 9 can press base end cleats
N	1	3/4 × 10-1/2 × 21 can press base (plywood)
P	4	3/4 × 6-1/2 × 9-1/2 jaw mounts (plywood)
Q	2	3/4 × 6-1/2 × 6-1/2 can press jaws (plywood)
R	1	1-1/2 × 3-1/2 × 5-3/4 jaw spacer
S	1	1-1/2 × 2-1/2 × 24 handle

CUTTING LIST (continued)		
KEY	**PIECES**	**SIZE/DESCRIPTION**
T	1	1-dia. × 3-1/2 pivot pin (dowel)
U	16	3/4 × 1-1/2 × 9-3/4 can receptacle frame members
V	8	1/4 × 10-3/4 × 20-1/2 can receptacle sides (plywood)
W	2	1/4 × 10-1/2 × 10-1/2 can receptacle bottoms (plywood)
X	8	3/4 × 1-1/2 × 17-1/4 glass receptacle frame end members
Y	8	3/4 × 1-1/2 × 19-1/2 glass receptacle frame side members
Z	4	1/4 × 11-1/2 × 18-1/4 glass receptacle end panels (plywood)
AA	4	1/4 × 11-1/2 × 20-1/2 glass receptacle sides (plywood)
BB	2	1/4 × 18 × 20-1/4 glass receptacle bottoms (plywood)

as shown in the drawings. Also, machine rabbets of the same depth and width along the inside edge of the upper face on each of these pieces to make room for the bottom panel. Fit the lower frame sides and ends together, checking for squareness and making sure the rabbets for the bottom panel are flush. Fasten the frame together using wood glue and 1-1/4" underlayment nails.

Before cutting the bottom panel (E), carefully measure the space inside the lower frame. Then cut the

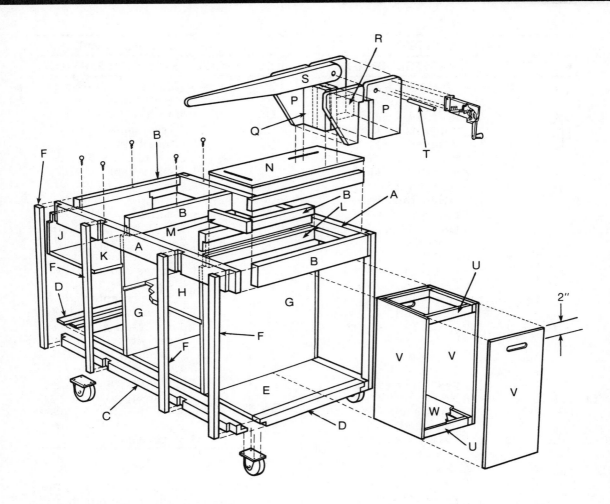

panel, adjusting its dimensions as necessary for a good fit. Fasten the panel in the lower frame using glue and 1-1/4″ underlayment nails.

Cut the vertical members (F) of the upper and lower frames to size. Insert four vertical members into the rabbets at the corners of the upper and lower frame assemblies, connecting the two assemblies together. Fasten with glue and 8d nails.

Cut the vertical panels (G) to size. Cut a notch 3/4″ wide × 1-3/4″ deep in the upper corners of the vertical panels so they will accept the lower inside edges of the upper frame sides.

Lay out and machine a 3/8″-deep × 3/4″-wide dado, 11-3/4″ from the base of each vertical panel to accept the bottle shelf (H). On the reverse side of one vertical panel, machine a second 3/8″-deep × 3/4″-wide

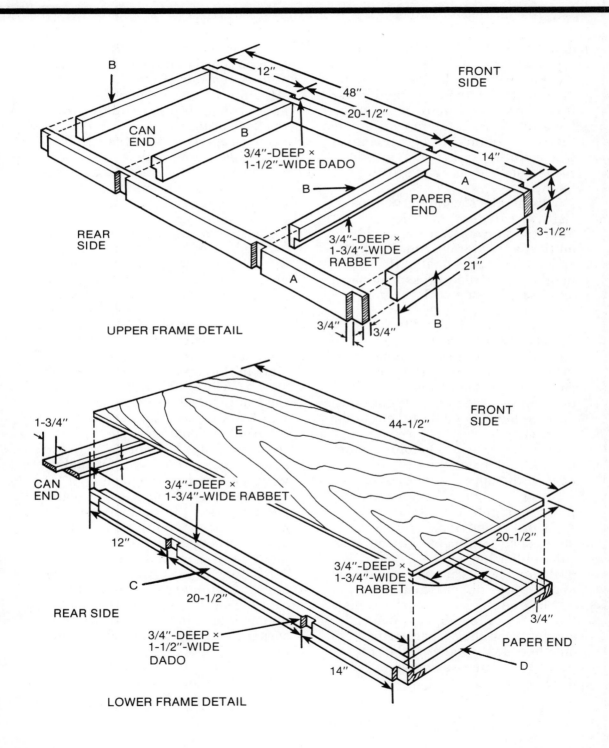

B

CAN
END

B

FRONT
SIDE

12"

48"

20-1/2"

3/4"-DEEP ×
1-1/2"-WIDE DADO

B

14"

A

PAPER
END

REAR
SIDE

A

3/4"-DEEP ×
1-3/4"-WIDE
RABBET

3-1/2"

21"

B

UPPER FRAME DETAIL

3/4"   3/4"

1-3/4"

CAN
END

E

FRONT
SIDE

44-1/2"

3/4"-DEEP ×
1-3/4"-WIDE RABBET

12"

C

20-1/2"

REAR SIDE

3/4"-DEEP ×
1-1/2"-WIDE
DADO

14"

3/4"-DEEP ×
1-3/4"-WIDE
RABBET

20-1/2"

3/4"

PAPER END

D

LOWER FRAME DETAIL

dado, 15-3/4″ from the base, to accept the paper shelf (K).

Fit the vertical panel (with one dado) between the upper and lower frame assemblies on the can receptacle end, resting the top end against the rabbet of one of the inside upper frame cross members and keeping the dadoed side of the vertical panel facing in.

Insert the second vertical panel (with two dadoes) between the upper and lower frame assemblies on the paper storage end. Fit the top end against the rabbet of the second inside upper frame cross member and keep the side with the lower dado facing in.

Cut the bottle shelf to size. Spread glue on the ends of the shelf and in the appropriate dadoes in the vertical panels. Slide the shelf between the vertical panels into the dadoes machined for it. Plumb the vertical panels and nail them to the inner cross members.

Fit the ends of the four remaining vertical members into the dadoes of the upper- and lower-frame sides provided for them. Fasten in place with glue and 6d nails.

Cut the end panel (J) and the paper shelf (K) to size. Lay out and cut a notch 3/4″ wide × 1-3/4″ deep in the upper corners of the end panel to accept the upper frame sides.

Fit the end panel flush against the rabbet of the upper frame end and between the corner vertical members at the paper end of the recycling center, as shown in the illustration.

Insert the paper shelf between the end panel and the vertical panel, sliding one side of the shelf into the remaining dado of the vertical panel and placing the other end flush with the base of the end panel. If the panels fit properly, fasten them in place with glue and 6d nails.

Now that the basic frame is assembled, build the can press. Start by cutting the can press base side cleats (L) and end cleats (M) to size. Fit the can press base cleats into the can end of the upper frame assembly, keeping the bottom edges of the cleats flush with the lower edges of the upper frame cross members and sides. Fasten in place with glue and 1-1/4″ underlayment nails.

Cut the can press base (N) to size. Lay out and machine two can slots in the can press base. Make the slots 1″ wide and 8-1/2″ long. Locate the front slot running across the width of the base, set back 1″ from the front and outside edges. Locate the second slot 1″ from the rear and inside edges of the base, parallel with the length of the panel.

Cut the stationary and movable jaw mounts (P) to size. Lay out and machine a 1-1/4″ radius on the two upper corners of each stationary jaw mount. Cut a notch 3/4″ deep × 6-1/2″ long in the lower inside edge of each stationary jaw mount to accept the stationary jaws. Drill a 1″-diameter hole in the upper inside corner of the stationary jaw mounts to accept the pivot pin (T).

Lay out and machine the movable jaw mounts as shown in the

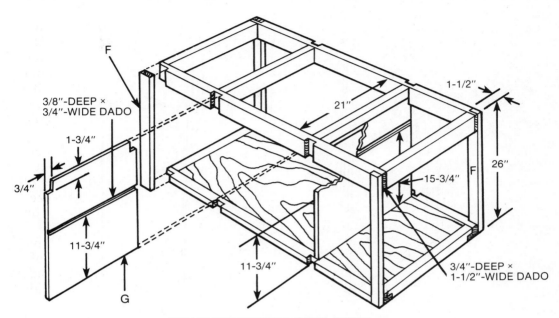

3/8"-DEEP ×
3/4"-WIDE DADO

1-3/4"

3/4"

11-3/4"

F

G

1-1/2"

21"

15-3/4"

26"

11-3/4"

3/4"-DEEP ×
1-1/2"-WIDE DADO

F

FRAME AND VERTICAL PANEL DETAIL

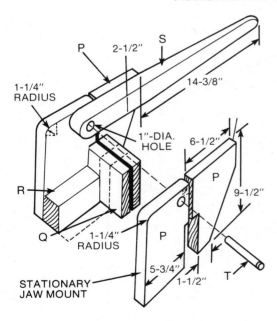

P

2-1/2"

S

14-3/8"

1-1/4"
RADIUS

1"-DIA.
HOLE

6-1/2"

R

P

9-1/2"

Q

1-1/4"
RADIUS

P

5-3/4"

1-1/2"

T

STATIONARY
JAW MOUNT

CAN PRESS DETAIL

can press detail. Cut a 3/4"-deep × 6-1/2"-long notch across the inside edge of each movable jaw mount to accept the movable jaw.

Cut the can press jaws (Q) and jaw spacer (R) to size. Cut the can press handle to size. Lay out and machine the handle beginning at a point 14-3/8" from one end and gradually decreasing the handle's thickness to 3/4" and width to 1-1/4". Machine the handle's other end to a 1-1/4" radius. Ease all sharp edges. Drill a 1"-diameter hole through the center of the handle head.

Cut the pivot pin to size. Chamfer the ends of the pin. Fit the jaw spacer (R) between the stationary jaw mounts. Fasten in place with glue and 6d nails.

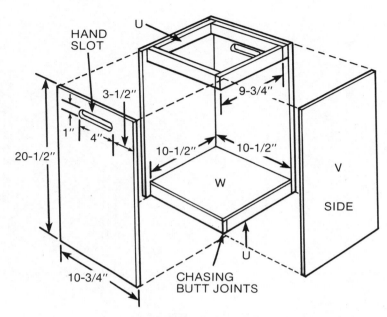

HAND
SLOT

U

3-1/2"

9-3/4"

1"

4"

10-1/2"

10-1/2"

20-1/2"

W

V

SIDE

10-3/4"

U

CHASING
BUTT JOINTS

CAN RECEPTACLE DETAIL

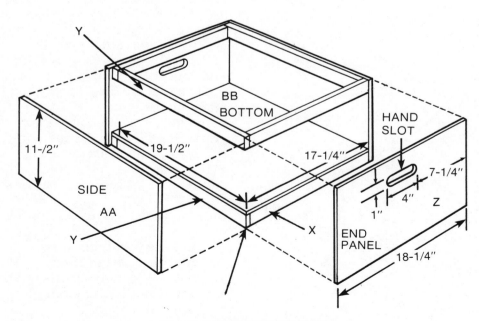

Y

HAND
SLOT

BB
BOTTOM

11-/2"

19-1/2"

17-1/4"

7-1/4"

SIDE

4"

AA

Z

1"

Y

X

END
PANEL

18-1/4"

GLASS RECEPTACLE DETAIL

Fasten the stationary can press jaw to the stationary jaw mounts with glue and 6d nails.

Using the head of the handle as a temporary spacer between the movable jaw mounts, position the movable jaw between the mounts and mark its location. Then fasten the jaw to the notched edges of the mounts using glue and 6d finishing nails.

Now set both jaw assemblies on a flat surface. Insert the head of the handle between the stationary jaw mounts and insert the pivot pin to fix it in place. Then set the movable jaw assembly next to the stationary assembly, leaving about 3/16" of space between the two jaws to make room for a flattened can. Drop the handle down between the movable jaw mounts until the upper edges of each are flush. Then fasten the jaw mounts to the handle using glue and 6d nails.

Position the stationary jaw assembly flush with the rear and outside edges of the can press base. Fasten with glue and 6d nails. When the glue is set, install No. 14 × 2-1/2" wood screws through the can press base and into the stationary jaw spacer.

Fasten the casters to the bottom of the assembled recycling center with No. 12 × 1" wood screws. Fasten the assembled can press base to the side cleats and end cleats on the upper frame with glue and 6d nails. Ease all sharp edges, fill voids, sand, and paint.

Fasten the five screw eyes to the paper end of the recycling center.

Thread a continuous strand of #24 twine through the five points before placing newspapers on the paper shelf. When the shelf is full, the twine can be pulled to the center of the pile and tied.

Mount the can opener on the side of the press.

The can receptacles should be constructed next. Cut the upper and lower frame members (U) and the sides (V) of the can receptacles to size.

Lay out and machine a 1" × 4" hand slot in four of the sides of the can receptacles.

Cut the bottoms (W) of the can receptacles to size. Fit four upper frame members together with the ends chasing one another (as shown in the can receptacle detail drawing). Assemble with glue and 6d nails. Fasten four lower frame members together in the same manner.

Fasten one of the bottoms to one of the lower frames with glue and 6d nails. Fasten four sides (including two with hand slots placed at opposite ends of the receptacle) to one upper and one lower frame assembly with the ends chasing one another. Assemble with glue and 18-gauge nails.

Ease all sharp edges, fill voids, sand, and paint. Repeat the preceding steps to assemble the second can receptacle.

Finally, make the two glass receptacles. Cut the upper and lower frame end members (X) and side members (Y) of the glass receptacles to size. Cut the end panels (Z) of the glass receptacles to size. Lay out and machine a 1″ × 4″ hand slot in each of the end panels of the glass receptacles, as shown in the glass receptacle detail drawing.

Cut the sides (AA) and bottoms (BB) of the glass receptacles to size. Fasten two upper frame end members to two upper frame side members (in alternating order), with the ends chasing one another. Assemble with glue and 6d nails. Fasten four lower frame members in the same manner.

Fasten one of the bottoms to one of the lower frames with glue and 6d nails. Fasten two sides and two end panels (in alternating order) to one upper and one lower frame assembly (with the ends chasing one another) with glue and 18-gauge nails. Ease all sharp edges, fill voids, sand, and paint. Repeat the preceding steps to assemble the second glass receptacle.

Section 6
Workshops

The projects in this section will keep your workshop running smoothly. Basic to any workshop is a sturdy work surface. This section provides you with plans for building a movable workbench loaded with storage compartments or a wall full of storage cabinets topped with a work surface. And there are cabinets for storing tools and fasteners, tool chests for the carpenter and master craftsman, bins and racks for storing lumber, and other projects that will make your workshop "storage-smart."

When planning storage for a workshop, keep two principles in mind: convenience and safety. Every tool should have a definite resting place so you can conveniently find it. Tools that are often used should be stored where they are quickly accessible. Tools used in related operations should be grouped together. For example, router bits, wrenches, and accessories should be kept in one cabinet and always returned there. Jigs and blades for the table saw should be hung on the same wall. Storage organized this way reduces nonproductive time in the shop.

Keep safety foremost in your plans as well. Walkways and work areas should be unobstructed. Power tools should be stored in cabinets out of the reach of children. Lumber and panel stock should be stacked in secured areas to avoid possible accidents.

GARAGE WORKBENCH AND WALL CABINETS

Transform one wall of your garage into the workshop of your dreams. Begin by insulating the stud wall and finishing it with 3/8" waferboard. Then, use sturdy 3/4" waferboard and 2 × 4 lumber to build cabinets and worktop surface to fill one wall. Add suspended cabinets and your favorite power tools and you are ready for business. These plans are for an eight-foot-long workbench/cabinet module and a four-foot-long suspended cabinet module. Modify them as needed to satisfy your workshop needs and space limitations.

Workbench Cabinets

Begin by cutting the base frame pieces (A, B, C) and the top frame pieces (D, E, F) to length. Using 10d common nails and carpenter's wood glue, fasten the pieces together. The two frames are basically assembled in the same manner. On both, the crosspieces fit between the front and back pieces, and the front pieces overlap the outer crosspieces by 3/4″ at each end. However, the center crosspiece on the top frame must be offset as shown in the top view drawing in order for the center divider (L) to fit on its right side as shown in the exploded-view drawing. The center crosspiece on the base frame can either be placed the same way or simply centered along the length of the frame.

Cut the cabinet sides (K) to size. Notch the front top corner 3-1/2″ × 1-1/2″ to accept the front member of the top frame. Notch the bottom front corner 3-1/2″ × 3-1/2″

MATERIALS LIST

2 × 4 × 10′ #2 pine
2 × 4 × 8′ #2 pine (4)
1 × 4 × 10′ #2 pine
1 × 4 × 8′ #2 pine
3/4″ × 4′ × 8′ waferboard (4 sheets)
1/8″ × 4′ × 8′ tempered hardboard
No. 8 × 1-1/4″ wood screws
No. 4 × 3/4″ wood screws
10d common nails
Wood glue

CUTTING LIST

KEY	PIECES	SIZE/DESCRIPTION
A	1	1-1/2 × 3-1/2 × 96 base frame front
B	1	1-1/2 × 3-1/2 × 94-1/2 base frame back
C	3	1-1/2 × 3-1/2 × 16-5/8 base frame crosspieces
D	1	1-1/2 × 3-1/2 × 96 top frame front
E	1	1-1/2 × 3-1/2 × 94-1/2 top frame back
F	3	1-1/2 × 3-1/2 × 18-5/8 top frame crosspieces
G	4	3/4 × 3-1/2 × 20-7/8 shelf cleats
H	4	3/4 × 3-1/2 × 10-3/8 lower risers
J	4	3/4 × 3-1/2 × 14-3/4 upper risers
K	2	3/4 × 22-3/8 × 37-1/8 cabinet sides (waferboard)
L	1	3/4 × 22 × 33-1/4 cabinet divider (waferboard)
M	1	3/4 × 37-1/8 × 94-1/2 cabinet back (waferboard)
N	1	3/4 × 21-5/8 × 94-1/2 cabinet bottom (waferboard)
P	2	3/4 × 20-3/4 × 46-3/4 shelves (waferboard)
Q	1	3/4 × 23-7/8 × 96 cabinet top (waferboard)
R	1	1/8 × 23-7/8 × 96 hardboard top
S	4	3/4 × 23-1/4 × 29-1/4 doors (waferboard)

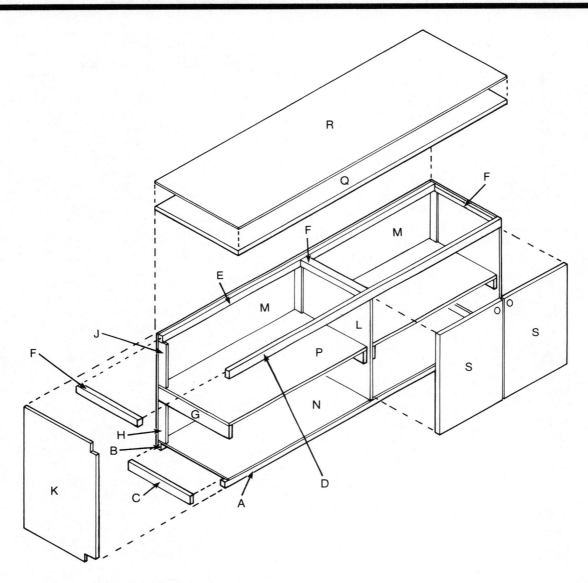

to accept the front member of the base frame and create a toe space.

Cut the cabinet divider (L) and bottom (N) to size. Machine a 3/4" × 3/8" dado centered across the bottom to accept the divider. Notch the upper front and rear corners of the divider to make room for the front and back frame members. The notch at the front should simply match the 3-1/2" × 1-1/2" size of the frame member. However, at the rear it must be 3/8" wider because the divider fits into a dado.

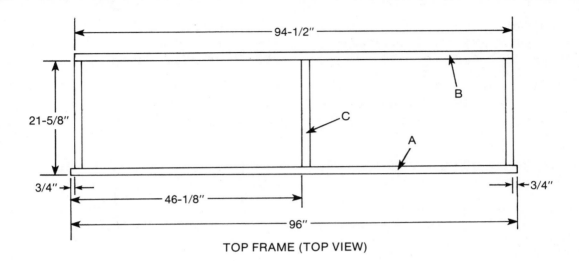

TOP FRAME (TOP VIEW)

Cut the shelves (P) and shelf cleats (G) to size. Position the cleats 3/4″ from the back edges of the side panels and 14-5/8″ from the bottom of the side panels. On the divider, position the cleats 3/8″ from the back edge and 10-3/4″ from the bottom edge. Drill and countersink holes, and fasten the cleats to the side panels and center divider with glue and No. 8 × 1-1/4″ wood screws.

Fasten the bottom panel (N) to the base frame using glue and No. 8 wood screws. Make sure the edges of the panel are flush with the outer edges of the frame and countersink the screws.

Cut the cabinet back (M) to size and machine a 3/4″ × 3/8″ dado across its center to receive the back edge of the center divider. Then fasten it to the rear of the base frame with glue and screws while holding their ends and lower edges flush.

Fit the side panels into place at the ends of the bottom and back panels with their notched lower corners sitting on top of the extended ends of the front frame member. Fasten the sides to the frame and the other panels using glue and screws. Then, cut two of the lower risers (H) to fit the spaces between the side panel shelf cleats and the bottom panel. Fasten these risers in place, setting them flush against the side and back panels.

Now set the top frame into place and fasten it to the back and side panels using glue and screws, while holding their upper edges flush. Spread glue in the bottom and back panel dadoes and on the right face of the top center crosspiece and fasten the center divider in place. Run a few screws through the divider into the crosspiece to further tie the two together.

Cut lower risers to fit beneath the shelf cleats on both sides of the center divider. Fasten them in place, then cut and install the shelves (P). After screwing the shelves to the shelf cleats, cut upper risers (J) and fit them between the shelves and the top frame in the four corners formed by the sides, divider, and back panels as shown in the exploded-view drawing.

Cut the countertop pieces (Q, R) to size. Screw the waferboard top to the top frame with No. 8 × 1-1/4" wood screws. Drill and countersink holes so that the screws lie flush with the surface of the top. Screw the 1/8" hardboard top to the waferboard top using No. 4 × 3/8" flathead wood screws. Countersink the screws.

Cut the doors (S) to size. Chisel hinge-mortises in the doors and the cabinet sides and center divider to accept the 2" leaf hinges.

Sand and finish the cabinet and doors with clear polyurethane varnish. Hang the doors and install magnetic latches and door pulls.

Wall Cabinets

Begin construction of the wall cabinet by cutting the sides (A) and top and bottom (B) to length from 1 × 8 stock. Cut a 1/8" × 3/8" rabbet along the rear inside edge of each piece to receive the edges of the back panel. Also, cut 3/4" × 3/8" rabbets across the ends of the side pieces to receive the ends of the top and bottom as shown in the drawing.

Assemble the cabinet frame with carpenter's wood glue and 4d finishing nails. Cut the back panel (C) to size, and glue and nail it to the back side of the frame assembly.

Cut three nailer strips (D) to length, and screw to the top and bottom of the cabinet using No. 6 × 1-1/2" wood screws. Countersink the holes so that the screws seat flush with the surface.

To build the doors, cut all the spacers (E, F) to length and the perforated hardboard door panels (G) to size. Glue and nail the spacer strips together and sandwich them between two panels. Glue and screw the panels to the spacers with No. 6 × 3/4" wood screws. Countersink the holes so that the screws seat flush with the surface.

Hang the doors on the cabinet with 1-1/2" butt hinges. Finish the

MATERIALS LIST

1 × 8 × 12' #2 pine
1 × 2 × 8' #2 pine (4)
1/8" × 4' × 8' perforated hardboard
No. 14 × 3" wood screws
No. 6 × 1-1/2" wood screws
No. 6 × 3/4" wood screws
4d finishing nails
1-1/2" butt hinges (4)
Magnetic latches (2)
Door pulls (2)
Wood putty
Wood glue

CUTTING LIST

KEY	PIECES	SIZE/DESCRIPTION
A	2	3/4 × 7-1/4 × 24 sides
B	2	3/4 × 7-1/4 × 47-1/4 top and bottom
C	1	1/8 × 23-1/4 × 47-1/4 back panel (perforated hardboard)
D	3	3/4 × 1-1/2 × 48 nailer strips
E	4	3/4 × 1-1/2 × 23-15/16 top and bottom spacers
F	4	3/4 × 1-1/2 × 21 side spacers
G	4	1/8 × 23-15/16 × 24 door panels (perforated hardboard)

cabinet as desired and secure it to the wall 12" to 15" above the workbench with No. 14 × 3" wood screws or the appropriate wall mounting hardware.

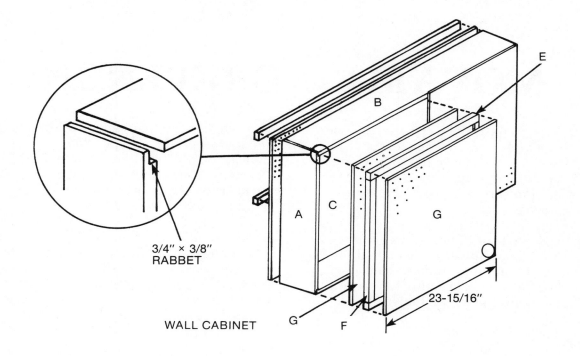

3/4" × 3/8" RABBET

23-15/16"

WALL CABINET

MOVABLE WORKBENCH

It's hard to be organized if you don't have enough space: space to work in and space to store whatever you're working with. Here's a cabinet that provides both work and storage area.

A two-sided cabinet forms the storage base. One side is shelved, to hold hand power tools and supplies. The other side contains variously sized drawers suitable for sandpaper, small tools, and miscellany.

Two sets of doors act as additional storage. The deeper doors have adjustable shelves for hanging a variety of mid-sized tools, while the narrow, shelf-lined doors put small tools within easy grasp.

The butcher block top work area is scaled to handle most projects comfortably. Clamps or woodworking vises can be attached to the extended edges at work level—a functional and unobstructive arrangement. (An optional four-gang receptacle can also be mounted on one of the cabinet's sides.)

Finally, if all of this organization is just what you have wanted but not where you need it, move it: The whole unit rests on casters. When you have found the right spot, two kickstands can be dropped to set the bench back on solid ground.

Cut the bottom panel (A) to size from a sheet of 3/4″ plywood. From the end of the same sheet of plywood, cut the center partition (B) to size. From the remainder of the sheet, cut off a 28-3/4″ × 48″ piece. Then cut this piece in half to form the two cabinet ends (C), each 28-3/4″ × 23-15/16″.

Machine a 3/4″ × 3/8″ rabbet on the bottom inside edge of each end piece to accept the bottom panel. Machine a 3/4″-wide × 3/8″-deep groove lengthwise down the inside center of each end piece. (The groove should be 11″ in from one edge of the cabinet.) Glue and nail the end pieces to the center partition, placing the center partition in the end piece grooves and keeping the top surfaces flush. Glue and nail the bottom panel to the assembled ends and center partition.

Cut the top mounting cleats (D) to size from 1 × 2 pine. Glue and nail the top mounting cleats into position. Butt the inner ends of the cleats against the center partition and keep them flush with the top surface of the cabinet.

Cut the shelf cleats (E) to size. From the remainder of the 3/4″-plywood, cut the 10-1/2″ × 47-1/2″ shelf (F) to size. In the 12″ side of the cabinet, determine the desired shelf position; then glue and nail the shelf cleats in place.

If you are going to mount a woodworking vise to run lengthwise on the workbench, cut a hole in one end piece to accommodate the vise.

Mount casters at all bottom corners of the cabinet, using 5/16″ T-nuts, 3/4″ hex-head bolts, and 5/16″ flat washers.

Cut the top and bottom (G) and intermediate drawer bases (H) to size. Cut all the drawer spacers (J, K) and sandpaper spacers (L) to size. Glue and assemble all the spacers and drawer bases, being careful to keep the spacers lined up equally (see illustration for dimensions) and keeping all outside edges flush.

NOTE: Start from the top and work down, layer by layer. You might have to toenail some of the drawer spacers.

Determine the desired position of the now assembled drawer cabinet and glue and nail it into the assembled workbench cabinet. Smooth ("break") all sharp edges, fill in all voids, sand and paint the workbench and drawer cabinets.

Cut to size the drawer fronts, backs, and sides (M, N, P, S, T). Drill a 7/8"-diameter finger hole in each drawer front. Machine a 1/4" radius on the inside and outside edges of the finger holes. Machine a 3/4" × 3/8" rabbet on both ends of all the front and back pieces. Machine a 1/4" × 3/8" rabbet on the lower edge of all pieces to accept the bottom.

Cut the drawer bottoms (Q, R, U) to size. Glue and nail the drawers together. Break all sharp edges, then sand and paint.

Cut the top and bottom kickstand pieces (V) to size. Rip a 3/4"-high, 30-degree angle lengthwise along the edges of two pieces. These will become the top pieces.

Measure in 3" from each end along the angled edge of the top pieces and machine a 5/8"-deep × 1-5/8"-wide dado through the angled edge. These dadoes will hold the kickstand catches.

Cut a 1-1/2" radius on the corners of the angled edge. Lay the bottom pieces flat; glue and screw the top pieces to them. Be sure that the angled edge of the top piece faces the inside and that all outside edges are flush. (Use five No. 10 × 3-1/2" flathead wood screws.)

Cut a 3/4" radius on the outside corner of the kickstand. Break all sharp edges, then sand and paint.

Mount three T-hinges on the top of the bottom piece, keeping the

MATERIALS LIST

3/4" × 4' × 8' AC plywood (1-1/2 sheets)
1/4" × 4' × 8' luan plywood
2 × 4 × 8' #2 pine
1 × 12 × 8' #2 pine
1 × 6 × 12' #2 pine
1 × 6 × 10' #2 pine
1 × 6 × 8' #2 pine
1 × 4 × 10' #2 pine (2)
1 × 4 × 8' #2 pine
1 × 3 × 12' #2 pine (2)
1 × 3 × 8' #2 pine
1 × 2 × 10' #2 pine
1-1/2" × 32" × 62" maple butcher block
6d finishing nails
No. 14 × 1-1/2" wood screws
No. 10 × 3-1/2" wood screws
5/16"—18 T-nuts (16)
5/16" I.D. flat washers (16)
5/16"—18 × 3/4" hex-head bolts (16)
2-1/2" casters (4)
Double-roller catches (8)
3' lengths of 3/8" nylon rope (2)
1-1/2" screw eyes (4)
3/4"-dia. × 4" hardwood dowels (2)
2" T-hinges (6)
3/4" offset hinges (8)
7" vise
Double receptacle box
Receptacles (2)
Plug
No. 16-3 wire (25')
1/4"-diameter shelf pins
Wood glue

CUTTING LIST

KEY	PIECES	SIZE/DESCRIPTION
A	1	3/4 × 23-15/16 × 48 workbench cabinet bottom (plywood)

CUTTING LIST (continued)

KEY	PIECES	SIZE/DESCRIPTION
B	1	3/4 × 28 × 48 workbench cabinet center partition (plywood)
C	2	3/4 × 23-15/16 × 28-3/4 workbench cabinet ends (plywood)
D	4	3/4 × 1-1/2 × 11 workbench cabinet top mounting cleats
E	2	3/4 × 1-1/2 × 10 workbench cabinet shelf cleats
F	1	3/4 × 10-1/2 × 47-1/4 workbench cabinet shelf (plywood)
G	2	3/4 × 10-1/2 × 47-1/4 drawer cabinet top and bottom
H	3	1/4 × 10-1/2 × 47-1/4 drawer cabinet intermediate bases (luan plywood)
J	10	3/4 × 2-1/2 × 10-1/2 drawer spacers
K	4	3/4 × 3-1/2 × 10-1/2 drawer spacers
L	6	3/4 × 3/4 × 10-1/2 sandpaper spacers
M	16	3/4 × 2-3/8 × 9-3/4 drawer sides
N	12	3/4 × 2-3/8 × 8-7/8 drawer fronts and backs
P	4	3/4 × 2-3/8 × 16-3/8 drawer fronts and backs
Q	6	1/4 × 8-1/8 × 9-3/4 drawer bottoms (plywood)

CUTTING LIST (continued)

KEY	PIECES	SIZE/DESCRIPTION
R	2	1/4 × 9-3/4 × 15-5/8 drawer bottoms (plywood)
S	6	3/4 × 3-3/8 × 9-3/4 drawer sides
T	6	3/4 × 3-3/8 × 14-5/8 drawer fronts and backs
U	3	1/4 × 9-3/4 × 13-7/8 bottoms (plywood)
V	4	1-1/2 × 3-1/2 × 24 kickstand tops and bottoms
W	4	3/4 × 5-1/2 × 28-1/2 deep cabinet door sides
X	4	3/4 × 5-1/2 × 23-1/2 deep door tops and bottoms
Y	2	1/4 × 23-1/2 × 27-3/4 deep door panels (plywood)
Z	1	3/4 × 5 × 27 deep door center partition
AA	2	3/4 × 5 × 22-5/8 deep door center partitions
BB	3	3/4 × 5 × 10-7/8 deep door shelves
CC	2	1/2 × 1-1/2 × 6 deep door shim
DD	4	3/4 × 1-1/2 × 28-1/2 narrow door sides
EE	4	3/4 × 1-1/2 × 23-1/2 narrow door tops and bottoms
FF	2	1/4 × 23-1/2 × 27-3/4 narrow door panels (plywood)
GG	3	3/4 × 1 × 22-3/4 bit holders

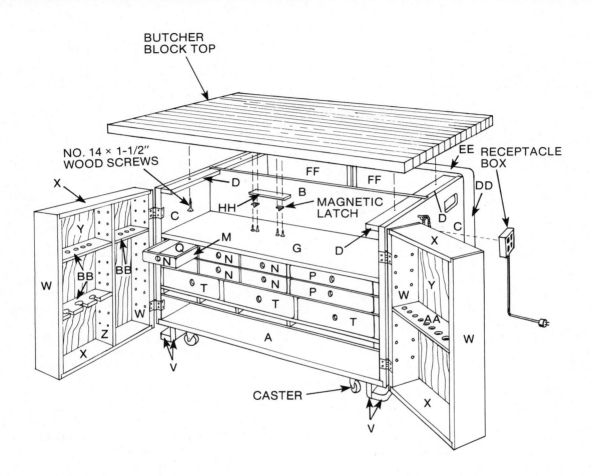

BUTCHER
BLOCK TOP

NO. 14 × 1-1/2"
WOOD SCREWS

EE RECEPTACLE
BOX

MAGNETIC
LATCH

CASTER

hinges flush with the outside edge. Mount the kickstands to the workbench.

The rope pull, designed to facilitate lifting the kickstand, is optional. To make it, screw in two 1-1/2" screw eyes for each kickstand: one in the center of each cabinet end, 2" from the top; the other into the center of the angled top piece of the kickstand. Cut two 4" lengths of 3/4"-diameter hardwood dowel and

drill a 3/8" hole in the center of each handle to accept the rope. Tie one end of the nylon rope to the screw eye on the kickstand and pass the other end up and through the screw eye in the cabinet end. Tie that end through the wooden handle. Fasten the catches and T-hinges to the kickstand and the cabinet ends.

Cut the sides (W) and tops and bottoms (X) to size for the 5-1/2"-thick doors. Machine a

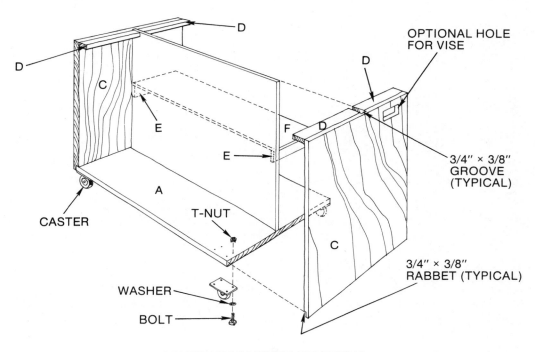

D

D

D

OPTIONAL HOLE
FOR VISE

C

E

F D

E

3/4" × 3/8"
GROOVE
(TYPICAL)

CASTER

A

T-NUT

C

3/4" × 3/8"
RABBET (TYPICAL)

WASHER

BOLT

WORKBENCH CABINET ASSEMBLY

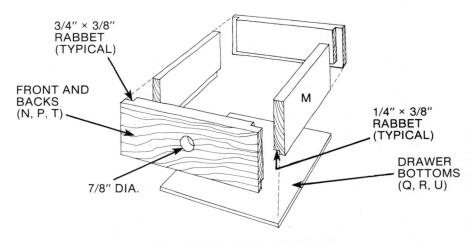

3/4" × 3/8"
RABBET
(TYPICAL)

FRONT AND
BACKS
(N, P, T)

M

1/4" × 3/8"
RABBET
(TYPICAL)

DRAWER
BOTTOMS
(Q, R, U)

7/8" DIA.

TYPICAL DRAWER ASSEMBLY

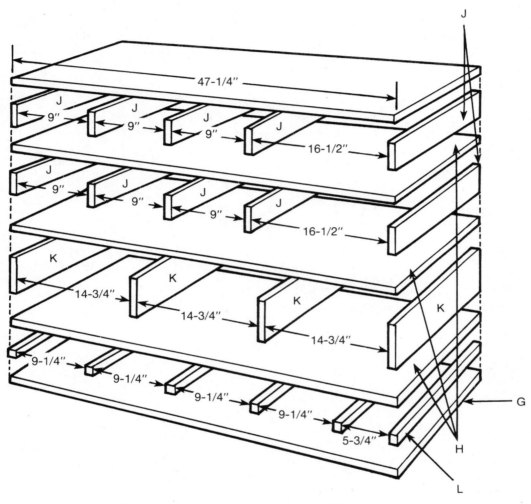

DRAWER CABINET ASSEMBLY

3/4″ × 3/8″-deep rabbet on both ends of the side pieces to accept the top and bottom pieces. Mark and drill several 1/4″-diameter × 1/2″-deep holes in the side pieces to accept the movable shelf pins. Machine a 1/4″-wide × 3/8″-deep groove lengthwise on all door pieces, 1/4″ in from the outside edge to accept the door panels.

Cut the door panels (Y) to size. Fasten the door pieces together with glue and 6d finishing nails.

Cut the center partitions (Z, AA) to size. Drill 1/4″-diameter holes through the center partition to line up with the holes in the sides of the door. Glue and nail the center partition in place.

Cut all the movable shelves (BB) to size. Break all sharp edges, then sand and paint doors.

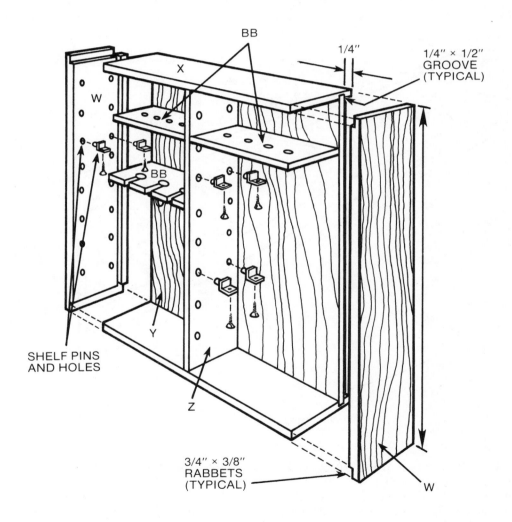

BB

1/4″

1/4″ × 1/2″
GROOVE
(TYPICAL)

X

W

BB

SHELF PINS
AND HOLES

Y

Z

3/4″ × 3/8″
RABBETS
(TYPICAL)

W

TYPICAL DOOR ASSEMBLY

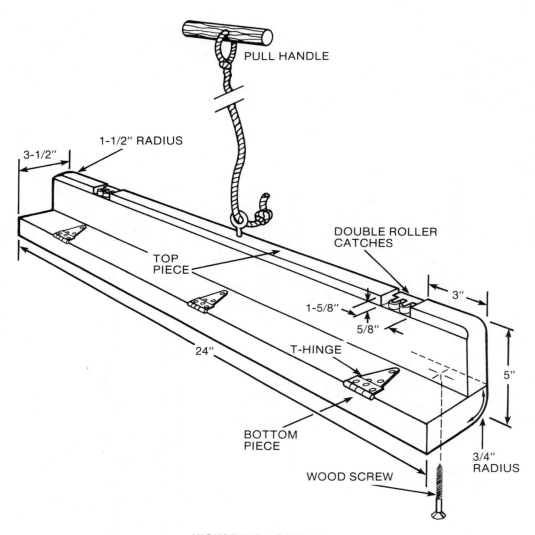

PULL HANDLE

1-1/2" RADIUS

3-1/2"

TOP PIECE

DOUBLE ROLLER CATCHES

24"

1-5/8"

5/8"

3"

T-HINGE

5"

BOTTOM PIECE

3/4" RADIUS

WOOD SCREW

KICKSTAND ASSEMBLY

Cut the narrow door sides (DD), tops and bottoms (EE), and door panels (FF) to size. Rabbet the sides and machine grooves in each piece as described for the 5-1/2"-thick door. Glue and nail the pieces together. Cut three pieces of 3/4" × 1" × 22-3/4" pine to be used as bit holders (GG) (spade bits, router bits, etc.) in the doors. Glue and nail

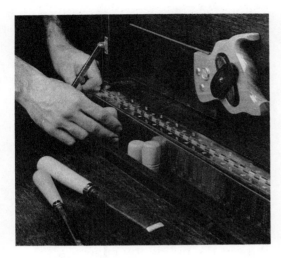

Chisel Compartment

the bit holders in the desired positions. Break all sharp edges, then sand and paint doors.

Mount the benchtop to the bench cabinet using No. 14 × 1-1/2″ flathead wood screws.

Mount the doors using two 3/4″-offset hinges per door. Keep the doors flush with the bottom of the cabinet.

Mount double-roller catches to the doors and benchtop. For best results, mount the catches to two 1/2″ × 1-1/2″ × 6″ pine blocks (HH) on the underside of the benchtop.

Attach a four-gang receptacle box with the desired length of power supply cord.

Mount a woodworking vise if desired. (The vise might require a clearance hole and can be mounted on the left side.)

WOOD-WORKER'S TOOL CHEST

Serious woodworkers will appreciate the utility and beauty of this tool chest. It is made of select mahogany hardwoods and plywood. It has separate compartments for chisels, screwdrivers, and squares, plus ten drawers to house a multitude of small, often misplaced tools and gadgets. Above the drawers, narrow compartments keep sandpaper flat and clean. Below the drawers are pullout shelves that provide safe storage for wood planes. Cutout holes allow for re-

trieving small, dropped items from inside the chest. When in use, the multifunctional lid holds two handsaws. When the work is done, it secures the front door panel and everything inside via two spring-loaded pins and a lock.

Begin construction by cutting all the vertical and horizontal members of the chest to size.

Lay out and machine a 1/4"-deep × 3/8"-wide rabbet on the inside edge of all the members of the end panels (A, B), the back panels (C, D), and the front door (G, H). Rabbet the inside top edge of all the members of the chest's lid (E, F) to accept the lid panel.

Lay out and cut half-lap joints on all the corners of the vertical and horizontal members of the end panels, the back panel, and the front door.

Lay out and cut 3/4"-wide × 3/8"-deep rabbets on the ends of the end members of the lid.

Cut the end panel pieces (L), the back panel (M), front door panel (N), lid panel and bottom panel (P) to size. Assemble, glue, and clamp the end panel sections, the back panel section, the front door section, and the lid section. (You will have five finished subassemblies.)

Lay out and machine a 3/8" × 3/4" rabbet along the vertical edges of each end panel to accept the front door and back panel sections.

Lay out and machine a 1/4" × 3/8" rabbet along the bottom edges of the end panels, back panel, and the bottom front rail (K) to accept the bottom panel.

Lay out and machine a 1/4″ × 3/8″ groove in the end panels and the top front rail (J) to accept the top inside tray (Q). Cut the top inside tray to size.

Glue and clamp the chest sections together (the end panels, the back panel, the front top and bottom horizontal members, the bottom, and the top inside tray).

Lay out and cut the chisel compartment panel (R) to size. Lay out and cut the two semicircular cutouts on the bottom of the panel.

Cut the bottom blocking (ends and center [S, T]) of the chisel compartment to size. Cut the chisel support (U) to size. Cut notches in the chisel support for chisels and framing and/or try squares. Drill holes for a set of screwdrivers.

Glue the bottom blocking in place. Then, glue the chisel support to the chisel compartment panel.

Glue the assembled inside panel and chisel support in place. (The assembled panel and support can be fitted through the front of the chest.) Cut the back support rail (V) of the top inside tray to size, and glue it in place at the rear edge of the top inside tray.

Cut the horizontal supports (N) for the drawers to size.

Cut the center divider (X) of the bottom tool compartments to size. Lay out and machine two 1/4″ × 1/4″ grooves on each side of the center divider to accept the pullout trays.

Cut all drawer dividers (Y, Z, AA) and the end supports (BB, CC, DD, EE, FF) to size.

Glue the bottom center divider and the bottom end supports in place. Then, lay out and glue in place all drawer and compartment supports and dividers.

Cut fronts, backs, and sides of the large and small drawers (GG–LL).

Lay out and drill a 3/4″-diameter finger hole in the front piece of each drawer. Rout a 3/16″ radius on both edges of the finger hole.

Machine a 1/4″ × 3/8″ rabbet along the bottom inner edge of the side and back pieces to accept the bottoms. Machine a 3/8″ × 3/4″ rabbet on each end of all front and back pieces of the drawers to accept the side pieces.

Cut all the drawer bottoms (MM, NN) to size.

Glue, clamp, and nail together all the drawers, using 7/8″, 18-gauge wire nails. Check that all drawers fit into the openings; adjust if necessary. Rout a 3/16″ radius on all the edges of the drawers.

Cut the pullout trays (PP) and plane-holding blocks (QQ, RR) to size. Lay out and drill a 1″-diameter finger hole in each tray. Using your plane as a positional guide, lay out and glue blocking pieces to the tray.

Attach the front door to the tool chest with a 1-1/2″ × 31″ piano hinge. Make adjustments so the door closes properly.

Mortise and install a recessed

finger catch into the door and frame.
Lay out and drill a 13/64″-wide hole completely through the top front rail and 5/8″ down into the top edge of the front door to accept the pins. Counterbore the 13/64″ hole with a 25/64″ drill to a depth of 1-1/4″ to accept the pin spring and top.
Cut two pieces of steel 3/16″ in diameter × 2-1/4″ in length for the locking pins. (A 20d common nail can be substituted.) Cut the wooden dowels to length for the locking pins. Lay out and drill a 3/16″-wide × 1/2″-deep hole in one end of

MATERIALS LIST

3/4″ select mahogany (35 board feet)
5/16″ select mahogany (3 board feet)
1-1/4″ select mahogany (1 board foot)
1/4″ × 4′ × 8′ mahogany plywood
No. 6 × 3/4″ roundhead brass wood
   screws (2)
3/16″ brass washers (2)
7/8″, 18-gauge wire nails
20d common nails (2)
1-1/2″ × 31″ piano hinge
1-1/2″ × 32″ piano hinge
1-1/4″ × 1-5/8″ brass half-mortised
   finger catch
Half-mortised chest lock
3/8″-dia. × 1-1/8″ hardwood dowels
   (2)
3/16″ light compression springs (2)
White vinyl glue
Brass lid support
Brass corner guard (8)

CUTTING LIST		
KEY	**PIECES**	**SIZE/DESCRIPTION**
A	4	3/4 × 2-1/2 × 17 end panel stiles
B	4	3/4 × 2-1/2 × 16 end panel rails
C	2	3/4 × 2-1/2 × 17 back panel stiles
D	2	3/4 × 2-1/2 × 31-1/4 back panel rails
E	2	3/4 × 2-1/2 × 16 lid ends
F	2	3/4 × 2-1/2 × 31-1/4 lid sides
G	2	3/4 × 2-1/2 × 31-1/4 front door rails
H	2	3/4 × 2-1/2 × 13-5/16 front door stiles
J	1	3/4 × 2-1/2 × 31-1/4 chest front top rail
K	1	3/4 × 1 × 31-1/4 chest front bottom rail
L	2	1/4 × 11-3/4 × 12-3/4 end panels (plywood)
M	1	1/4 × 12-3/4 × 27 back panel (plywood)
N	1	1/4 × 9 × 27 front door panel (plywood)
P	2	1/4 × 15-1/4 × 31-1/4 lid and bottom panels (plywood)
Q	1	1/4 × 12-5/8 × 31-1/4 inside tray (plywood)
R	1	1/4 × 14-7/8 × 30-1/2 chisel compartment panel (plywood)
S	2	3/4 × 2-1/4 × 2-3/4 bottom blocking ends
T	1	3/4 × 2-1/4 × 6 bottom blocking center

CUTTING LIST (continued)		
KEY	**PIECES**	**SIZE/DESCRIPTION**
U	1	3/4 × 2-1/4 × 30-1/2 chisel support
V	1	3/4 × 3/4 × 30-1/2 back support rail
W	5	1/4 × 12 × 30-1/2 horizontal drawer divider supports (plywood)
X	1	3/4 × 5-1/4 × 12 bottom tool compartment center divider
Y	1	3/4 × 2-1/2 × 12 drawer center divider
Z	2	3/4 × 1-3/8 × 12 sandpaper compartment center dividers
AA	5	3/4 × 1-1/2 × 12 drawer center dividers
BB	2	5/16 × 2 × 12 bottom compartment end supports
CC	2	5/16 × 2-1/2 × 12 drawer end supports
DD	2	5/16 × 1-3/8 × 12 sandpaper compartment end supports
EE	2	5/16 × 3 × 12 tool compartment end supports
FF	6	5/16 × 1-1/2 × 12 drawer end supports
GG	4	3/4 × 2-7/16 × 14-3/8 drawer fronts and backs

CUTTING LIST (continued)		
KEY	**PIECES**	**SIZE/DESCRIPTION**
HH	4	3/4 × 2-7/16 × 11-1/4 drawer sides
JJ	4	3/4 × 1-7/16 × 14-3/8 drawer fronts and backs
KK	12	3/4 × 1-7/16 × 9-3/8 drawer fronts and backs
LL	16	3/4 × 1-7/16 × 11-1/4 drawer sides
MM	4	1/4 × 11-1/4 × 13-5/8 drawer bottoms (plywood)
NN	6	1/4 × 11-1/4 × 8-5/8 drawer bottoms (plywood)
PP	2	1/4 × 12 × 15 pullout trays (plywood)
QQ	1	3/4 × 1 × 12 plane-holding blocks
RR	2	3/4 × 1 × 3 plane-holding blocks
SS	1	3/4 × 2-1/4 × 14-1/2 saw rack
TT	1	1-1/4 × 1-1/4 × 3 saw handle block
UU	1	1-1/4 × 2-3/8 × 3-3/4 saw handle block

each dowel pin to accept the steel locking pin. Glue the pieces together.

Machine a 5/32"-deep × 5/8"-wide rabbet along the bottom back edge of the chest lid to accept the piano hinge. Attach the lid to the chest with the 32"-wide hinge.

Install a half-mortise lock to secure the lid to the chest.

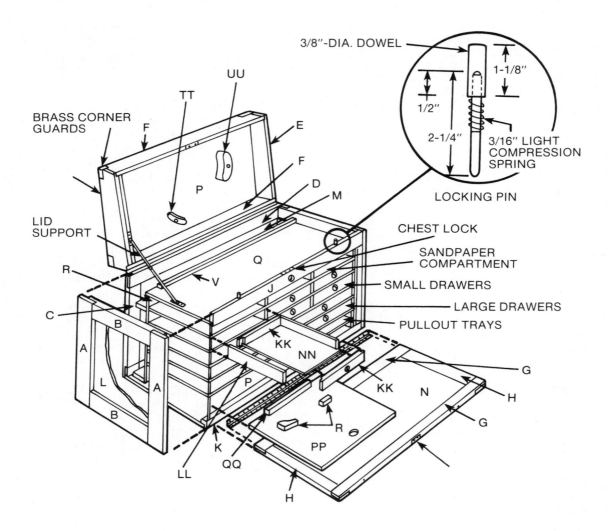

BRASS CORNER GUARDS

TT

UU

F

E

F

P

D

M

3/8"-DIA. DOWEL

1-1/8"

1/2"

2-1/4"

3/16" LIGHT COMPRESSION SPRING

LOCKING PIN

CHEST LOCK

LID SUPPORT

SANDPAPER COMPARTMENT

R

V

Q

J

SMALL DRAWERS

LARGE DRAWERS

C

B

KK

NN

PULLOUT TRAYS

A

L

A

P

KK

N

G

B

R

H

K

PP

G

LL

QQ

H

Cut the saw rack (SS) to size. Lay out and cut slots in the saw rack to fit the blades of your handsaws. Glue the rack in place. Lay out and cut blocks (TT, UU) to fit through the saw handles. Cut the blocks 1/16" wider than the thickness of the handles. Cut a 1/4"-thick piece of mahogany the same shape as the block to secure the saws in place. Lay out and glue the blocks in place. Screw the 1/4" turnbuckles to the blocks using brass wood screws.

Stain the tool chest to the desired color, and finish with three coats of brushing lacquer. Then, install a lid support and the corner guards on the chest corners.

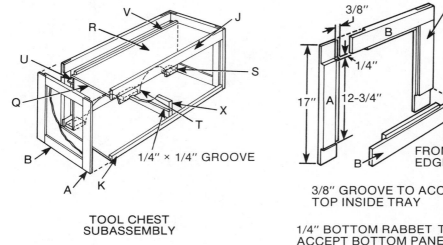

V
R
J
U
S
Q
X
B
T
A
K

1/4" × 1/4" GROOVE

**TOOL CHEST
SUBASSEMBLY**

3/8"
A
B
1/4"
17"
A   12-3/4"
B
3/4"   1-7/8"
B
1/4"
B
FRONT
EDGE
END
PANEL
(INSIDE)
A
B
3/8"

**3/8" GROOVE TO ACCEPT
TOP INSIDE TRAY**

**1/4" BOTTOM RABBET TO
ACCEPT BOTTOM PANEL**

END PANEL ASSEMBLY

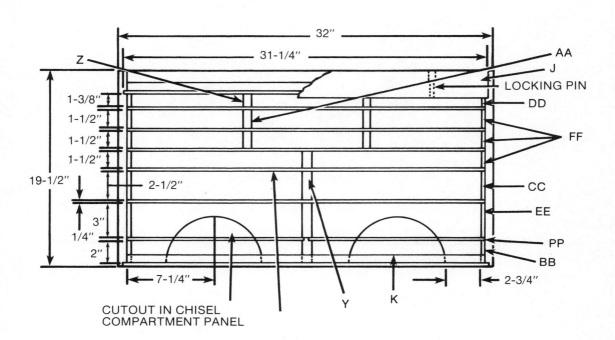

32"
31-1/4"
Z
AA
J
LOCKING PIN
1-3/8"
DD
1-1/2"
1-1/2"
FF
1-1/2"
19-1/2"
2-1/2"
CC
EE
3"
1/4"
PP
2"
BB
2-3/4"
7-1/4"
Y   K

**CUTOUT IN CHISEL
COMPARTMENT PANEL**

CHEST FRONT, CUTAWAY

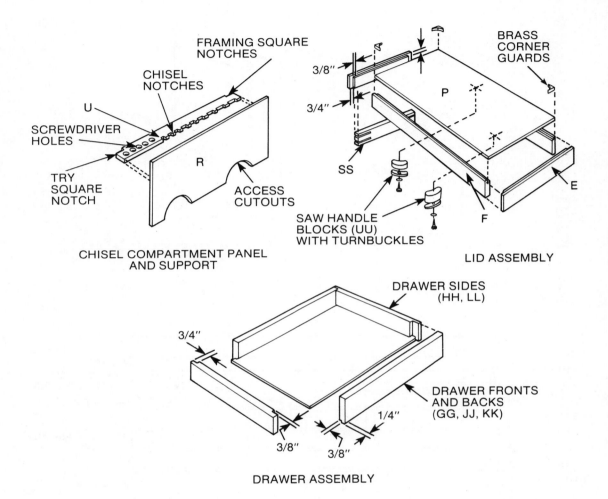

FRAMING SQUARE NOTCHES

CHISEL NOTCHES

U

SCREWDRIVER HOLES

TRY SQUARE NOTCH

R

ACCESS CUTOUTS

CHISEL COMPARTMENT PANEL AND SUPPORT

3/8"

3/4"

SS

P

BRASS CORNER GUARDS

E

F

SAW HANDLE BLOCKS (UU) WITH TURNBUCKLES

LID ASSEMBLY

DRAWER SIDES (HH, LL)

3/4"

DRAWER FRONTS AND BACKS (GG, JJ, KK)

1/4"

3/8"

3/8"

DRAWER ASSEMBLY

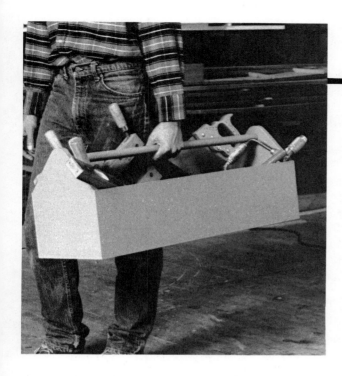

TOOL TOTE

If organization is one of the keys to success, then every do-it-yourselfer needs a tool tote. Built with sturdy 3/4" and 1/4" interior plywood and designed with a hand-saw compartment, this tool box is large enough to carry all the hand tools you will need for fix-up projects around the house or construction jobs outside.

Begin building the tool tote by laying out and cutting the end panels (A) to size. Also, lay out and drill a 1"-diameter hole through each end panel to accept the handle.

Machine a 3/4" × 3/8" rabbet across the bottom inside edge of each end panel to accept the bottom.

Cut the bottom (B) to size. Machine a 1/8" × 3/8" groove 1-1/2"

from one side in the upper face of the bottom to accept the saw compartment side panel.

Cut the handle (C) and sides (D) to size. Also cut the saw compartment end blocks (E), saw rests (F), and side panel (G) to size.

Lay out and drill two 9/64"-diameter mounting holes near the upper edge of the saw compartment

MATERIALS LIST

3/4" AC interior plywood (1/4 sheet)
1/8" tempered hardboard (1/4 sheet)
1 × 2 × 13" #2 pine
1"-dia. hardwood dowel (3')
6d cement coated box nails
1" underlayment nails
No. 6 × 3/4" roundhead wood
  screws (2)
Wood glue

CUTTING LIST

KEY	PIECES	SIZE/DESCRIPTION
A	2	3/4 × 10 × 12 end panels (plywood)
B	1	3/4 × 10 × 31-1/4 bottom (plywood)
C	1	1-dia. × 32 hardwood dowel handle
D	2	1/8 × 7-1/4 × 32 sides (hardboard)
E	2	3/4 × 1-1/2 × 4-3/4 saw compartment end blocks
F	2	3/4 × 1-1/2 × 1-1/2 saw rests
G	1	1/8 × 5-1/8 × 30-1/2 saw compartment side panel

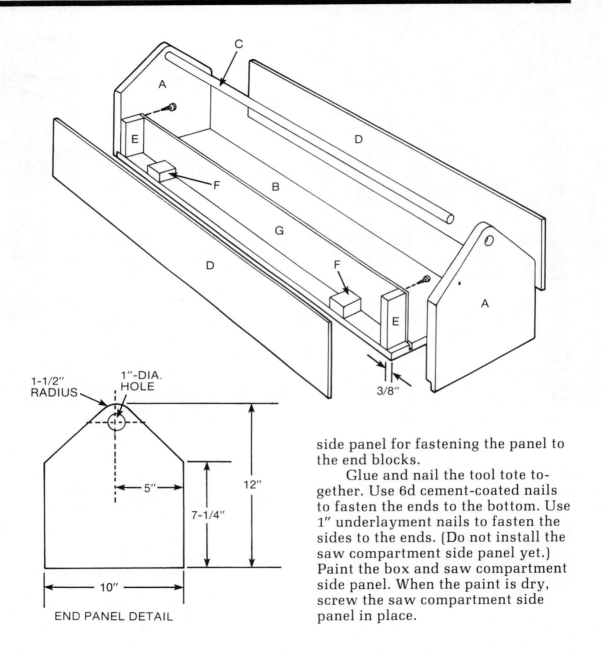

C

A

E

D

F

B

G

D

F

E

A

3/8″

1-1/2″
RADIUS

1″-DIA.
HOLE

5″

7-1/4″

12″

10″

END PANEL DETAIL

side panel for fastening the panel to the end blocks.

Glue and nail the tool tote together. Use 6d cement-coated nails to fasten the ends to the bottom. Use 1″ underlayment nails to fasten the sides to the ends. (Do not install the saw compartment side panel yet.) Paint the box and saw compartment side panel. When the paint is dry, screw the saw compartment side panel in place.

OVERHEAD
LUMBER RACK

Lumber storage is a very important consideration, especially in a small workshop. Lumber must be kept dry and straight to avoid warpage and stored where it will not be an obstacle to work or movement. These objectives are met in the overhead storage rack pictured here. The rack is made of 2 × 4s and 2 × 6s

and hung from overhead floor joists or trusses.

The rack is quite simple to make. Cut the 2 × 4 and 2 × 6 pieces to length for the vertical and horizontal supports (A, B).

To minimize the chances of lumber slipping off the sides of the rack, taper the upper edge of each horizontal support from full height at each end down to 1″ below full height at the middle. This will give these edges the flattened V-shape visible in the drawing and photo. Once those cuts are completed, fasten the vertical supports to the horizontal supports using carriage bolts or glue and nails. Before fastening, make sure the pieces are perpendicular to each other and that the vertical piece is centered along the length of the other piece.

The racks can be nailed or bolted to the overhead trusses or joists.

MATERIALS LIST
2 × 6 × 4′ #2 pine
2 × 4 × 6′ #2 pine
12d nails

CUTTING LIST		
KEY	**PIECES**	**SIZE/DESCRIPTION**
A	2	1-1/2 × 3-1/2 × 35-7/8 vertical supports
B	2	1-1/2 × 5-1/2 × 23-1/2 horizontal supports

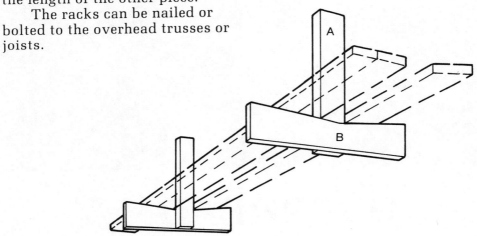

PLYWOOD AND LUMBER RACK

If you are a serious do-it-yourselfer, you want a place to store lumber and panel products—a place that will keep your materials organized, dry, and straight. This combination plywood and lumber rack might be just what you need. As you can see from the photo and drawing, this rack is made more sturdy by extensive use of rabbet and dado joints in the assembly of the 2 × 4 frames.

Begin the construction of the rack by cutting the 2 × 4 frame pieces (A, B, C, D) to length. Cut 1-1/2"-wide and 1/2"-deep rabbets across the inner faces of the six supports (A) at their upper ends. Cut dadoes of the same dimensions across their inner faces 2" above their lower ends as shown in the drawing. Cut an additional pair of dadoes on each of three supports and a matching pair of dadoes on one face of the dividers to receive the center rails (D) on the lumber side of the rack. Space these dadoes 16" apart as shown in the drawing.

Assemble the three frames using carpenter's wood glue and 10d common nails.

Attach a 3/4" square strip along one long edge of a 4' × 8' sheet of 1/4" plywood (either luan plywood or an inexpensive sheet of paneling). The strip (E) will protect and support the top edge of the plywood. Screw the plywood panel to the panel storage side of the center dividers in the three frames. Use No. 8 × 1" wood screws.

Cut the panel storage floor (F) to width and length from 3/4" plywood. Nail the floor in place with 6d common nails.

Because of the hard use a scrap bin must take, leave it unfinished.

MATERIALS LIST

2 × 4 × 10' (5)
2 × 4 × 8' #2 pine
3/4" × 1' × 8' CD interior plywood
1/4" × 4' × 8' luan plywood
No. 8 × 1" wood screws
10d common nails
6d common nails
Wood glue

CUTTING LIST

KEY	PIECES	SIZE/DESCRIPTION
A	6	1-1/2 × 3-1/2 × 56 supports
B	3	1-1/2 × 3-1/2 × 51 divider
C	6	1-1/2 × 3-1/2 × 26-1/2 top and bottom rails
D	6	1-1/2 × 3-1/2 × 13 center rails
E	1	3/4 × 3/4 × 96 spacer strip
F	1	3/4 × 11-5/8 × 96 panel storage floor
G	1	1/4 × 48 × 96 plywood divider

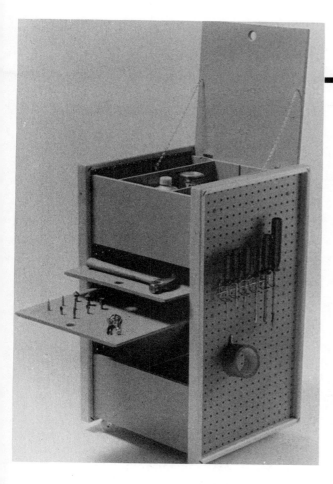

TOOL TABORET

This multipurpose rolling cart was designed to organize everything from sewing supplies to shop tools.

Two boxes form the storage modules. Each box has three removable dividers so the space can be organized to meet your needs. The dividers can also be made in various heights.

The boxes are sandwiched between two pegboard sides. This simple arrangement allows the boxes to be fastened with screws run through the pegboard holes. The pegboard sides also provide a great deal of space which can be used to hold part trays and tools.

Two sliding shelves mount under the top storage box. These shelves can be modified to hold everything from router bits to spools of thread and pads of paper. The shelves also provide access from both sides of the cart.

Begin by cutting the horizontal and vertical side members (A, B) to size.

Lay out and cut 45-degree miters on each end of the side members. Lay out and cut a 1/8"-wide × 5/16"-deep saw kerf on the mitered ends to accept a spline.

Cut a 1/4"-wide × 3/8"-deep groove on the inside face of each side member to accept the side panel. Locate the grooves 1/2" from the outside edges as shown in the exploded view.

Cut the splines (C) to size.

Cut the side panels (D) to size. Trim each corner of the side panels to allow clearance for the splines. Sand and paint the panels.

Assemble each side unit using wood glue and clamps. Machine a 1/4" radius along all edges of each unit and apply a clear finish to the frames.

Cut the sides (E) of the upper and lower box units to size. Cut a 1/4"-deep × 1/2"-wide rabbet on one end of each box side to form chasing rabbet joints and along the bottom

MATERIALS LIST

1 × 2 × 10' select pine (2)
1/2" × 4' × 8' AC interior plywood
1/8" × 5/8" × 1-5/8" walnut splines
  (8)
1/4" × 4' × 4' pegboard
No. 14 × 3/4" panhead screws (24)
No. 12 × 1/2" panhead screws (16)
No. 6 × 1/2" wood screws (12)
No. 6 × 1/2" eye screws (4)
1" × 1-1/2" brass hinges with
  screws (2)
1-1/2"-dia. swivel casters (4)
14"-long jack chains (2)
1/4"-dia. hardwood dowel (36")
Assorted pegboard tool holders
Wood glue
Latex paint
Brushing lacquer

CUTTING LIST

KEY	PIECES	SIZE/DESCRIPTION
A	4	3/4 × 1-1/2 × 18 horizontal side members
B	4	3/4 × 1-1/2 × 32 vertical side members
C	8	1/8 × 5/8 × 1-5/8 splines (walnut)
D	2	1/4 × 17-1/4 × 31-1/4 side panels (pegboard)
E	8	1/2 × 8 × 16-1/4 box unit sides (plywood)
F	2	1/2 × 16 × 16 box unit bottoms (plywood)
G	1	1/2 × 14-7/8 × 16-1/2 box unit lid (plywood)
H	4	1/2 × 5/8 × 16-1/2 guide spacers (plywood)
J	4	41/64 × 1/2 × 16-1/2 tray guides (aluminum channel)
K	2	1/2 × 15-5/16 × 16-1/2 sliding trays (plywood)
L	3	1/4 × 5 × 15-7/8 dividers (pegboard)
M	3	1/4 × 7-1/2 × 15-7/8 dividers (pegboard)
N	18	1/4-dia. × 1-7/8 spool holders (dowel)

edge of each box side to accept the bottom piece.

Lay out and cut three 3/16"-deep × 5/16"-wide grooves in two side members of each box unit to accept the dividers.

Cut the bottoms (F) for the upper and lower box units to size. Then assemble each box unit using glue and clamps.

Lay out and cut recesses in the top edge of the back panel in the upper box unit to accept the lid hinges.

Cut the guide spacers (H), tray guides (J), and sliding trays (K) to size. Drill and countersink the tray guides for No. 6 × 1/2" wood screws. Ease all sharp edges.

Drill a 1"-diameter hole near the front and back edges of each of the sliding trays to create finger pulls. Machine a 1/8" radius around each hole.

Machine a 1/16"-deep × 7/16"-wide rabbet along the two side

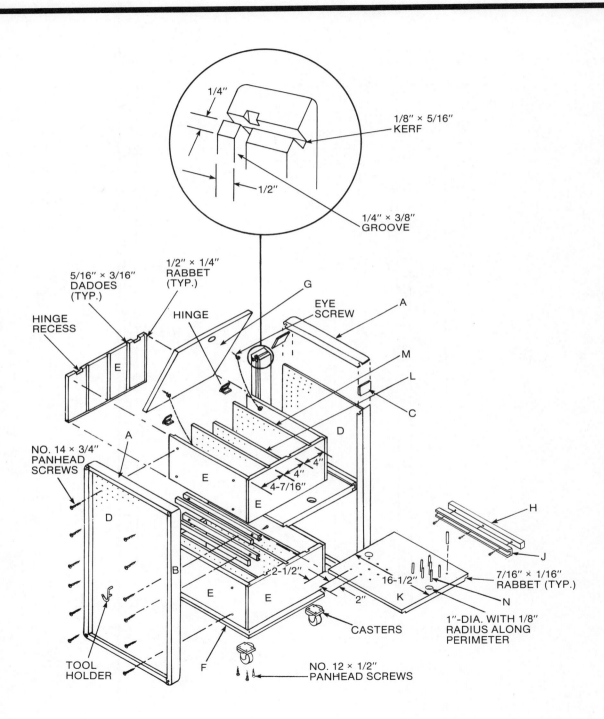

1/4"

1/8" × 5/16"
KERF

1/2"

1/4" × 3/8"
GROOVE

1/2" × 1/4"
RABBET
(TYP.)

5/16" × 3/16"
DADOES
(TYP.)

HINGE

EYE
SCREW

G

A

HINGE
RECESS

M

L

C

E

D

NO. 14 × 3/4"
PANHEAD
SCREWS

A

H

E

4"

4"

4-7/16"

E

J

D

7/16" × 1/16"
RABBET (TYP.)

B

2-1/2"

16-1/2"

N

E

E

2"

K

TOOL
HOLDER

F

CASTERS

1"-DIA. WITH 1/8"
RADIUS ALONG
PERIMETER

NO. 12 × 1/2"
PANHEAD SCREWS

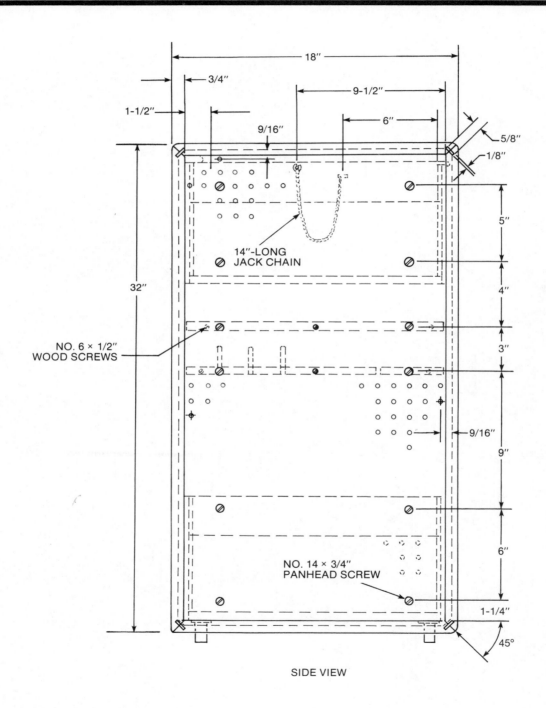

18"

3/4"

9-1/2"

1-1/2"

6"

9/16"

5/8"

1/8"

5"

14"-LONG
JACK CHAIN

32"

4"

NO. 6 × 1/2"
WOOD SCREWS

3"

9/16"

9"

NO. 14 × 3/4"
PANHEAD SCREW

6"

1-1/4"

45°

SIDE VIEW

edges of each sliding tray to provide clearance in the tray guides.

Lay out and drill eighteen 1/4"-diameter holes in one sliding tray to accept 1/4"-diameter shank router bits or the spool holders.

If the tool taboret will be used to store sewing supplies, cut the spool holders (N) to size and glue them into the holes in the sliding tray.

Cut the dividers (L, M) and the box unit lid (G) to size. Center and drill a 1"-diameter hole near the front end of the box unit lid. Machine a 1/8" radius around the hole.

Paint the box units, dividers, sliding trays, and lid.

Attach the box units and the guide spacers to the side units at the locations shown in the side view drawing. Use No. 14 × 3/4" panhead screws. Predrill a 3/16"-diameter hole for each screw. Note that the face of the sides with the least amount of frame overhang goes inside the assembled unit.

Attach the tray guides to the guide spacers using No. 6 × 1/2" wood screws.

Fasten the casters to the underside of the bottom box using No. 12 × 1/2" panhead screws.

Place the dividers in the box units, distributing the two sizes as you see fit.

Fasten the hinges to the upper box unit's top back edge and lid.

Locate and install four eye screws to accept the lid stops. Cut the lid stop chains to length. Open the end links of the lid stops and close each end link around an eye screw.

Insert the side panel tool holders in place.

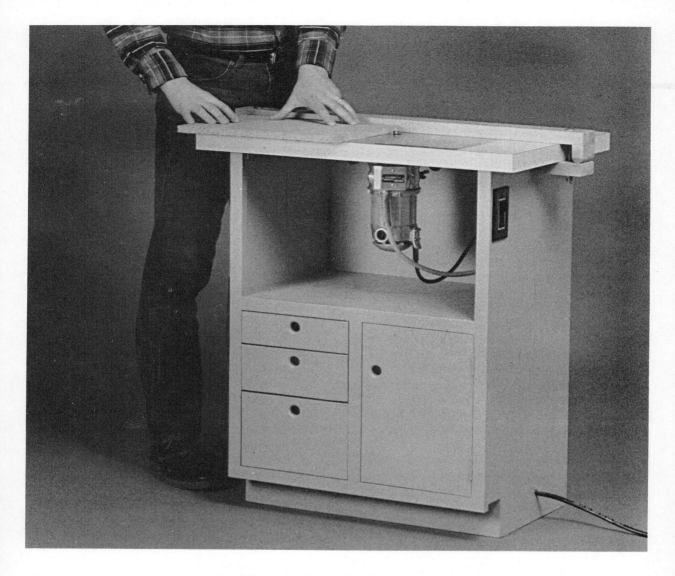

ROUTABOUT CABINET

A cleanly shaped edge is a sign of professional craftsmanship. You don't have to buy an expensive shaper to create smooth edges, however. This routabout cabinet will transform your router into a sta-tionary shaper as well as provide a roomy work surface and plenty of storage space.

In this design, the router is turned upside down and mounted vertically to the bottom side of the cabinet's top, with the bit extending up. This way, you move the wood past a stationary router, instead of trying to steer your machine freehand or with inadequate clamp-on guides. For very long cuts or grooves, our cabinet features a generous overhang for attaching a full-sized fence or other accurate guiding device.

Two pullout trays and a large drawer provide organized storage of your router bits and accessories while a closeable storage compartment protects other tools, plans, and workbooks from dust.

The routabout cabinet is equipped with an electrical switch so you can safely turn the router on and off from outside the cabinet without having to reach in and around a running power tool.

When you want to use your machine's freehand capabilities, remove four screws and the router is demounted.

Cabinet Body

Begin by cutting the cabinet body side panels (A) to size. Cut a 3″ × 3-1/2″ notch in a bottom corner of each panel to create a recessed toe space.

Cut the shelf and bottom (B) and the divider and filler (C) panels to size. Using glue and 6d finishing nails, fasten the bottom to the sides, the filler panel to the side panel, the divider to the bottom, and the shelf to the filler, divider, and sides.

Cut the back panel (D) to size. If the cabinet will sit on an uneven floor, cut a 1″-high arc from corner to corner on the bottom edge of the back panel to improve floor clearance and stability of the cabinet. Or, simply cut the back panel 1/2″ short. Glue and nail the back panel in place.

Cut the back and side mounting rails (E, F) to size. Glue and nail the rails flush with the tops of the side and back panels as shown.

MATERIALS LIST

3/4″ × 4′ × 8′ AC interior plywood
3/4″ × 4′ × 4′ particleboard
1/4″ × 2′ × 4′ plywood
1 × 8 × 4′ #2 pine
1 × 4 × 8′ #2 pine (2)
6d finishing nails
1″ underlayment nails
No. 8 × 1-1/2″ wood screws (4)
No. 8 × 1″ wood screws (4)
1/2″ panhead sheet metal screws (4)
24″ × 36″ plastic laminate
1/8″ × 15″ × 18-3/4″ sheet aluminum
1″ × 2″ cabinet hinges (2)
Magnetic door catch
2″ × 4″ receptacle box (1)
2″ × 4″ shallow wall box (1)
Single pole switch and mounting plate
14-gauge 3 conductor cord, type SJT (25′)
Romex wire nuts (3)
Grounded duplex receptacle (1)
Duplex plate (1)
Grounded male plug (1)
Contact cement
Wood putty
Wood glue

CUTTING LIST		
KEY	**PIECES**	**SIZE/DESCRIPTION**
A	2	3/4 × 16 × 32-1/2 cabinet side panels (plywood)
B	2	3/4 × 16 × 22-1/2 cabinet shelf and bottom (plywood)
C	2	3/4 × 14-3/4 × 16 cabinet divider and filler panels (plywood)
D	1	1/4 × 24 × 32-1/2 cabinet back panel (plywood)
E	1	3/4 × 3-1/2 × 22-1/2 back mounting rail
F	2	3/4 × 3/4 × 12-1/2 side mounting rails
G	1	3/4 × 3-1/2 × 24 kickplate
H	2	3/4 × 2-5/8 × 16 top runners
J	2	3/4 × 3-5/8 × 16 middle runners
K	2	3/4 × 2-5/8 × 16 bottom runners
L	2	3/4 × 1-1/2 × 29-1/2 face frame stiles
M	2	3/4 × 1-1/4 × 21 face frame rails
N	1	3/4 × 1-1/4 × 14-1/4 center stile
P	1	3/4 × 2-7/8 × 9-3/4 top tray front
Q	1	3/4 × 4-1/8 × 9-3/4 middle tray front
R	1	3/4 × 6-13/16 × 9-3/4 drawer front
S	2	3/4 × 4-1/8 × 15-7/8 drawer sides
T	1	3/4 × 4-1/8 × 8-1/4 drawer back

CUTTING LIST (continued)		
KEY	**PIECES**	**SIZE/DESCRIPTION**
U	3	3/4 × 9-3/4 × 16-1/4 tray and drawer bottoms (plywood)
V	1	3/4 × 9-3/4 × 14-1/8 cabinet door (plywood)
W	1	3/4 × 1-1/2 × 14-3/4 doorstop
X	2	3/4 × 19-3/8 × 28-7/8 cabinet top (particleboard)
Y	1	1/8 × 15 × 18-3/4 router mounting plate (sheet aluminum)

NOTE: *The back mounting rail is mounted with its 3-1/2" surfaces horizontal.*

Predrill the mounting rails for the later screw mounting of the cabinet top.

Cut the kickplate (G) to size. Glue and nail the kickplate in place as shown.

Cut the front frame's stiles (L), rails (M), and center stile to size. Glue and nail the frame together; then glue and nail the assembled frame to the front of the cabinet body.

Cut the doorstop (W) to size. Glue and nail the doorstop to the front edge of the divider panel (be-

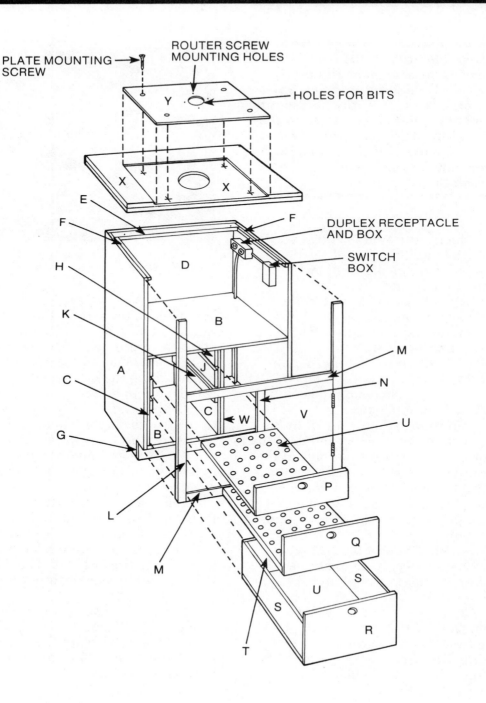

PLATE MOUNTING SCREW

ROUTER SCREW MOUNTING HOLES

HOLES FOR BITS

DUPLEX RECEPTACLE AND BOX

SWITCH BOX

Pullout Tray

hind the front frame's central vertical member). The edge of the door-stop will extend slightly beyond the edge of the front frame.

Lay out and cut a hole in the side panel to accept the electrical switch box. Mount the switch box and switch in the hole, with the switch itself on the cabinet's exterior. Mount the receptacle box and duplex receptacle inside the cabinet next to the switch box.

Determine where you want the wire to exit the cabinet, and drill the appropriate holes for passage of the wire. Wire the switch and receptacle with 14-gauge, three-conductor wire. Snake the remaining wire through the holes drilled in preceding steps.

Install cover plates on the switch and receptacle. Install a grounded (three-prong) male plug on the loose end of the wire.

Construct the pullout trays next. Cut the tray bottoms (U) to size first. Then, cut the top and middle tray front (P, Q) to size. Lay out and drill a 1"-diameter finger

hole in each tray front. Rout a 1/4" radius on both sides of the finger holes to eliminate sharp edges.

Cut a 3/8"-deep × 3/4"-wide rabbet along the bottom edge of the tray fronts to accept the tray bottoms. Glue and nail the tray bottoms to the fronts. Lay out and drill holes in the tray bottoms for storing router bits. (Size and number of the holes depends on type and number of bits to be stored.)

Cut the drawer bottom (U) and front (R) to size. Lay out, drill, and rout a finger hole in the drawer fronts. Rout a 1/4" radius on both sides of the finger holes. The drawer hole should line up with the tray holes.

Cut a 3/8"-deep × 3/4"-wide rabbet along the bottom edge of the drawer front to accept the drawer bottom. Glue and nail the drawer bottom to the front.

Cut the drawer sides (S) and back (T) to size. Glue and nail the sides and back in place.

Cut the top, middle, and bottom pairs of runners (H, J, K) to size. Lay out, glue, and nail the runners in place. The top pair of runners mounts against the underside of the cabinet shelf. Typical spacing between adjacent runner pairs is 7/8", adjust as needed to fit your pullout trays and drawer.

Cut the cabinet door to size. Lay out, drill, and rout a finger hole as described above. Measure your hinges; then chisel or rout the door and frame to fit. Mount the hinges and hang the door.

Set all exposed nails and fill with wood putty. Sand the assembled cabinet and paint with two coats of paint. Install a magnetic catch to hold the door closed.

The cabinet top (X) is made of two 3/4"-thick panels glued together. Cut the two top layers to size. Glue the layers together to create a single 1-1/2"-thick top. Cover the top surface and all four edges with plastic laminate.

Cut the aluminum router mounting plate (Y) to size.

Rout a 1/8" × 15" × 18-3/4" rectangle in the laminate-covered cabinet top to accept the aluminum mounting plate. The routed area should be centered at the front edge of the cabinet top.

Lay out and cut a hole in the center of the routed area. Size the hole to provide the router's base with adequate clearance for easy mounting and demounting.

Lay out and drill a hole in the aluminum mounting plate large enough to accept your largest router bit or accessory. The hole should be centered within the larger hole cut in the cabinet top.

Drill and countersink one hole in each corner of the mounting plate, for screwing the plate to the cabinet top. Also, drill and countersink holes in the mounting plate for screwing the router to the plate. The number, location, and size of the holes is determined by the factory predrilled mounting holes in the router's base.

Screw the mounting plate to the cabinet top, using flathead screws, so the screw heads are flush with the mounting plate's surface. Screw the cabinet top to the body, using the predrilled holes in the cabinet's mounting rails. Screw the router, upside down, to the underside of the mounting plate, using flathead screws, so the screw heads are flush with the surface of the mounting plate.

Plug the router into the cabinet's receptacle. Turn on the router's built-in switch; turn off the cabinet's switch. Plug the cabinet's cord into a grounded wall outlet, and you are ready for routing.

Section 7
Outdoors

Outdoor storage is in a class by itself. Outdoor storage usually means a shed, lean-to, bin, or some other structure providing protection from the elements. The basic function of outdoor storage is to keep stored items dry, secured, and/or out of sight. With suitable outdoor storage facilities, you could rid your garage and basement of lawn mowers, game equipment, trash cans, sleds, gardening tools, building supplies, Christmas decorations—there is no end to the list of things that could be stored outside if a secure, dry spot were available.

In this section, you will find plans specially designed for storing trash cans and gardening supplies. Everything else must go in a storage barn, for which you will also find plans in this section.

Do not make the mistake of associating outdoor projects with amateur craftsmanship. The projects in this section demand careful attention to detail. Build two strengths into all of your outdoor storage projects: protection and longevity. Protection means that the construction is tight and the structure is sealed against weather and intruders. Loose construction joints will allow wind and rain to seep into the structure and invite unwanted insects and vermin.

Longevity is a result of using the right building materials, proper construction techniques, and exterior finishes. Use only pressure-treated lumber for structural members in ground contact. Exposed untreated wood should be painted or finished with an exterior stain. Cover rooftops with shingles and drip caps.

STORAGE BARN

What's the next step after squeezing every possible inch of storage space from your basement, attic, and garage? Build one of the storage barns shown here. You will create space for bicycles, lawnmowers, garden supplies, tools, sports equipment, camping gear, sleds, spare furniture, Christmas decorations, and so on. This storage barn can be built in only a few weekends. Not only will it give you years of service, it will also add to the appearance and value of your home. It has an especially attractive gable roof and barn door design and deluxe optional features—such as skylights—you are not likely to find on "store bought" storage barns.

Begin construction of the barn by leveling the building site. Then, lay two pressure-treated 12'-long 4 × 4 runners (A) parallel and 5'4" apart. These runners will hold the floor framework and allow air to circulate under the barn.

Cut the floor joists (B) and header joists (C) to size. Lay out the locations for the floor joists along an edge of one of the header joists. All but the two end joists should be placed on 16" centers. Each of the end joists must be brought in 3/4" so the floor sheathing will completely lap them. Begin the layout by hooking your tape on the left end of the header and stretching it to the right along the edge of the board. Square a line across the header at 15-1/4" and every 16" thereafter, then place a big X to the right of the line.

Set the second header up against the marked header, face-to-face and ends flush, and extend the layout lines across its upper edge as well. Then spread the headers apart and fit floor joists between them— one joist flush with each end and the rest at the positions marked. If there is a crook in any of them, turn the pieces crown up. Drive a pair of 16d nails through the headers into each end of each joist.

With the help of a friend, lift the floor frame and place it on the 4 × 4 runners, turned so that the floor joists cross the runners and overlap them 12" on each side.

Measure diagonally across the frame in both directions. Square the frame by adjusting it until both measurements are equal. Then, toe-nail the joists to the runners.

Snap a chalk line across the center of the floor joists. Measure the distance between each of the thirteen joists and cut twelve pressure-treated 2 × 4 bridging blocks (D) to fit between them. Nail the blocks in staggered fashion on either side of the centerline. String the length of a joist occasionally to make sure that the cumulative effect of the added bridging is not bowing the joists. Measure and cut the blocks for the outer joists last to avoid bowing the end joists.

Floor

If possible, use pressure-treated 1/2" sheathing plywood for the floor panels (Q, R). If that's not available, coat both sides of the sheathing plywood with two coats of a clear wood preservative. Cut one panel (Q) in half.

Lay the plywood on top of the floor joists, the long dimension parallel to the 4 × 4 runners. Stagger the end joints as shown in the floor detail drawing.

Leave a 1/8" gap around the edges of the plywood to allow for expansion. Most plywood panels used for floor sheathing are slightly undersized to compensate for the spacing, but measure the panels you are using and trim them, if necessary. Attach the plywood floor to the floor joists with 6d common

MATERIALS LIST

3/4″ × 4′ × 8′ APA-rated sheathing
  plywood (6 sheets)
5/8″ × 4′ × 8′ rough-sawn T1-11
  siding plywood (7 sheets)
1/2″ × 4′ × 8′ APA-rated sheathing
  pressure-treated plywood
  (3 sheets)
4 × 4 × 12′ pressure-treated
  lumber (2)
2 × 4 × 12′ pressure-treated
  lumber (3)
2 × 4 × 8′ pressure-treated
  lumber (13)
2 × 4 × 12′ (6)
2 × 4 × 8′ (36)
1 × 4 × 8′ #2 pine (17)
Self-sealing fiberglass square butt
  strip shingles (6 bundles)
Saturated felt underlayment or
  black felt paper (1 roll)
16d common nails (5 lb)
16d galvanized nails (5 lb)
8d galvanized siding nails (5 lb)
6d common nails (5 lb)
4d finishing nails
3/4″ or 7/8″ galvanized roofing
  nails (10 lb)
No. 6 × 1-1/2″ wood screws
3″ T-hinges (3 pairs)
24″ × 24″ skylights (2) (optional)
6″ × 12″ air vents (2)
Door latch or safety hasp
Exterior stain or acrylic latex paint
Construction adhesive

nails spaced 6″ apart along panel
edges and 10″ apart down the center
rows. It helps to snap chalk lines
across the floor 12″ on center as
guidelines before nailing.

CUTTING LIST

KEY	PIECES	SIZE/DESCRIPTION
A	2	3-1/2 × 3-1/2 × 144 runners (pressure-treated)
B	13	1-1/2 × 3-1/2 × 93 floor joists (pressure-treated)
C	2	1-1/2 × 3-1/2 × 144 header joists (pressure-treated)
D	12	1-1/2 × 3-1/2 × 10-1/2 (approx.) blocks (pressure-treated)
E	14	1-1/2 × 3-1/2 × 42 truss members (part 1)
F	14	1-1/2 × 3-1/2 × 34-1/4 truss members (part 2)
G	20	1-1/2 × 3-1/2 × 41-1/2 side wall studs
H	4	1-1/2 × 3-1/2 × 144 side wall top plates
J	2	1-1/2 × 3-1/2 × 144 side wall bottom plates
K	4	1-1/2 × 3-1/2 × 81 end wall studs
L	2	1-1/2 × 3-1/2 × 89 end wall bottom plates
M	4	1-1/2 × 3-1/2 × 19 end wall blocking
N	1	1-1/2 × 3-1/2 × 91-1/2 back wall center stud
P	2	1-1/2 × 3-1/2 × 48 door headers
Q	2	1/2 × 47-15/16 × 48 floor panels
R	2	1/2 × 48 × 96 floor panels
S	6	5/8 × 47-15/16 × 48 side wall panels

CUTTING LIST (continued)		
KEY	**PIECES**	**SIZE/DESCRIPTION**
T	4	5/8 × 48 × 96 end walls
U	2	3/4 × 35 × 96 roof sheathing (plywood)
V	2	3/4 × 35 × 47-15/16 roof sheathing (plywood)
W	2	3/4 × 44 × 96 roof sheathing (plywood)
X	2	3/4 × 44 × 47-15/16 roof sheathing (plywood)
Y	36	3/4 × 6 × 12 gussets

Trusses

Use the completed floor and the truss layout to help you assemble the roof trusses.

Square a line across the width of the floor 39″ from one end. Square another line aross the floor 48″ from the same end. We will call the first line "Y" and the second line "Z" as shown in the truss layout drawing. The centerline will be the small gap between plywood sheets. We will consider that line "X."

Consider the corner of the floor point A and the midpoint of line Z as point C, as shown in the layout drawing. To locate point B, measure

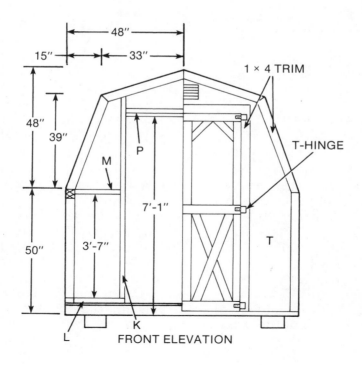

FRONT ELEVATION

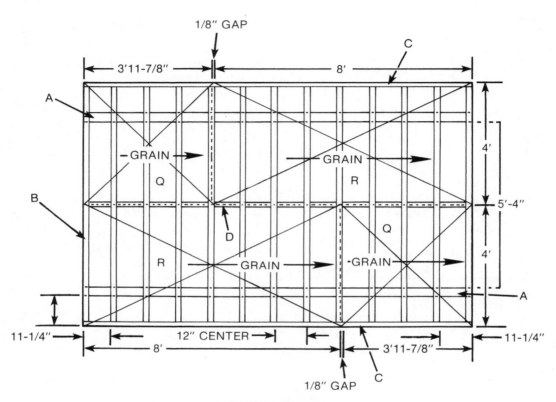

FLOOR DETAIL

15" from the side of the plywood deck along line Y. Snap chalklines between points A and B and points B and C. Then lay an 8' length of 2 × 4 facedown on the deck on the inside of the first of these lines with its edge placed against the line. Make a mark alongside its other edge to complete the profile of the board. Repeat the process with the other chalkline. Where these two lines intersect is point D. Connect points B and D to identify the joint between parts 1 and 2 of the truss.

Now using this layout as your guide, cut the 2 × 4 into a part 1 piece and a part 2 piece. If your layout and cutting are accurate, when you have completed the point B to point D cut on part 1 of the board, all you should have to do with the part 2 section is flip it over, line up its angled edge with the point B—point D line, then mark it for trimming at point C.

Once you have completed cutting a part 1 and part 2 piece according to the layout on the deck, use

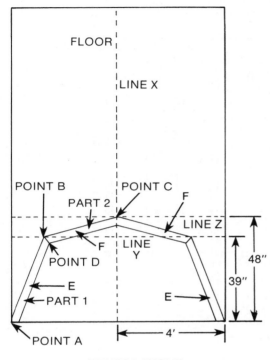

TRUSS LAYOUT

them as patterns for cutting the remaining thirteen pairs of truss parts.

Cut thirty-six 6″ × 12″ strips from a sheet of plywood. These will act as gussets (Y) when you assemble the trusses.

To assemble a truss, lay out two sets each of parts 1 and 2 on the floor as indicated in the illustration. Fasten a gusset to each side of each joint. Let the top corners of the gussets overlap the trusses. Trim the gussets flush with the top of the truss, using a handsaw or saber saw. (Use one trimmed gusset as a template for cutting the rest.)

NOTE: When making the front and rear trusses, use gussets on one side only.

Make a jig for assembling the remaining trusses by nailing 2 × 4 blocks to the floor about halfway along each part 1 and part 2.

Walls

Use the floor as a work surface to frame the two side walls. Cut twenty wall studs (G) out of 2 × 4 stock, making each 41-1/2″ in length. Use 12′ lengths of 2 × 4 for the top and bottom wall plates (H, J).

Lay out the locations for the wall studs along an edge of one of the top plates. All but the two end studs should be placed on 16″ centers. Each of the end studs must be brought in 3/4″ so the wall sheathing will completely lap them. Begin the layout by hooking your tape on the left end of the plate and stretching it to the right along the edge of the board. Square a line across the plate at 15-1/4″ and every 16″ thereafter, then place a big X to the right of the line.

Set the bottom plate up against the marked plate, face-to-face and ends flush, and extend the layout lines across its upper edge as well.

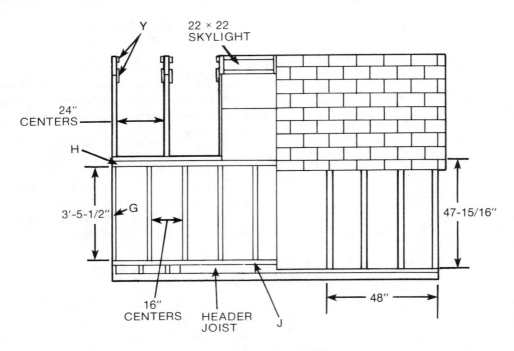

SIDE ELEVATION

Then spread the plates apart and fit wall studs between them—one stud flush with each end and the rest at the positions marked. Drive a pair of 16d nails through the plate into each end of each stud. When all the studs are properly fastened, place the second top plate over the first one and nail them together. Repeat the layout and framing process for the second wall.

Lay out the truss locations on the top plate of each wall, placing the intermediate trusses 24″ on center while using 3/4″-narrower spacing for the front and rear trusses. When the layout is complete, raise the walls into place, fastening them to the deck, joists, and joist headers using 16d galvanized nails. Plumb the walls and secure them with temporary braces while installing the trusses.

With the side walls secured in place, toenail the roof trusses to the top plate. The front and rear trusses should be turned so their gussets face in.

The barn described here was designed for a warm climate. If you live in an area with heavy snowfall, we recommend strengthening the roof structure by running 2 × 4 collar beams between two or three of the trusses at the center of the barn. Set the beams at about the same

height as the top of the door to provide adequate head clearance and
make your plywood gussets large
enough to simultaneously stiffen the
truss joint and tie the truss to the
collar beam.

Cut a 2 × 4 to 89″ in length for
the bottom plate (L) of the front end
wall. Mark off 48″ in the center of
the plate for the doorway, then set
the plate in proper position on the
deck—only pushed a couple of
inches in from the edge of the deck—
for checking the height of the wall
studs. Set a stud on the plate next to
the area marked for the doorway,
plumb it, and mark its upper end
where it intersects the roof truss. Do
the same for the other stud, then cut
the studs to length at the appropriate angle. (The length should be
about 81″ and the angle 75 degrees.)
Check the fit again, then fasten the
studs to the plate. Move the plate into position and nail it to the deck,
avoiding the area that must be cut
out for the door. Plumb the studs
and toenail their upper ends into the
roof truss, then use a handsaw to
cut out the doorway section of the
plate.

Lay out the back end wall. Cut a
bottom plate and pencil the stud locations on it. Center the outer studs
21-7/8″ from the side walls and the
center stud (N) in the end wall center. The outer studs must be cut to
fit the roof angle, and the center
stud must be beveled in both directions. For the best possible fit, hold
the studs in position and plumb.
Mark the angle of the truss on the

stud and cut to fit. Nail the plate to
the base of the studs and the top of
the studs to the truss. Cut two 2 × 4
blocks to fit between the studs level
with the side wall top plate and nail
them in place.

Cut two 19″ lengths of 2 × 4 to
use as blocking for the front end
wall. Fasten the blocking horizontally between the side wall top plates
and the studs framing the doorway.

Siding and Roof Plywood

Cut the plywood roof panels (U,
V) and rough-sawn T1-11 panels
(S) to size. Attach the 3/4″ plywood
roof sheathing using construction
adhesive and 6d common nails. Install the upper panels first. Then
butt the lower panels against the
overhanging upper panels. Be sure
to maintain the 24″ on-center spacing along the ridge. The grain should
be perpendicular to the trusses.
Stagger the joints as on the floor.
Space the adjoining ends of the
plywood 1/8″ apart. Space the nails
6″ apart on the panel edges and 12″
apart on the intermediate supports.
After the roof sheathing has been
installed, nail the siding to the side
walls first, using galvanized 8d siding nails. The cut edge of the panels
should be flush against the overhanging roof panels.

On the front and back walls,
tack the panels (T) in place and
trace the outline of the trusses on
the backside of the panels. Remove
the panels and cut along the outline

Nail the end panels to the barn following the nailing instructions given for the side panels.

Carefully measure and mark the plywood panels to be cut for the front door opening. Drive a long finishing nail through the four corners of the door opening and draw or snap lines connecting the holes. Cut along the lines with a saber saw to cut out the doorway. The cutout plywood will become the doors.

On the front and back walls, cut 6″ × 12″ openings for the vents and install them with the manufacturer's supplied hardware.

If skylights are to be installed, frame the openings between the trusses approximately 22″ square. (Check the skylight for actual dimensions.) After framing, cut the opening in the roof using a saber saw. Attach skylights to roof sheathing according to the manufacturer's instructions.

Attach the 1 × 4 trim to corners, around the door frame, and along the roof edge. Measure and cut as you go so that each joint is tight.

Plane and sand the edges of the doors smooth and face with 1 × 4 trim in a traditional barn door design. Carefully measure and cut as you go. Nail to the door panels with 4d finishing nails or No. 6 × 1-1/2″ wood screws.

Hang the doors in the opening, using three 3″ T-hinges for each door. Install the door latch.

Cut the black felt paper into 12′ lengths. Starting at the bottom of the roof, align the paper with the bottom edge of the roof sheathing and tack it in place. Overlap each successive layer at least 2″. (For greater weather resistance, nail roof flashing over the felt along the roof edges.)

Shingle the roof with self-sealing fiberglass shingles. Follow the manufacturer's installation instructions, which are usually printed on each bundle. Use 3/4″ or 7/8″ galvanized roofing nails, long enough to penetrate through the roof sheathing. Make ridge caps to shingle the ridge by cutting the shingles in quarters and overlapping them 50 percent as you nail them to the sheathing.

The Materials List includes sufficient 1 × 4 stock to trim the building as shown in the photograph. Measure and cut to fit as you go, starting with the gable trim and working out and down. Use 6d pan-head siding nails and drive the nails into trusses and wall studs.

Finish the storage barn with a solid color stain or paint of your choice.

TRASH CAN BIN

Nobody likes to take out the garbage—especially when the cans have been knocked over again. Although you cannot make garbage chores go away, you can eliminate knocked over cans and spilled trash. This easy-to-build trash can holder is big enough to hold two standard size trash cans.

The unit shown is set on a concrete pad, but if yours will be set on the ground, elevate it on 4 × 4 pressure-treated sleepers.

Begin by cutting the 2 × 4 side frame members (A, B, C, D) to length. As shown in the side frame detail drawing, miter the top end of the front members and the front end of the top members 53 degrees to the inside. Also cut a 75-degree bevel across the back end of the top members.

Cut a 3-1/2"-wide × 1-3/4"-deep rabbet in the lower inside edge of the front members and in the back upper edge of the bottom piece.

NOTE: Because of variations in materials and in the accuracy of settings on a saw, greater precision can be achieved by cutting the frame members to length, cutting the rabbets in pieces B and D, and dry assembling the frames. Then mark the miters and bevels on pieces A and B.

MATERIALS LIST

2 × 4 × 12′ (5)
3/4″ × 4′ × 8′ CD plywood (2 sheets)
5/8″ × 4′ × 8′ T1-11 plywood
  (2 sheets)
4″ T-hinges and screws (4)
Double roller catches (with springs)
  (2)
12d galvanized common nails
8d galvanized common nails
6d galvanized panhead siding nails
Construction adhesive

Finally, cut the bird's-mouth notch in the back end of the top member to accept the upper end of the rear member. Fasten the side frames together, using 8d galvanized nails. Make sure that the frames are square.

Cut the five braces (E, F) to length. Rip a 15-degree bevel on the two braces that will fit at the front and rear between the upper part of the side frames. Cut a 1-1/2″-wide × 1-5/8″-deep notch out of the upper edge at each end of the longer center brace, as shown in the exploded-view drawing.

Set the two rear braces 3/4″ in from the back edge and align the inner faces of the two front braces with the inner edges of the front frame members. Set the bottom braces flush with the bottom of the frames and the beveled top braces 1-7/8″ below the upper edges of the frames. As its name implies, the center brace goes in the center as shown in the drawings. Fasten the braces in place by driving a pair of 12d galvanized nails through the frames into each end of each brace.

CUTTING LIST

KEY	PIECES	SIZE/DESCRIPTION
A	2	1-1/2 × 3-1/2 × 29 side frame top members
B	2	1-1/2 × 3-1/2 × 36-3/4 side frame front members
C	2	1-1/2 × 3-1/2 × 39-3/4 side frame members
D	2	1-1/2 × 3-1/2 × 26-1/4 side frame bottom members
E	4	1-1/2 × 3-1/2 × 61-3/4 top and bottom braces
F	1	1-1/2 × 3-1/2 × 64-3/4 top center brace
G	1	1-1/2 × 2-1/2 × 61-1/2 hand grip
H	2	3/4 × 1-1/2 × 34-3/4 back cleats
J1	1	5/8 × 29 × 48 top panel (T1-11)
J2	1	5/8 × 29 × 13-3/4 side top panel (T1-11)
K	2	5/8 × 25-1/2 × 41 side panels (T1-11)
L	1	5/8 × 32-1/4 × 61-1/2 door panel (T1-11)
M	1	3/4 × 41 × 61-3/4 back panel
N	1	3/4 × 25-1/2 × 64-3/4 floor panel
O	2	1-1/2 × 3-1/2 × 22-1/2 floor brace blocking

Cut 2 × 4 blocks (O) to fit between the lower braces. Space them evenly between the side frames and nail them to the lower braces.

Cut 1 × 2 cleats (H) to length. Using construction adhesive and 6d siding nails, fasten them to the side frames between the rear braces, set

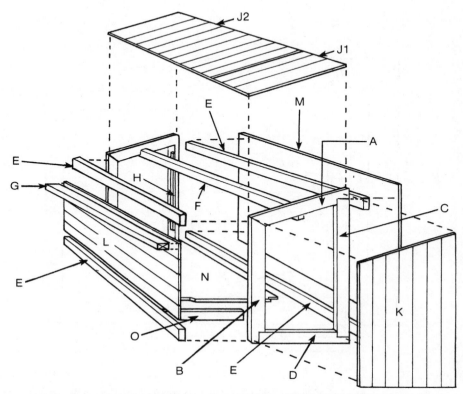

TIPS: SET CIRCULAR POWER SAW BLADES TO CUT THROUGH
AND CLEAR PLYWOOD BY 1/8" TO CONFINE SPLINTERING.

back 3/4" from the rear edge of the frames, setting their lower ends 3-5/8" above the bottom of the frames.

Cut the top panels (J-1, J-2) to size. Bevel the front and rear edges of the panels 75 degrees. Extrude a bead of construction adhesive on the top edges of the upper braces. Place the panels in position and fasten them with 6d siding nails.

Cut the back panel (M) to size and position it against the rear braces with its top edge flush against the bottom face of the top

panel. Using construction adhesive and 6d siding nails, fasten it to the braces and cleats.

Cut the side panels (K) to size and bevel the top edges 75 degrees to the front edge. Locate the panels 3/4" in from the back edges and 1-1/4" down from the top edges of the side frames. Fasten them to the side frames.

Cut the door grip (G) to length and rip it to 2-1/2" wide. On the bottom face of the handle, rout a 1/2"-wide V-groove along the front edge of the board. This groove will

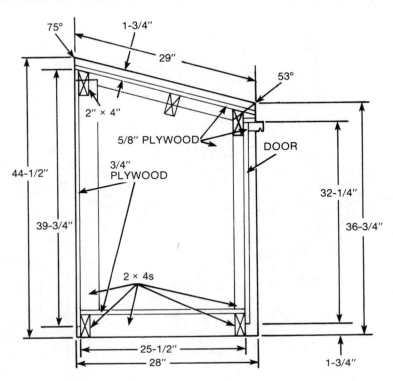

act as a finger hold and keep water from running back under the handle and down the face of the door panel.

Cut the door panel (L) to size. Using nails and construction adhesive, fasten the grip to the outer face of the panel, flush with the upper edge.

Cut the floor panel (N) to size and notch the four corners to fit around the 2 × 4 side frames. Spread construction adhesive on the top edge of the side frame bottom members and on the floor brace blocking, set the floor in position, and nail it in place.

Attach the four T-hinges to the door panel and to the lower front brace.

NOTE: To avoid placing excessive stress on the hinges, attach them as close as possible to the bottom edge of the brace so that the bottom edge of the door rests on the ground when the door is open.

Stain the bin to suit your taste. Install two double roller catches for the door, and you are ready to take out the garbage.

PORTABLE GARDEN TOOL CART

This project does double duty. Not only does it keep your gardening tools safely stored, it also can be wheeled wherever the tools are needed. Large or long-handled tools are stored on the front of the cart in individualized grooves and held secure with elasticized cord. Smaller tools and miscellaneous items (seeds, stakes, string) are tucked away in bins on the back of the cart.

Everyone's tool collection varies, so you'll have to determine the specific groove dimensions for tool placement. The cart has been designed for balance and therefore is easy to pull, but to facilitate its portability, use wheels no smaller than 10″ in diameter. The axle is located so that the cart will sit upright. But the lower back edge of the sides is rounded so that a slight, backward pull on the handle will cause the cart to lift off the ground onto the wheels for rolling. If wheels larger than 10″ in diameter are used, adjust the design accordingly.

Start by laying out and cutting the two side panels (A) to size (see the panel layout drawing). Do not round the corners of the sides until the nailer cleats (H) and bearing blocks (K) have been installed and the holes for the handle and axle have been drilled.

Cut the 1 × 3 bearing blocks (K) to size. Position the blocks parallel to and centered 5″ above the bottom edges of the sides, their tail ends flush with the back edges of the sides. Note that if a different wheel diameter is used, the location of these blocks must be adjusted so their horizontal centerline matches the centerline for drilling the axle holes. Make sure the blocks are placed on what will become the inside face of each side, then fasten them in place.

Fasten the side nailer cleats to the side panels using waterproof glue and 1″ ring nails. Make the bot-

MATERIALS LIST

3/4" × 4' × 8' exterior plywood
(1/2 sheet)
1/2" × 4' × 8' CD exterior plywood
(2 sheets)
2 × 6 × 6' construction grade spruce
1 × 3 × 2' #2 pine
1 × 2 × 5' #2 pine
6d galvanized common nails
1" ring nails
1"-dia. hardwood dowel (3')
Light-duty 2" T-hinges (4)
24" shock cord (1)
5/8" screw eye (3)
1/2" × 31-5/8" steel rod
1/2" flat washers (4)
1/8" × 1" cotter pins (2)
1-3/4" × 10" wheels (2)
Latex paint
Resorcinol wood glue

CUTTING LIST

KEY	PIECES	SIZE/DESCRIPTION
A	2	1/2 × 22 × 60 side panels (plywood)
B	1	1/2 × 26 × 56 back panel (plywood)
C	1	1/2 × 14 × 26 bottom panel (plywood)
D	2	3/4 × 6-3/8 × 26 storage bin bottoms (plywood)
E	1	1/2 × 8 × 26 storage bin front (plywood)
F	1	1/2 × 12 × 26 storage bin front (plywood)
G	2	3/4 × 7-1/8 × 25-3/4 storage bin lids (plywood)
H	2	3/4 × 1-1/2 × 13-1/4 side nailer cleats
J	1	3/4 × 1-1/2 × 26 back nailer cleat
K	2	3/4 × 2-1/2 × 7 bearing blocks
L	1	1-1/2 × 5-1/2 × 26 tool rack
M	1	1-1/2 × 3-1/2 × 26 tool rack
N	1	1-1/2 × 1-1/2 × 26 retaining bar
O	1	1-dia. × 27 handle

tom edges of the cleats and panels flush and set the inner ends of the cleats at least 8-1/4" in from the rear edges of the panels so that after fastening the back nailer cleat to the back panel you will be able to properly fit that panel between the bearing blocks and the side cleats.

Center and drill 1/2"-diameter holes through the bearing blocks and sides, 1-1/2" from the back edges and 5" from the bottom edges of the sides, to make room for the wheel axle. As mentioned earlier, this location is designed for mounting 10"-diameter wheels. If a different size of wheels is used, adjust the location of the axle holes so that the bottoms of the wheels will be flush with the bottom of the cart when it

is upright. To get the holes perfectly aligned, stack the panels (outside face against outside face) and drill both holes at once.

Center and drill 1"-diameter holes through the side panels 2" below their upper edge as shown in the panel layout drawing. For good

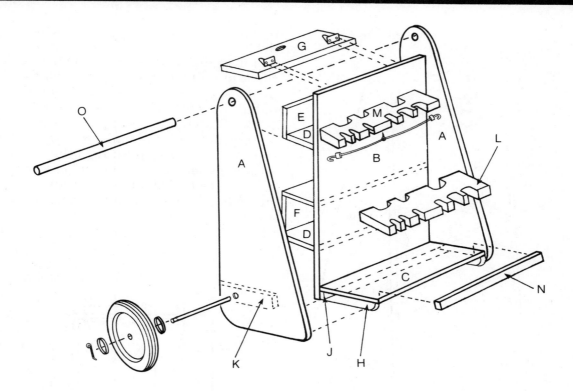

alignment, stack the panels and drill both at once.

Lay out and cut radii on the corners of the side panels. Round the top on a 4-1/2″ radius, the lower back corner on a 4″ radius, and the lower front corner on a 1-1/2″ radius. When radiusing the two lower corners, be prepared to partially round the outer ends of the bearing blocks and side nailers as well.

Cut the back panel (B) and the back nailer cleat (J) to size. Fasten the cleat to the panel, making the bottom edges of each flush, using waterproof glue and 1″ ring nails. Fit the panel between the sides and

against the inner ends of the bearing blocks, its nailer cleat facing toward the front. Make sure the edges of the three panels are flush and that the back panel is perfectly parallel with the back edges of the side panels; then, fasten the side panels to the back panel, using waterproof glue and 6d galvanized common nails.

Cut the bottom panel (C) to size and bevel its front edge 13 degrees to conform with the sloping front edges of the side panels. For a neat job, you will probably find it necessary to first rip the panel a bit wide, set it in place on top of the side nailer cleats so you can mark where its

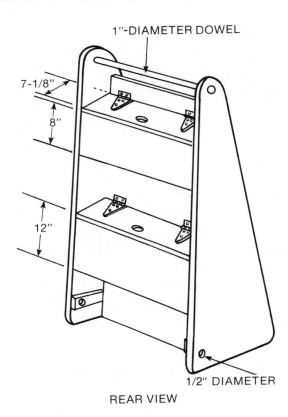

1"-DIAMETER DOWEL

7-1/8"

8"

12"

1/2" DIAMETER

REAR VIEW

this piece so that when you place the bar between the side panels and on top of the bottom panel, the front edges of all these pieces can be made flush. While beveling the bar, also reduce its width to approximately 1-1/2". Fasten the bar in place using waterproof glue and nails. Run the shorter ring nails up through the bottom panel into the bar and one or more of the 6d nails through each side panel into an end of the bar.

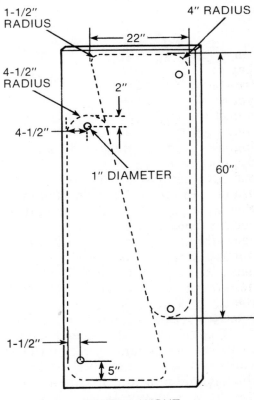

1-1/2" RADIUS

4" RADIUS

22"

4-1/2" RADIUS

2"

4-1/2"

1" DIAMETER

60"

1-1/2"

5"

PANEL LAYOUT

front edge intersects the sides, then rip it to the precise width with your saw blade tilted to produce the bevel required. Fasten the panel to the nailer cleats using waterproof glue and 1" ring nails. Drill a few holes through the bottom panel so that any moisture that accumulates inside the cart can drain off.

Cut a piece of 2 × 6 to 26" in length, then rip it to a width of 3-1/2". Save the 3-1/2" piece for the upper tool rack (M), and use the narrower ripping for the retaining bar (N). Bevel the ripped edge of

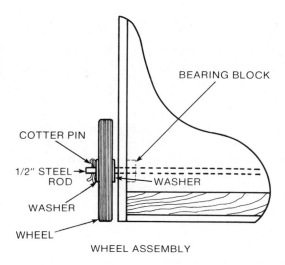

COTTER PIN

1/2" STEEL ROD

WASHER

WHEEL

BEARING BLOCK

WASHER

WHEEL ASSEMBLY

Cut a piece of 2 × 6 to 26" in length for the lower tool rack (L). Lay out and cut notches out of the front edge of the piece sized to fit your hoe, rake, and other long-handled garden tools. Then, use this piece as a pattern for cutting matching notches in the front edge of the upper tool rack. Slope the back of the notches in each piece so that when they are installed in the cart the tools lean from the lower, wider rack back into the higher, narrower rack. If you wish, cut matching notches out of the back edges of each rack so that other tools can be held there. Just remember to arrange the notches so different tools do not interfere with each other.

Fasten the tool racks in place using waterproof glue and 6d galvanized nails. Run the nails through the back panel and side panels into the racks. There is no precise height

required for the racks, but the lower one should be placed approximately 20" and the upper one approximately 40" above the bottom of the cart.

Cut the bin bottoms (D), fronts (E, F) and lids (G) to size. When cutting the lids, rip parallel 10-degree bevels on each side edge and drill a 1"-diameter finger hole at the center near the front edge of each. Round over the edges of the finger holes using sandpaper or a router so they will not splinter easily.

Lap each bin front over one of the bottoms as shown in the drawings. Fasten them together using waterproof glue and 6d galvanized nails driven through the fronts into the bottoms.

Before installing the bins, sand and paint them and the rest of the cart as well. After the paint has dried, take each bin front/bottom assembly in turn and fit it between the side panels in the place you want to locate the bin. Make sure the rear end of the bottom is square against the back panel, then drive 6d galvanized nails through the side panels into the edges of the paired bin parts.

Fasten the bin lids to the back panel using light-duty, 2" T-hinges. Set the lids at a height that will allow their back edges to be fairly flush against the back panel when they are closed. Also, when fastening the lids in place, make sure they are centered between the side panels, so that any later racking of the panels will not prevent the lids from opening and closing.

Cut a piece of 1/2″-diameter steel rod to 31-5/8″ in length for the axle. Drill a 1/8″-diameter hole through each end of the rod to receive a cotter pin. Run the axle through the cart side panels and fit a washer on each end. Then install the wheels, a second set of washers, and cotter pins to hold the assembly together.

Cut a piece of 1″-diameter hardwood dowel to 27″ in length for the cart handle. Fasten the handle in the holes drilled for it using waterproof glue. Either leave the handle unfinished or coat it with linseed oil or some other type of oil that will help it weather well.

Finally, install screw eyes on the insides of the side panels and beneath the upper tool rack so that you can stretch a shock cord between them to hold your tools in place.

Credits

Georgia-Pacific Corp. (133 Peachtree Street NE, Atlanta, Georgia, 30307): Family Room Desk and TV Cabinet with Bookshelves; Room Divider Shelves; Computer Desk with Shelves; Library Cabinet; Soffit Storage; Dining Room Display Shelves; Closet Pantry; Kitchen Niches; Broom Closet; Headboard Storage; Wall Shelf; Stackable Beds; Vanity; Sewing Center; Shaker Desk; Magazine Rack; Storage Barn; Trash Can Bin.

Louisiana-Pacific Corp. (111 SW Fifth Avenue, Portland, Oregon, 97205): Electronic Media Center; Laundry Room Cabinet; Overhood Storage; Stud-Mounted Storage; Sports Equipment Storage; Garden Storage Center and Tool Rack; Garage Workbench and Wall Cabinets; Overhead Lumber Rack.

Rodale Press, Inc. (33 E. Minor Street, Emmaus, Pennsylvania, 18098): Movable Storage Center; Home Finance Center; Home Office; Kitchen Island; Spice Organizer; Pack-It-In Pantry; Wooden Pot Rack; Platform Bed; Modular Closet Organizer; Bedroom Desk; Home Recycling Center; Movable Workbench; Plywood and Lumber Rack; Woodworker's Tool Chest; Tool Tote; Routabout Cabinet; Tool Taboret; Portable Garden Tool Cart.

The Know Place. (4038-128 Avenue SE, Suite 176, Bellevue, Washington, 98009): Entertainment Center; Stacking Bookcases; Garden Center; Wall Shelf with Mirror; Display Stand; Matching Freestanding and Wall-Hung Bookcases; Spice Rack; Toy Chest; Book Rack; Bathroom Storage Cabinet; Mirrored Wall Cabinet.

Western Wood Products Assn. (Yeon Building, 522 SW Fifth Avenue, Portland, Oregon, 97204): Stackable Storage.

Rodale Press, Inc., publishes RODALE'S ORGANIC GARDENING®,
the all-time favorite gardening magazine.
For information on how to order your subscription,
write to RODALE'S ORGANIC GARDENING®, Emmaus, PA 18098.